D1563743

THE GLOBAL PR REVOLUTION

THE GLOBAL PR REVOLUTION

How Thought Leaders Succeed in the Transformed World of PR

MAXIM BEHAR

ALLWORTH PRESS
NEW YORK

Allworth Press books may be purchased in bulk at special discounts for sales promotion, corporate gifts, fund-raising, or educational purposes. Special editions can also be created to specifications. For details, contact the Special Sales Department, Allworth Press, 307 West 36th Street, 11th Floor, New York, NY 10018 or info@skyhorsepublishing.com.

23 22 21 20 19 5 4 3 2 1

Published by Allworth Press, an imprint of Skyhorse Publishing, Inc. 307 West 36th Street, 11th Floor, New York, NY 10018. Allworth Press® is a registered trademark of Skyhorse Publishing, Inc.®, a Delaware corporation.

www.allworth.com

Cover design by M3 Communications Group, Inc.
Front cover illustration by Yana Georgieva

Library of Congress Cataloging-in-Publication Data

Names: Behar, Maxim, author.
Title: The global PR revolution: how thought leaders succeed in the transformed world of PR / Maxim Behar.
Description: New York, NY: Allworth Press, [2019] | Includes index.
Identifiers: LCCN 2019008429 (print) | LCCN 2019010717 (ebook) | ISBN 9781621537175 (eBook) | ISBN 9781621537151 (hardcover: alk. paper)
Subjects: LCSH: Public relations. | Social media. | Internet in public relations.
Classification: LCC HD59 (ebook) | LCC HD59 .B377 2019 (print) | DDC 659.2—dc23
LC record available at https://lccn.loc.gov/2019008429

Hardcover ISBN: 978-1-62153-715-1
eBook ISBN: 978-1-62153-717-5

Printed in the United States of America

CONTENTS

INTRODUCTION

July 2019, London, United Kingdom

"What are you doing, man?"

"Writing a book."

"About what?"

"Public relations, of course. That's what I've been doing for the past twenty-five years. That's what I know well."

"Good, good. Then write about everything that's happening in the modern world today. Everything! Fake news, black PR, bloggers, trolls, haters . . . Write about Brexit and about Trump . . . PR only. No politics, no business, no human relations. Just PR. You know all of this much better than I do."

"You've just made my point."

October 1995, Sofia, Bulgaria

It all happened with a simple email. Just a couple of lines.

Two centuries ago, this would have happened with a letter brought on horseback; a century ago, via a letter by mail; decades ago, via fax machine.

Today, it may happen with a message on Facebook or Snapchat.

But nearly twenty years ago, there was an email in my inbox. Short and clear.

> Mr. Behar, in WPP we've heard about your operation in Bulgaria and will be interested to cooperate. I think Hill & Knowlton might be your logical partner. Please contact, on that matter, Mr. Howard Paster.
>
> —Martin Sorrell

Who was this guy?

I was sitting in my office in downtown Sofia—a tiny room with a slightly bigger kitchen, where my secretary's desk was, and I was trying to figure out who Martin Sorrell was. Then I called Elka Koleva, who ran Young & Rubican's office in Sofia, and asked: "Elka, have you ever heard the name Martin Sorrell? I just got a strange mail from him." Elka was silent for a few seconds and then very slowly said, "Max . . . how come Sir Martin knows who you are and you don't know who he is?"

Of course, I also did not know that 2018 would become "the year of Martin Sorrell" and that his resignation as chief executive of WPP, the world's largest advertising-and-marketing conglomerate, would turn the whole corporate PR business upside down (at least this is my current prediction).

How come, indeed? I did not know that this email would change my life, many other lives, and from a certain point of view the PR industry in Bulgaria.

And all over the world.

PR IN THE DAYS OF REVOLUTIONS

> "If I would ask customers what they want, they certainly would tell me: faster horses."
>
> —Henry Ford, explaining why he invented the so-called fast production line for gasoline cars

Henry Ford will be mentioned again in this book, especially when we discuss the threats of *modern* social media.

I started writing this book many times. Then I would stop and start all over again. For months. On the plane, at the airport, big and small hotels, during forums, conferences, and summits, sometimes even in small coffee shops surrounded by couples in love. I was watching them very, very carefully, as I was and I am still in love—with the extremely dynamic business that is changing every day called Public Relations. What will its name be tomorrow?

PR is everything and everywhere. PR is the King and the Slave, the Game Changer and the Boss, the *revolution*! Indeed, the Global PR Revolution!

The reason I stopped and started this book over and over was that the industry kept changing so dynamically, within a matter of days, hours, and minutes, that what I had written seemed obsolete already.

The PR environment has been changing like a taximeter on a high-speed highway, and I could hardly fix the price—not the financial one, but the creative and the communications one. It had been changing literally every week, day, and hour.

It is quite important to know when you read this book that I was writing and stopping, starting, deleting, adding . . . Then it hit me that in the time of social media revolution, this is precisely the essence of the industry called "public relations"—the most dynamic, creative, and captivating business in the world over the past two decades.

It will always be like that. Ever changing.

I have been a part of the International Communications Consultancy Organisation (ICCO), the leading global organization of PR consultancies, for over ten exciting years now.

From ICCO board member, to treasurer, to vice president, and now as president, I have had the opportunity to witness with my own eyes how the PR revolution, brought about by social media, has played out in over fifty countries. I have been discussing it with my colleagues and their clients and partners.

I still do this. Every day, almost every hour. Every minute, even.

In 2014, my lecture in front of hundreds of professionals at the World Economic Forum in Davos, Switzerland, was entitled "PR Man Never Gives Up." I believed in that sentiment from the very first moment in the business, back in 1994, and the more time I spend in PR, the more I know in my gut that it is true. The next year, the organizers asked me to make a similar lecture, which I titled "PR Man Never Grows Old." Indeed, this captures the demands and aspirations of PR professionals all over the world today.

My fellow PR professionals and I would have endless arguments on how our industry has actually changed. We would cite who said what in some presentation somewhere around the world. We would fall out, make up, and then, after some more bottles of wine, we would agree: what we do today in the PR industry has not much to do with what we used to do yesterday, and it's all because of social media.

I am not a professional writer of books (although the first three I wrote had many editions in many countries) but have spent almost a quarter century in the public relations business, solved hundreds of crises, managed almost six thousand projects, and met PR colleagues from at least fifty countries. This has given me the energy to try to formulate what has happened in our business for the past couple of years, in 2017 particularly.

Exactly 100 years ago plus one (history sometimes makes such jokes), a political revolution in Russia divided the world into two camps. Luckily, one century later, the PR revolution is going to unite it.

How?

It is simple—technology and social media.

2017. The year of miracles for public relations. The first year of Mr. #45's (Donald Trump's) era and the last year of Harvey Weinstein's glory, the year of the biggest PR boom in the whole history of this business. You will see why later in this book.

I'm not sure how I ended up in the PR business, I mean before Sir Martin's email and before I met the legendary Terence Billing (then-executive vice president of Hill & Knowlton, which was later rebranded to Hill+Knowlton Strategies, and one of the greatest names in the PR industry at that time). Looking back, I realize that I had actually always aspired toward it—even in the years when it was unthinkable or unknown.

When I was fifteen, I published ten issues of a neighborhood daily newspaper produced on a typewriter. Later, I defended a thesis on marketing and advertising, the first senior thesis to tackle this topic in the history of the Prague University of Economics. That was ten years before Communism collapsed, bringing a free market.

After twenty successful years in journalism, I left it, vividly remembering that "You can achieve a lot with journalism, but you should know exactly when to quit." Somebody told me that was a quote by the legendary British Prime Minister Winston Churchill. Although I've never managed to confirm he ever said that, it does sound like something he might have said, and at the end of the day, it didn't even matter—I liked the quote so much that it has stayed in my mind ever since.

I started a business in downtown Sofia, as if by a miracle. I didn't know what was hiding behind the two magical letters of "PR," but I realized that public communication was my love, and once I fell in love, it was for good.

I started my business full of ideas and energy—of which I have even greater quantities today—but I think that I have never really moved away from journalism.

Freedom of speech is priceless to me. So is the freedom of expression of thoughts and beliefs as an expression of yourself, the freedom of showing that you are different, the freedom of being the force motivating people around you, and the freedom of being motivated by the successes of others.

The freedom of speech is the mother of all those freedoms in the modern democracy. This freedom has completely conquered the new communication technologies.

It has also, to a great extent, influenced the dynamic development of this marvelous and ever less predictable industry still known by the name of "public relations" (though probably not for long).

If you decide that some of the ideas or arguments in this book could have been put differently or explained in greater detail, or if you just want to comment on something, do not hesitate: get in touch with me through social media or drop me an email at max@maximbehar.com with the subject "PR Revolution."

I look forward to hearing your thoughts.

Talk to you soon. Very soon, I hope.

—Maxim Behar
August 2019

CHAPTER 1

PR REVOLUTION 101

Public Relations? Three billion people who are on social media are dealing with "relations," and everything has become "public."

THE NEW "SOCIAL MEDIA" NORMAL

3.8 billion.

That was the number of active social media users on Planet Earth as of late fall 2018!

Mind-blowing as it is, that number is no longer accurate. It will have grown well beyond that by the time you are reading this book.

Yet it's a momentary snapshot that's overwhelming: the Earth's population at the time was estimated at 7.66 billion people.

Half of humanity is now actively engaged on social media.

Close to four billion human beings plugged into social media might be difficult to absorb, but its implications for everything, PR included, are way more profound than the impressive number itself.

Up until ten years ago, freedom of speech was primarily in the realm of the professional journalists; but today, with well over three billion users of various social media, freedom of speech has grown into entirely different dimensions.

For instance, a taxi driver with a secondhand laptop sitting in an old garage could actually become a lot more well known and tell a lot more truths than a journalist on TV.

We are observing ferocious efforts to wield control over the media, especially television, everywhere in the world.

In the very cradle of free speech, the United States, the election of Donald Trump as president has ignited a Punic War among different TV networks. His personality, in particular, has undeniably emerged as a litmus test among the media, who are trying to prove how much they are for or against Trump.

Similar media upheavals—or outright efforts to keep a lid on free speech—can be observed in most other countries around the globe.

Yet, at the end of the day, if TV cameras are brought under control, and the traditional media and even online media are under excessive pressure, social media cannot be controlled. This is where the true leaders of speech and communication emerge nowadays.

At the very beginning, when the PR industry was invented, some 110 years ago, about 95 percent of the relations in politics and in business were hidden from the public—only the convenient information was made available, no more than 5 percent.

Business people and politicians would hire people, former journalists more than anyone else, to manage that 5 percent of public communications for them. Everything else was decided in private, in muddled talks behind closed doors.

In the century since PR's humble beginnings, the share of political and business decisions that remained closed to the public has been declining, but a good deal still remained rather secret.

In 2019, however, there is nothing left from that: the revolutionary advent of social media has now reached its full swing, and 100 percent of all deeds, thoughts, deals, and acts in our lives are public. Social media's almightiness has brought about many things, but the main one is transparency. Total transparency everywhere and for everyone.

As a result, social media have shaken up the PR industry beyond recognition. In fact, social media have caused the first and only real PR revolution in the industry's more than 100 years of history.

Regardless of how the PR business may have developed over the years, we always used to be a transmission, a sort of bridge, between our clients and their clients.

Ten years ago, the PR formula was overwhelmingly simple.

The client would show up, knock on the door or ring the bell, and say, "Mr. PR expert, good morning, it's very nice to meet you. I make these nice cars (or chairs, or whatever). I would like the people to know more about my goods. How should we go about doing that?"

We would reply, "Of course, Mrs. Client, that would cost you one thousand dollars!"

Back then, we had a specific set of tools. It was the same set that we had for decades, and it was the same one all over the world.

We would send out a press release, stage a press conference, organize a breakfast with reporters, organize a media trip, or take the journalists to show them the products in order to convince them how great those products really are. We would avoid talking about the competition, and we would only emphasize the strengths and advantages of our clients' products, and so on, and so on.

Nowadays, all of that is almost entirely gone. First, because the client would come to us with an entirely different query.

The client would come in and say, "Mr. PR expert, I produce *X* products, and they are great products!"

That part is the same, but the next sentence makes all the difference: "I've got media, and I don't know what to do with it!"

PR businesses used to try to convince the media how fabulous a product was, so they would publish or broadcast as many materials about it as possible. Today, thanks to the social media revolution, clients actually own media and consequently a platform to express themselves.

In many cases, we would tell that new client, "We're going to think about Facebook . . ."

"No, no, don't touch it, my secretary is doing a great job with Facebook."

"Then what do you have in mind?" we would ask.

"Well, if you could come up with something interesting so that I can become more popular . . . but please, it really shouldn't be very expensive, because my secretary already does a lot of the work, you know . . ."

That would be a huge mistake, of course, because of the revolutionary changes in PR brought by social media that have already matured in 2015–2017.

One implication is that we, the people who have been known as PR experts—and still go by that title—have now turned into a combination of publishers, reporters, and editors.

We are publishers because we own media. We control the social media profiles and pages of our clients. We have their blogs and their websites.

We are reporters because we have to fill up all those media channels with relevant content.

We are editors because that content has got to be created, designed, arranged, structured, and presented in the best way possible so that it can be convincing, attention-grabbing, and—most important—efficient.

Our PR business today has increasingly less in common with the business that we used to do just ten years ago, let alone a hundred years ago. Pretty soon, it will look nothing like its former self.

This book explores in detail the numerous arguments I have for this claim as I delve, with input from some of the world's top PR professionals, into the various aspects of the first and only real PR revolution so far—social media—that has swept our industry.

Not like the first press release sent out by Ivy Lee in 1906. The press releases we used to send just five years ago were meant for the media.

Today, the press release (or whatever is left of it) and the new types of messages, tweets, and posts that have replaced the traditional press release, mostly target the end consumer.

A medium-sized influencer on Twitter in the United States has between 1 and 1.2 million followers! There simply isn't any other medium that has that large a circulation. There probably aren't that many TV viewers who would see something on TV and remember it.

In that sense, I am inclined to think that "Public Relations" is not the best name anymore for the industry that we are in.

We do need these two words, "public" and "relations"—and, of course, those words are still extremely important.

However, those 3 billion people who are social media users are all dealing with "relations," and everything has become "public"!

With social media, everything has been "public" for quite a while now; there is nothing "nonpublic" anymore.

My current definition of PR is "telling the truth in a way that people understand," plain and simple.

In the next chapter, I will discuss how I have arrived at this definition, because I have spent a good deal of time researching and contemplating it. But I am now firmly convinced that telling the truth in such a way that people will understand it is the essence of PR, especially in this time of social media revolution.

"FROM CRISIS POINT TO TURNING POINT": THE BELL POTTINGER CASE

This book is going to delve into ethics, morality, accuracy, and transparency—but the fact is that the gist of our job has always been to tell the truth, and this is what we've been doing in our everyday lives.

Nothing proves this point better than the giant scandal that shocked the UK, South Africa, and the entire global PR community, culminating in September 2017, just as I was starting and restarting this book: the Bell Pottinger case.

Bell Pottinger is a PR agency founded in 1987 by Lord Bell, Margaret Thatcher's favorite PR adviser, whom I know personally, and Piers Pottinger.

Lord Bell is a great personality in modern PR, and it is a pity that he got entangled in what has become not only South Africa's biggest political scandal since the end of apartheid, but also a landmark case for PR in the world of total transparency.

In January 2016, Lord Bell led a Bell Pottinger delegation to South Africa to pitch for business from the wealthy and powerful Guptas, the Indian-born family said to be connected to South African President Jacob Zuma.

Bell Pottinger stood to gain 100,000 pounds (UK) per month from the Guptas' company, Oakbay Investments, for a campaign for "economic emancipation." The campaign, however, stirred up anger over so-called "white monopoly capital" and "economic apartheid," thereby spurring racial tensions in order to divert attention from the Guptas, who had been accused of benefiting financially from their links to Zuma.

Leaked emails and documents and subsequent journalistic investigations have revealed that Bell Pottinger used a fake blog and Twitter account, and other questionable tactics such as misleading journalists during the campaign.

Lord Bell went live on the BBC to allege that he had nothing to do with the negotiated contract. To prove it, he resigned from Bell Pottinger.

By September 2017, the Bell Pottinger firm itself had all but collapsed after it was expelled from Britain's Public Relations and Communications Association (PRCA) in an unprecedented move, underscoring better than anything else how crucial ethics, morality, and transparency are in today's PR industry.

Paul Holmes, the founder of the website The Holmes Report, had some scathing criticism to offer in the 2018 Global Communications Report of the USC Annenberg School for Communication and Journalism, aptly titled "The Evolution of Ethics":

> When British PR man Lord Tim Bell told the New York Times earlier this year that "morality is a job for priests, not PR men," he demonstrated just how far the PR profession—or at least an element of it—had fallen from its true purpose.
>
> Lord Bell belonged to a generation of PR people—and a school of PR, with its roots in rough-and-tumble, anything-goes politics—for whom morality took a back seat to pragmatism. But these days, morality and pragmatism are no longer in conflict; they are, instead, synonymous. Or, to look at the issue from a slightly different perspective, good public relations provides the pragmatic justification for ethical decision-making.

PRCA Director General Francis Ingham explains the cataclysmic ramifications of the Bell Pottinger case:

The Bell Pottinger case, handled by the PRCA, was a defining moment for our industry. The moment when the world saw that we have high ethical standards and that we are prepared to uphold them, no matter how famous an agency might be.

There was nothing wrong in an agency working for Oakbay Capital. What was wrong was the nature of the work that was delivered, breaking as it did a number of clauses in the PRCA Professional Charter and the PRCA Public Affairs Code of Conduct.

No industry association can prevent every single practitioner from doing the wrong thing—but it can set powerful precedents when it expels them for doing so. And the PRCA did just that.

The reaction in the UK and internationally was simply astonishing. Our action generated literally thousands of television, newspaper, and magazine pieces, along with vast amounts of online coverage.

It also garnered massive amounts of industry support—of practitioners saying that they were delighted to be associated with us, and we're proud that we had done the right thing in taking decisive action.

It led directly to the Helsinki Declaration launched by ICCO under Maxim Behar's presidency, a new gold standard of ethical professionalism around the world. Quite simply, it turned what could have been a crisis point for our industry into a turning point.

As Francis points out, many people deem the Bell Pottinger case to be both an incredible precedent and a milestone in the PR industry. For the first time, there has been an information leak from a PR company trying to use dishonest and subversive means to the benefit of their clients, and the industry reacted in the most honorable way.

The Bell Pottinger affair is certainly going to be a lesson for all, bringing our industry even further down the road of total transparency—a point that goes back to my plain and simple definition of PR as telling the truth so people can understand it.

Ten years ago, my definition of PR had more to do with "telling the truth in such a way that people will like it." Things have changed. It isn't so much about liking any more as it is about understanding, since we are all obliged to tell the truth.

In all those years in the PR business, I have rejected the demands of dozens, maybe even hundreds of clients to send out press releases that may have been inaccurate, or even just a tiny bit too liberal with the truth. I have refused to organize press conferences for people whom I suspected of wishing to misrepresent reality.

At the end of the day, the age of total transparency generated by the social media is only going to make our industry "cleaner," and our role will be reduced to conveying our clients' messages to their own clients in the most creative way possible. Hence my notion of the PR agencies as something like editorial teams.

TRADITIONAL MEDIA: FROM ENDANGERED TO EXTINCT

The perception of PR agencies as editorial teams in the years of social media revolution is all the more relevant given that traditional media are no longer just endangered species, but are actually going extinct.

Back in 1999, in an interview with Bulgarian online media expert Justin Toms, I declared that print newspapers will be gone by 2025.

What followed was a tsunami of indignation on behalf of many press professionals. At least 100 former colleagues and friends of mine called me or wrote me with anger.

"Max, you're going against your livelihood—you started in the press, with the printing press and newspaper ink!" they would rant.

"Don't make fools out of yourselves!" I would reply, insisting on my forecast. This was in 1999, twenty years ago. The upcoming extinction of the press had been clear for a long time, and many people had predicted it back then, so it's nothing to claim credit for. But I think I have been proven right. Why is that?

First of all, the word "newspaper" doesn't really exist anymore, because the first part, "news," is gone from it. What's left is only "paper."

Some PR professionals have been slow to grasp the scope of the paradigm shift brought by the social media revolution in our industry. Many who have grasped it have been slow to keep up-to-date with it.

Many of their colleagues from traditional media, however, have been even slower. They have often been lagging desperately behind.

A case demonstrating that mindset was the 2010 meeting of the International Press Institute in Bratislava, Slovakia. At the meeting, a couple of hundred people, mainly old-school journalists, reporters, editors, and publishers from around the world, mostly from print media, were greeted by the prime minister of Slovakia, Iveta Radičová, who told them that newspapers were never going to die.

Other speakers' most convincing argument was as follows: "I like how the paper feels, I like the smell, I like touching and smelling the newspapers! You can never get that from online media!"

There have been thousands of similar stories of reporters, journalists, publishers, editors, and plain old-fashioned readers desperately clinging to the old, traditional media, especially the press.

And by "press" I don't just mean newspapers, but also the actual printing press. As discussed below, the fate of printed books will be the same as the fate of print newspapers—it is just going to take some more time to go all digital.

The big issue with newspapers is not with the smell, the touch, the feel, or any other sensations—or the lack thereof. If one has a newspaper fetish, they can easily keep several newspaper issues on their nightstand, or when the press finally truly goes extinct, they can have it here just for themselves so that they can smell it, touch it, and feel it as much as they like.

The big issue with newspapers is that there is no one to fund them anymore. Nobody can support them and bear the costs in the new environment of public communications revolutionized by online media and even further by social media.

It's not that the press was or is bad journalism. It's a matter of financing. It has been a long time since newspapers have been able to sustain themselves through sales revenues alone.

The other reason for the demise of the press, as already mentioned, is the fact that "news" is now gone from what once used to be NEWS-papers.

It is hard to possibly fathom why some people are still buying newspapers. Maybe mine is some kind of a professional sickness, but it is really hard for me to read actual newspapers. It's the same thing with printed books. I am unable to read those, either.

The moment they are downloaded to my Kindle, reading is extremely fast and pleasant for me. Printed books are beautiful, they are great to look at on your bookshelf at home, but they, too, are set for extinction.

It is madness for someone to drag a suitcase full of books for their summer beach vacation, or a business trip, instead of just getting the Kindle in their back pocket and downloading 20,000–30,000 books.

Not to mention that the function I most often use and like best on Kindle is to pick quotes and put them in notes. Therefore, when I think of a book that I've read, I just go over the quotes I have selected.

Yet while electronic devices and software have already been beating hard copies for a long time now, in some cases, I find it is better to do without them.

I might be one of the few business presenters in the industry who never uses PowerPoint, Prezi, or other presentation programs for keynote speeches, lectures, etc. I never use visuals.

There is one other person I know who never does that—and I have copied that from him. That is my good old friend, teacher, and mentor Paul Holmes, CEO and founder of the Holmes Report.

There was one single time when I used PowerPoint for a presentation, back in 2009 at the Communication on Top forum in Davos.

I gave my presentation and showed my slides with all of my charts and graphs and short videos. When I sat down, I said to myself, "God, how could I be such an idiot! There are intelligent people from around the world sitting here, and I was showing them slides rather than just speaking to them!"

Whenever you are showing presentation slides, you unwillingly start verbalizing whatever is written on them. "No way, I am not doing that anymore!" I said.

Paul Holmes was the keynote speaker in the same forum. I recently had lunch with him in Casablanca, and I told him, "You know, I got a light bulb idea as I was listening to you back then. I thought, 'God, this person speaks so freely, as if he speaks to students or somebody on the street, while the rest of us are torturing ourselves and the others with slides and long presentations!'"

He replied, "Max, it's also made an impression on me that I have never seen you with a PowerPoint presentation since then."

"Because you set an example for me," I said.

"Oh, I am so happy because that's what happened to me, too. I used PowerPoint once, and then I was ashamed of myself for doing that," he said.

So when I am about to give a speech, I resort to the hand-brain connection. I jot down notes on my notepad, half a page, and when they go through my hand and pen, there seems to be a better link to the memory. Once I do my notes, I don't even need to look at the paper anymore; I just know the sequence of my arguments.

I do use flip charts to demonstrate my ideas, but flip charts also have to do with your own handwriting. Oftentimes in those flip charts, you are coming up with the things on the spur of the moment—you don't have them prepared in advance, as you would in presentation slides.

While thousands of people had been aware that newspapers would go extinct, nobody had really imagined certain disturbing developments in the new media, and more specifically in social media.

This has been a little like the collapse of Communism. In 1989, we were all jubilant, and so was the entire world. In Eastern Europe, we knew nothing about democracy and how culturally and mentally things should fall into their places in a free society. We thought that the great freedom had arrived, and we could do whatever we liked. It turned out to be much more complex than that.

In the same way, when newspapers began to die and social media started its supreme reign, we didn't imagine the risk of fake news. We didn't think that when media is freely in the hands of billions of people, they will do with it as they please. We didn't suspect that social media profiles could be stolen and fake personalities would come up. We didn't know that there would be fake profiles, pretenders, bots, and other ill-minded actors whose only goal would be to carry out some political or business manipulation agenda so they could destroy some company or boost another that didn't have what it takes.

ALWAYS PREPARED: THE LESS-THAN-10-MINUTES RESPONSE RULE

All these things have affected our industry so dramatically that PR experts must be excellently trained and prepared for all kinds of contingencies.

Nowadays, some 60–70 percent of our clients turn to us as PR consultants—and it seems to be exactly the same everywhere in the world—for two main reasons: crisis management and reputation management.

The two often overlap. Not always, though. Sometimes an organization has no reputation whatsoever but strives to become popular and established. Today, that is the easiest thing to do—you create your social media profiles, hire professionals, they start writing about you or on your behalf and work on professionally engaging with the organization's target audience.

PR experts need to be brilliantly trained and prepared. That's not just good sense—there are very concrete and powerful reasons for that.

First, a mere ten years ago, we used to have plenty of time on our hands to solve a crisis. Usually, we used to enjoy almost an entire day to do that.

You'd get up in the morning, grab the newspaper, and see that someone had written something against a client of yours.

You would give your client a call and say, "Well, here is a bad article about you." They would reply, "Come to my office so we can figure out how to handle it."

Then you would go and have lunch with the client. In the afternoon, you would issue a press release. At 5 or 6 p.m., you would meet with reporters to tell them that what had been written was not true, and so on.

We used to have between ten and twelve hours to solve a crisis.

Now we don't even have ten minutes!

The moment a client of ours suffers a blow somewhere, we have to respond immediately. We do that every single day in our office by monitoring social networks, even at 5 a.m. If any of our clients have been affected in any way, we've got to react. If the client has done wrong, we have to apologize on their behalf, quite naturally. If the client has been wronged, we have to disprove whatever false allegations or perceptions there might be about them.

This requires an entirely different mindset, training, and level of preparedness.

It requires an understanding that there is no difference between PR and social media anymore. From the point of view of a top-notch PR expert, they have become one and the same thing.

Many people come to our office and say, "I don't want social media. What I want from you is traditional PR!"

"What do you understand by traditional PR?" we ask.

"Well, more traditional, you know, classical PR!"

You can guess our response.

"There is no such thing anymore, it's all social media now!"

The findings of the 2018 World PR Report by the International Communications Consultancy Organisation (ICCO) demonstrated that beyond any doubt, based on the survey of ICCO's members.

Roughly half of the respondents, 44 percent, said they saw the most growth in 2017 in social media community management. Multimedia content creation and senior counsel remained second and third with 37 percent and 31 percent, respectively.

According to the survey, social media community management scored the highest growth in almost all world regions—Africa, Asia-Pacific, Eastern Europe, Latin America, the Middle East, the UK, and Western Europe. The only exception is North America, where multimedia content creation came in first with social media management being a close second, a result that probably reflects the maturity and certain other specifics of the said market.

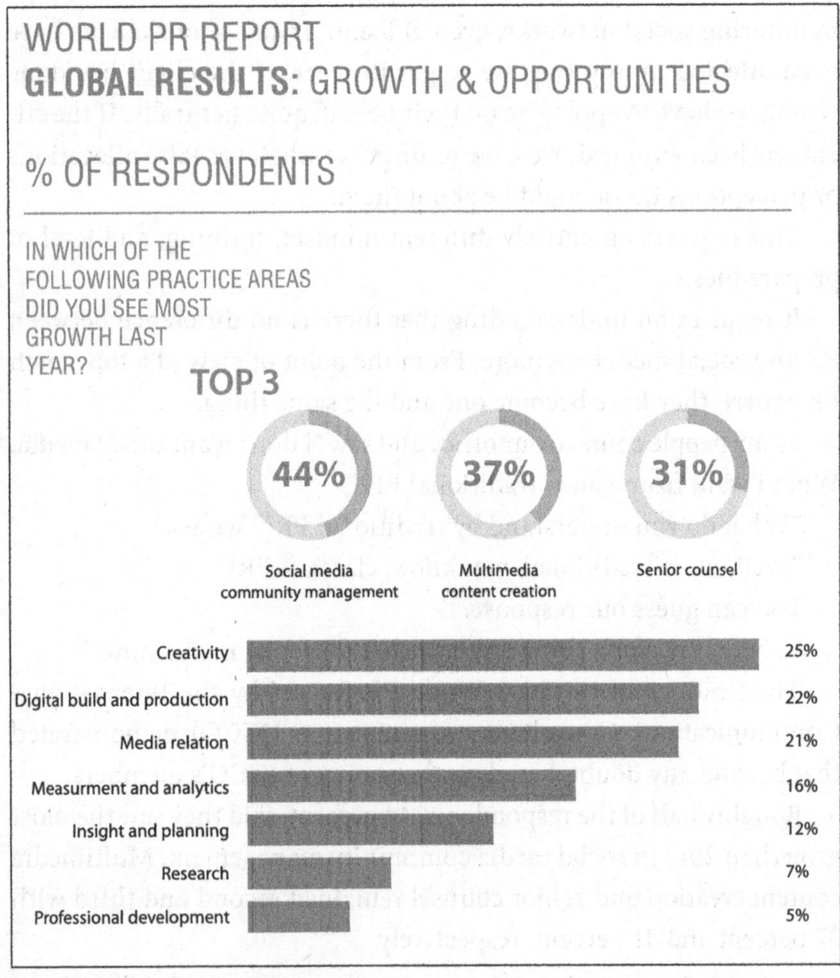

Source: 2018 World PR Report by the International Communications Consultancy Organisation (ICCO).

Social media community management was also the leader, at 43 percent, in terms of the areas with expected increase in investment in 2017. Multimedia content creation and digital build and production again came in second and third, with 41 percent and 35 percent, respectively.

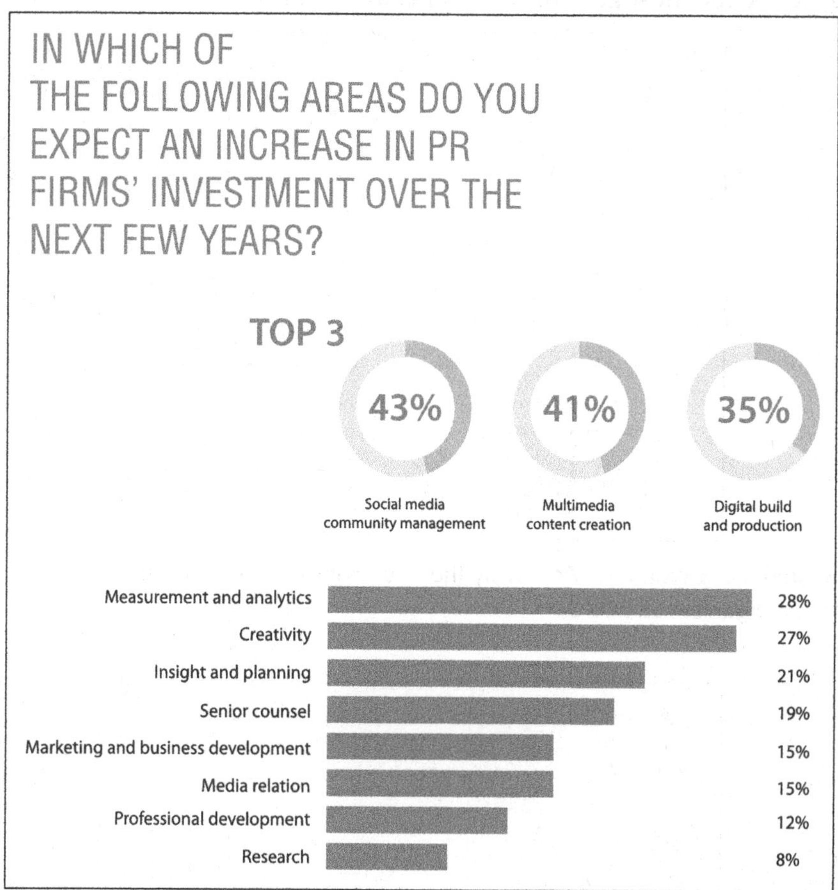

Source: 2018 World PR Report by the International Communications Consultancy Organisation (ICCO).

A good 64 percent of the ICCO members said they saw the most growth in 2016 in digital and online communications from among the other communications functions, and 48 percent of the respondents said they expected that particular communications function to generate the most growth in the upcoming years.

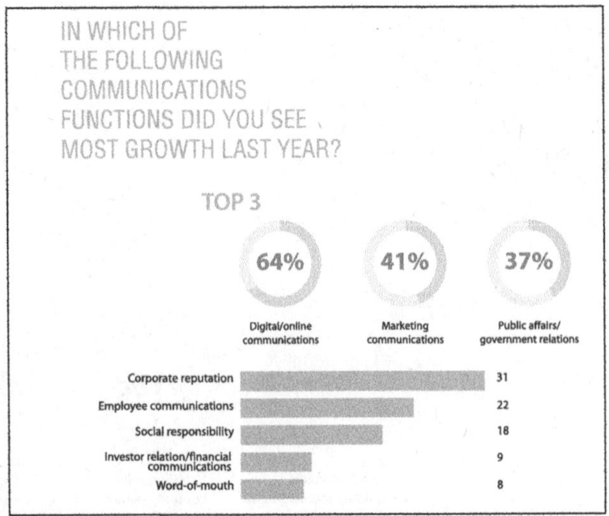

Source: 2018 World PR Report by the International Communications Consultancy Organisation (ICCO).

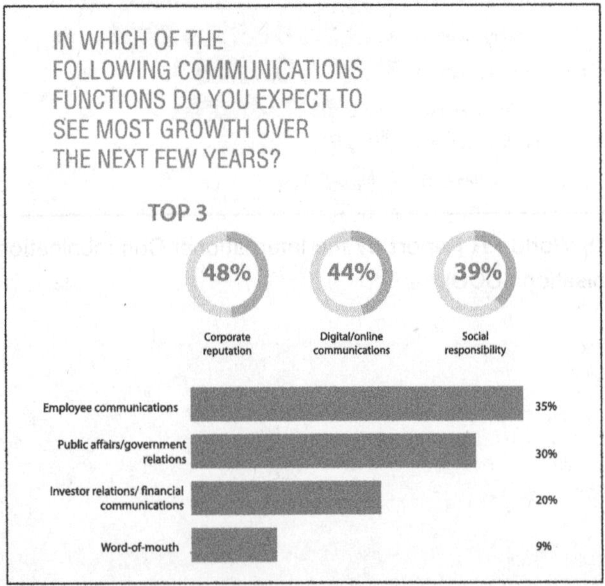

Source: 2018 World PR Report by the International Communications Consultancy Organisation (ICCO).

Social media community management also features prominently on ICCO members' lists when it comes to the skills deemed to be the most relevant for PR executives in the next decade. It shares the top positions with closely related skills crucial for the era of the global PR revolution, namely, crisis counseling, creativity, and multimedia content creation.

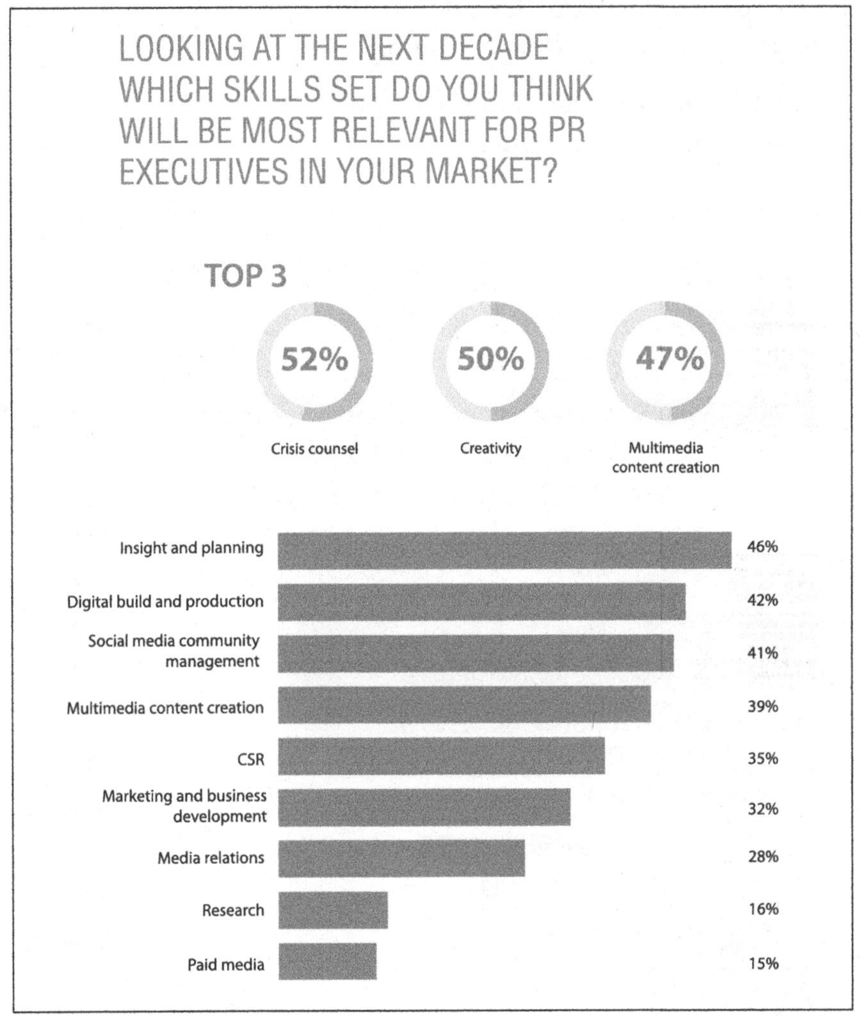

Source: 2018 World PR Report by the International Communications Consultancy Organisation (ICCO).

Social media is one of the top four choices, together with strategic planning, leadership, and written communication, among the skills necessary for a PR organization's success, according to the 2018 Global Communications Report of the USC Annenberg School for Communication and Journalism.

PR professionals believe, in the next five years, the following skills will be necessary for their organization's success:

STRATEGIC PLANNING	89%
LEADERSHIP	84%
WRITTEN COMMUNICATIONS	84%
SOCIAL MEDIA	83%
MULTIMEDIA CONTENT DEVELOPMENT	79%
DATA AND ANALYTICS	78%
CRISIS MANAGEMENT	77%
VERBAL COMMUNICATIONS	75%
EMPLOYEE COMMUNICATIONS	68%
RESEARCH	67%
BUSINESS LITERACY	66%
MEDIA RELATIONS	63%
INFLUENCER MARKETING	62%
ETHICS COUNSELING	52%
REAL-TIME MARKETING	46%
ARTIFICIAL INTELLIGENTCE	35%
SOFTWARE PROGR.	24%
ADVERTISING	21%
MEDIA BUYING	21%

Source: 2018 Global Communications Report of the USC Annenberg School for Communication and Journalism.

According to the 2017 report on "The Evolution of Public Relations" from the US Association of National Advertisers (ANA) and the USC Center for Public Relations at the Annenberg School for Communication and Journalism, expertise in digital and social media is ranked among the top four reasons why organizations work with outside PR agencies, alongside expertise in specific practice areas, strategic insights, and expertise in media relations.

Reasons for Working with Outside Public Relations Agencies

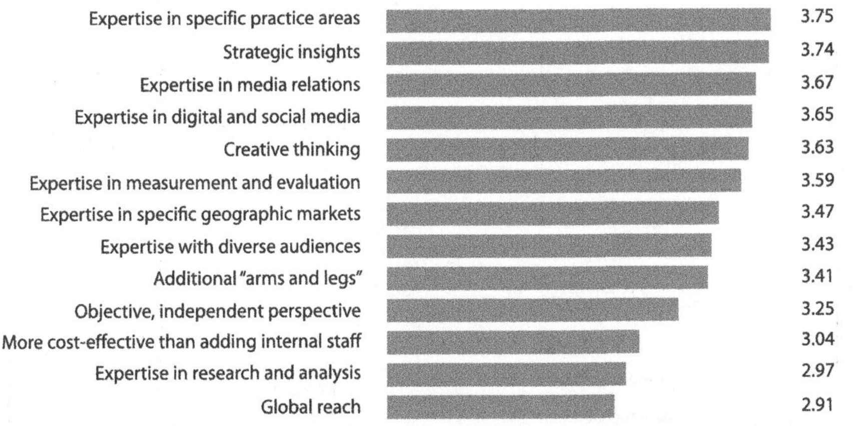

Scale: 5 = Exstremely Important; 4 = Very Important; 3 = Moderately Important; 2= Slightly Important; 1 = Not Important

Q. How important are the following reasons for your organization to work with outside public relations agencies?
Please select an answer ranging from Not Important to Extremely Important.

Source: 2017 Report on the Evolution of PR by the US Association of National Advertisers (ANA) and the USC Center for Public Relations at the Annenberg School for Communication and Journalism.

The bulk of the global PR industry certainly has no illusions about the complexity of the shift brought about by the social media revolution, with digital and new technologies topping the list of the greatest challenges for PR firms.

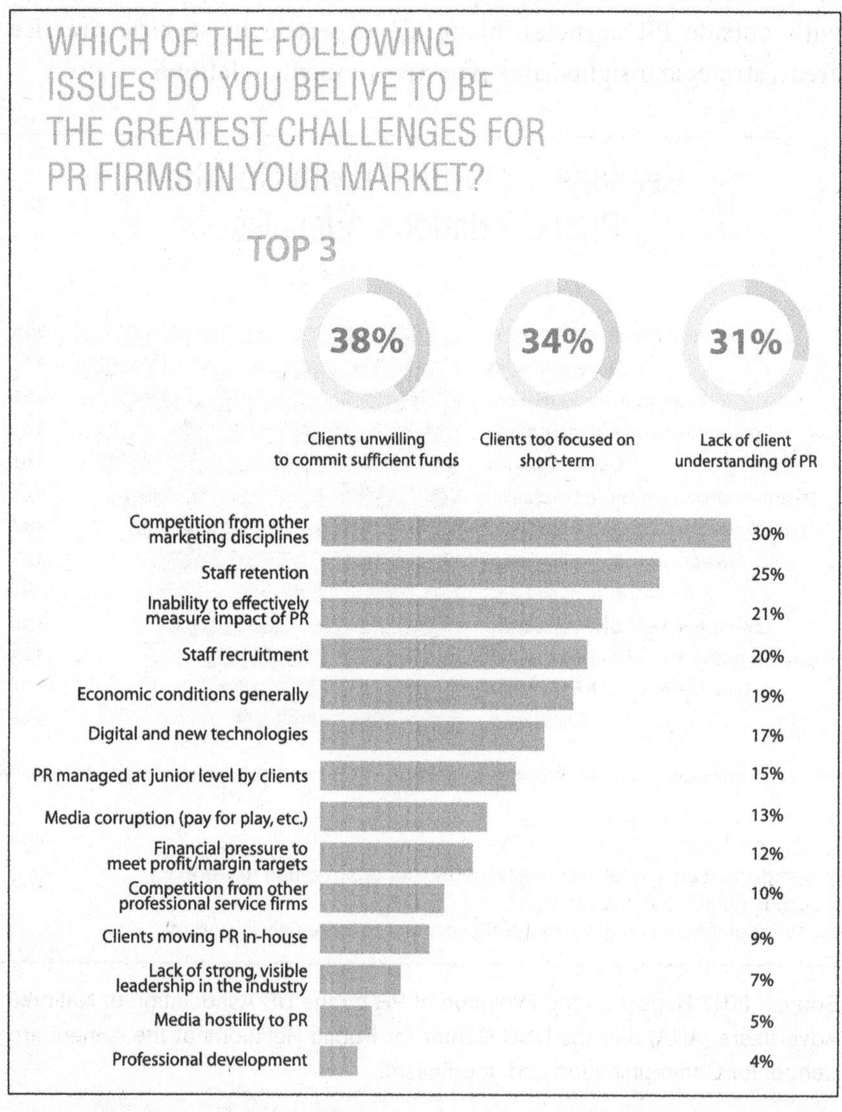

Source: 2018 World PR Report by the International Communications Consultancy Organisation (ICCO).

As the 2018 World PR Report demonstrates, the majority of ICCO members have a keen awareness of both the preeminence of social media and the countless challenges for the industry posed by them.

THE "CREATIVE LIAR" NOTION: BOUND FOR EXTINCTION, TOO

Unfortunately, in many countries, PR as an industry and profession has a negative connotation for the general public.

"This is only PR!" people might say, using the phrase as a euphemism for lying and deception.

Several years ago, I was in a cab in New York City. The driver, an immigrant from the Indian subcontinent, asked me, "What's your job, sir?"

"I am in business," I said.

"What business exactly? What's your job?" he insisted.

"Public relations," I said, yielding.

Then he turned around and said, "Oh, so you are a creative liar!"

This is probably the most accurate expression of the bad connotation of our profession worldwide: a good PR expert is a creative liar.

This perception implies that, on the one hand, you misrepresent the facts, but on the other hand, you do that in the most creative way possible.

If the PR industry suffers from this negative reputation, it is because many people associate our profession with politicians and businesspeople who use various contrivances and tricks to conceal or whitewash their flaws and wrongdoings.

Nevertheless, the perception of the PR expert as a "creative liar" is going to die over the next few years. It will dissolve as a notion in the public mindset, because liars simply cannot exist in modern PR life.

The moment a person lies somewhere (online), ten others are going to show up to expose the lie, wherever it might be, on any social media platform.

Regardless of this forecast, however, we still must take into account the fact that many people used to lack a decent understanding of our profession, and many still do.

FROM "PR" TO ". . . LIVE . . ."

During my two-year mandate as president of ICCO, I toured countries all over the world. In some of them, there were two or three PR associations.

In those cases, a rival association would state, "We do traditional PR, we don't use social media. We do press conferences and all that." The others, their competitors, would declare proudly, "We do social media."

However, in practice, they often happen to do one and the same thing. It is all part of the PR revolution brought by social media.

That is part of the new definition of public relations that has not been invented yet. When it does emerge in a clear-cut fashion, it is going to require—and receive—a new name because the name "PR" categorically isn't going to exist in five or ten years.

"Eighty-seven percent of PR executives believe the term Public Relations won't accurately describe the work they will be doing in five years. About half of them believe PR needs to be more broadly defined, while the rest think the name should be changed," stated the 2017 Global Communications Report of the USC Annenberg School for Communication and Journalism.

Whatever the new name of the industry might be, this book makes the case that it will contain the word "live" in it.

Live communication, *live* contact, and *live* presentation are becoming increasingly dominant in our lives, let alone in our business. So everything that's not "live" is doomed to quickly become already known, obsolete, and boring.

The essence of our industry is to be able to present something to somebody in the most concise form and in the quickest way possible.

Moreover, it must be something that nobody knows. Here once again, we overlap with the journalistic profession and the news industry.

Our instruments of communication have changed, our ways of communication have changed, and, most important, the ownership of media has changed—because now we all own media.

If that's not a revolution, one that has unraveled in just five to ten years, what else might be?

In 5 Years, the Term "Public Relations" Will...

87%

of professionals say that the term "Public Relations" will not describe the work they will do in five years

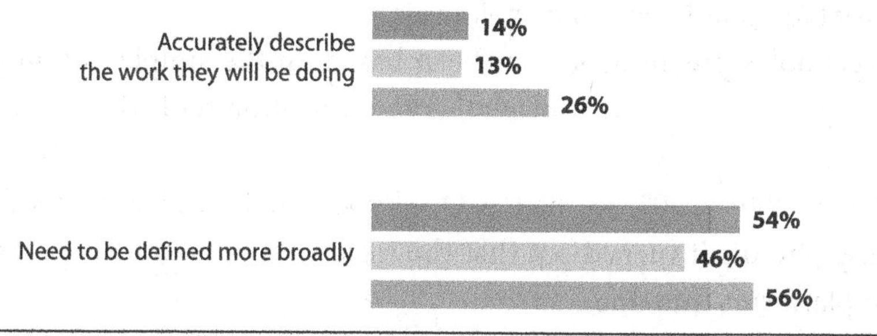

Source: 2017 Global Communications Report of the USC Annenberg School for Communication and Journalism.

The language has changed, as well. Things that we used to say in entire pages in a newspaper now must be said in 140 characters.

My previous book, *Generation F*, published in 2013, tackled the modern-day issue with language.

Eventually, the dominant and maybe even only spoken language will be broken English (yes, we are not all native). That might turn out to be the language all of humanity uses to communicate. It is already rapidly becoming so.

Social media platforms are increasingly consolidating, even though they seem to keep their differing structures and messages. There are several big players, but they don't interfere with one another.

Different social media networks are used for different communication to the extent that the written word still prevails over visuals. However, in the future, it will be other way around.

Facebook continues to be the most popular social media outlet because it is able to combine text and visuals in a great way. Instagram and Pinterest are dominated by visuals, whereas Twitter is still dominated by text.

Twitter's success—not so much in terms of numbers, but in terms of delivering breaking news, brevity, and efficiency—could have been predicted easily years ago precisely because it is based on text.

One hundred and forty characters are telling more than a photo. Nobody has time to read long texts anymore, nor does anyone have time to stare at a photo and guess what is depicted.

Sure, sometimes it is interesting to see a nice image. It helps explain the story. But political messages cannot be sent out through a photo only. And if you want to a promote a product with a photo, it is essential to include text that explains it.

Facebook's preeminence has been based on the simple notion of bringing to one single platform all communication tools that existed before it.

Before 2004–2007, we had ICQ, Skype, email, and websites for posting photos. It turned out that the easiest thing is to merge all of those platforms into one.

Facebook might or might not develop further on from here, but it will indisputably remain the main medium for brand presence for at least a decade, because it provides an opportunity for businesses to reach a vast number of their target audience.

LinkedIn's development has been very interesting as well, yet it is a narrowly targeted medium in which business messages are a lot more textual than visual. This is why it is uncertain whether it will develop beyond its current function as a platform for business contacts.

FROM MEASURING RULERS TO TRULY MEASURABLE

For a modern-day PR expert, it is absolutely essential to know social media platforms in detail: not just because of the tremendous, revolutionary communication tools they provide for our industry, but also because for the first time, our business has become truly measurable. It was never like that before the arrival of social media.

Back in the day, fifteen or twenty years ago, clients would say to us: "We have invested 10,000 dollars with you, Mr. or Mrs. PR Expert. How much would it have cost us if we had purchased advertising space instead?"

We would then pull out a ruler and start measuring. Literally, we operated with rulers. We would measure up the space that the articles about the client occupied in the paper and say, "If this amount of press space had been purchased as an ad, it would have cost you this much."

Of course, this made no sense whatsoever. It was complete nonsense, because an advertisement is viewed in one way, and an editorial text, an article, is perceived totally differently.

Yet the client had no other way of knowing if their money had gone to waste—and had no other way to justify their spending before the governing board of the company.

Even as recently as six or seven years ago, we in the PR industry adopted the so-called Barcelona Declaration, which declares explicitly that comparing PR articles with advertising value is total nonsense.

PR companies have even been banned from doing that by industry organizations and trade bodies. The Bulgarian Association of PR Agencies (BAPRA) has also adopted such a ban, along with many other PR organizations, due to the fact that clients continue to pressure us for such evaluations.

In the pre-social media revolution era, our clients might also say, "Oh, this press article is very nice. How many people have read it?"

"Well," we would reply, "the newspaper has a circulation of 30,000. Four or five people on average read one issue—so 150,000 people have read the article."

This was complete BS as well, because that article might have been at the bottom of page nine, on the left, and you could never prove how many people actually read it, or even if anyone noticed it.

Today, the PR business is 100 percent measurable. You can demonstrate with utmost accuracy who read what, when they read it, what gender they are, what education they have, what country they are from—we have all kinds of data to the smallest detail. That, too, is related to the transparency of our business.

This new world of total transparency and the previously unimaginable abundance of data is the level playing field in which only true PR professionals really stand out based on how they can position a client's messages in the most efficient and beneficial way.

CULTURAL DIFFERENCES OR ENVELOPE JOURNALISM?

My observations from the large number of countries I have toured as president of ICCO have led to the generalization, conditional as it may be, that no more than 25 percent of the communication in a given country is defined by local relations, customs, traditions, etc., and 75 percent of the communication is defined by whether the media are "for sale," that is, if media and journalists can be bribed.

This does not necessarily pertain to countries where the government controls the media, because they can be considered as special cases in that regard.

However, for a large number of countries with free and strong market economies, the question of whether you can buy (i.e., bribe) the media is crucial.

This makes all the difference, because if you can go to some journalist and say, "Here are 1,000 dollars; print this article," that's one type of business.

If you go to some journalist and say, "Here is a great news story that will sell your media, newspaper, TV, radio, or even online media," and then the journalist decides to run the story—that is a whole other thing.

In the second case, you have done real PR, since you have taken the time and put in the effort to creatively formulate the news story and pitch it to the journalist, making it interesting, making it real, and communicating the right messages about your clients.

Of course, there are special cases such as Bulgaria, where for some reason it is forbidden to mention brands in the media, a ban unseen anywhere else in the free world.

Thus, very often you may watch a fifteen-minute report on TV about a certain product without learning what it is.

This restriction has its history. Advertising agencies in Bulgaria, which had a lot of influence in the media, thought that when the government banned the media from mentioning brands in their coverage—for example, Nestlé sweets or Dannon yogurt—the brands would have to come to them and buy advertisements, because otherwise they wouldn't be featured in the media at all.

This has led to all kinds of absurdities. For instance, there were recently TV reports about products containing toxic substances, and the TV stations wouldn't announce the brand that produced it. When asked why, they would say, "It will be construed as advertising."

At the end of the day, the true watershed between different countries and cultures in our business is the so-called envelope journalism: that is, whether journalists and media can be bribed to publish something.

Every country in the world probably has them, and if you pay them, they will run whatever you like. The million-dollar question is how many of those are there in the country where you operate.

Envelope journalism has evolved somewhat by acknowledging the content that was paid for by a third party with a specific symbol or in a specific section—the so-called PR articles, paid supplements, branded business surveys, or sponsored content.

This is the huge difference in various free markets as far as PR's relations with the media are concerned. This topic warrants in-depth research, which is why PR experts from around the world were interviewed for this book and were asked specifically about this.

GLOBAL MERGING: PR ON TOP

One of the most important consequences of the social media revolution appears to be a future gigantic merger of the three main parts of the communications industry—public relations, advertising, and digital communications—which is already under way.

Since this merger began, there has been a tough competition over which one of the three will emerge as the leader of the future merged industry: advertising, PR, or digital companies.

"Without us, you are lost. We have the media shops, we own the media, we stack up the large budgets, we direct the media," advertising agencies would argue.

That is indeed the case in many countries. The advertising agencies' rationale would go, "Whatever we tell the media, and especially TV channels, that's what they'll do, because otherwise they will be losing millions of dollars from lack of advertising at the end of the month."

The digital industry, which is getting more influential and more specialized by the minute, also claims supremacy: "We will be managing this future merged industry because you can't cope without us—you can't do anything without digital communications, without people to write your programs and apps and feed you various interesting software solutions."

Each of the three parties might have its arguments, but it is my strong conviction that the PR business will emerge on top in this future merger of the three industries.

Regardless of what is done in the wider communications industry, PR will always be linked to content creation. And that content remains textual, first and foremost.

Of course, a large share of the content is visual, and that is why more and more agencies around the world do hire people who deal with social media, but also with graphic design and web design. Visuals are becoming an inseparable part of our work as PR experts.

Yet at the end of the day, we, the PR experts, are the people who manage content. We are the masters of content, whether it's textual or visual.

Second, clients are increasingly coming to us for the two reasons I already mentioned: crisis management and reputation management.

These are matters that no advertising agency and no digital communications company can handle.

If there were no social media, our industry would have remained exactly the same as before, because we would be working entirely with traditional media, and we would have the exact same business share as ten, twenty, or even a hundred years ago.

However, social media is here, it is in full swing, and it is omnipotent. As a result, the industry is entirely different now. The revolution is ongoing, this is the first and only true PR revolution so far, and it is perplexingly gigantic.

CHAPTER 2

INTO THE REVOLUTION

HOW I GOT INTO THE PR BUSINESS

When I entered the PR business back in the mid-1990s, the most logical thing to do when one parted with journalism was to take up a profession that had something to do with the press.

The most obvious choice was advertising—everybody was starting up advertising agencies. It somehow made the most sense when I decided to quit journalism. The quote from Churchill (or whoever might have said it) certainly applied to me when I quit journalism.

I got home one night and said, "I am done with journalism, I am starting up an ad agency." Back then, everything was about advertising, but I had no idea how and where to begin.

I went to the American Cultural Institute in Sofia, which back then was the only source of relevant information. There was no Google. The internet existed, but accessing it was hard, with dial-up modems and MS-DOS computers.

Long after I had started my business, we still had just one telephone line in the office, which we used for both phone conversations and checking email via dial-up.

One day, I was in the office. Someone else was on the phone, but I wanted to check my email. "Give me a line, give me a line!" I shouted.

A young intern came to me and handed me a string.

"What the heck is that for?" I asked, astonished.

"You were shouting you wanted 'a line'!" she replied, even more so.

That was the level of communication we had to deal with back in those days.

It was totally normal for me to try out advertising, although back then, advertising everywhere in Eastern Europe, not just in Bulgaria, often boiled down to making branded souvenirs—pens, business cards, forms, calendars, etc.

My first order was for a large number of calendars for some Lebanese businessmen I had met at an event at the Sheraton. They asked me what I did, and I said I had an ad agency.

"That's awesome, we need an ad agency to make the annual calendars." And they ordered 2,000 calendars. This was back when we had no money.

We designed them, printed them, and I loaded them in my car and took them to the client. As soon as I delivered them, they said, "There is a mistake!" There was a spelling mistake.

So I loaded the calendars back in my car, and instead of making $2,000, I lost $5,000.

Every successful businessman has experienced such events in their career.

One day, Peter van Gompel, a friend of mine and food-and-beverage manager of Sheraton Sofia, called me: "Max, there is an American guy here who has rented the entire presidential apartment as his office and wants me to find him an advertising agency that can print out his business cards."

I went there, and the guy first ordered business cards, then brochures, then leaflets. Then he called me one day and asked, "Max, do you know what PR is?"

He was from the largest American oil company at the time, Amoco Corporation (originally Standard Oil). They had decided to try to make a breakthrough in Eastern Europe. They tested out Poland, they tested out Russia, and they also tested out Bulgaria, since they wanted to split the European market with British Petroleum. Later, BP bought them and remained in Europe, and Amoco remained in the US.

But back when I was starting up my business, all that mattered was that Amoco was trying to make a breakthrough in Eastern Europe.

So this guy called me one day and asked me if I knew what PR was.

"I do," I said.

It was the time when we couldn't afford to say "No." It is the same in our company today—whatever you are asked by a client, you say "Yes," and you find a way to do it. If you are asked if you can bring five watermelons from the marketplace, you say, "Sure, that will cost ten dollars," for example.

If anybody shows up at our door and asks, "Can you make some business cards for me?" we will do it even though we will probably make only twenty cents. But we will start a new partnership with future potential. So there is never a "No" with our company.

So I told that guy I knew what PR was.

"I have here a man from Chicago [where Amoco was based]. We are looking for a PR agency. Are you OK to participate in a tender?"

"Sure," I said. We met, and this man from Chicago asked, "Can you give me an overview of the Bulgarian press?"

For me, that was a piece of cake. I went back to my tiny office, bought all the newspapers from the kiosk across the street, brought all the papers to him, and gave him an overview.

"I am very impressed!" he said.

"What is this guy impressed about?" I thought, because for me that was nothing.

Then the same guy from Amoco, Jim Shields, called me and said, "We need to sign a contract." I replied that was not a problem. However, that contract turned out to be 120 pages.

"I need to sit down and read it through," I said. For all the business card orders, we had been signing one- or two-page contracts.

"Max, don't read it, you won't understand it anyway," he told me.

"Why do we need this contract?" I asked.

"Because you've won our tender for a PR agency!"

My reaction was utter astonishment. "Jim, you are kidding! I have a small office with a kitchen, how is that possible? Are you telling me that you have declined offers from big firms with luxury marble-plastered offices?"

"That's the thing, Max. We've decided that not only are you qualified for the job, but the money that we are going to pay for you won't go to glossy offices and luxury cars but will help you develop, it will help you do good things!"

That's how we started working with Amoco Corporation.

But before that happened, when I was submitting my bid for Amoco's tender, we were required to submit a PR strategy.

I opened a huge book titled *Contemporary Advertising* that I had bought from the American Cultural Center in Sofia. I still have it. It was the only relevant book that I could find.

And it was all about advertising. Only at the end of the book were there some three or four pages on PR. I absorbed them, reading all night to draft this strategy. I was alone at the office and had no employees back then.

After I had read the book's tiny section on public relations, I exclaimed to myself, "Such an industry cannot exist in Bulgaria!"

That may have been my first definition of PR: "An industry that cannot exist in Bulgaria."

That was how I entered the PR business with Amoco. Then came other clients such as Microsoft, Cisco, Dannon, TNT Worldwide, and many others.

Throughout all those years, we have been working with our clients in the exact same way.

What really gave my PR career a boost was a month-long trip to the United States in 2000 that was organized by USAID, the US development agency.

They no longer operate in Bulgaria, but back then, they were very active in the country. They offered to help with my training if I could cover my transportation expenses. My accommodation was covered by local convention centers. They drafted a very busy program for me. That was when I went for the first time to Hill & Knowlton, Manning Selvage & Lee, Burson-Marsteller. I toured about twenty cities in the States within a month. That was when I understood what PR really is.

In Los Angeles, they had set up a meeting for me with the PR director for the actress Jane Fonda. We had lunch in a beach restaurant in Santa Monica.

"Do you have any problems in your business?" he asked me.

"Nothing major. Although I do have one issue."

"What is that?"

"Every single client wants to work with me. They don't want to work with my employees, but only with me personally." I said.

"That's not a problem, forget about it! That's not a problem! That's your job!" he told me.

This was a real wake-up call for me, because all of a sudden I came to realize that this is a consultancy business.

It's not like any other business in which only your employees are working for you and you just stay there and get the credit for it. Even today, a CEO would say, "I have twenty people working for me," or "I have a hundred people working for me!" That has never been our concept at M3 Communications Group, Inc.

One day in 2003, we were organizing the visit of the Belgian King Albert II to Bulgaria. I met one of his closest advisers, coming to a so-called "advance mission" at the airport, and then we both came to my office to meet the team responsible for the organization of His Majesty's visit. The adviser went all over the rooms, then we sat in the conference room, where he took a cup of coffee, smelled it, and asked, "Max, how many people work here?"

"About forty-five," I replied. That was how many people we had on staff back then.

"And you work for all of them?" he asked.

These words took me further down the road Jane Fonda's PR expert had set me on with the truth that he shared with me.

I did and do work for all of them, because this is a consultancy business, and when you are not around, things don't flow as smoothly.

That seems to be the reason a huge number of the global consultancy agencies bear the names of their founders. That's the case with Hill+Knowlton Strategies, Burson-Marsteller, Edelman, Cohn & Wolfe, Ogilvy, Young & Rubicam, and many others. Based on the genesis of this business, it is understood that those were the founders and managers of these companies, who generate business. M3 Communications Group's name has a similar origin, but it is not directly called "Behar," because Bulgaria doesn't have that kind of tradition.

The comment by Jane Fonda's PR Director in LA was the real eye-opener for me. Following my meeting with the king's adviser, I said to myself that I should not be relying on having many people at the office working for me. Rather, I should be the face of the company and the person who generated the ideas.

After I came back from my trip to the US, I picked up some flip charts, brought my staff together, and told them what I had seen. I also told them what I wanted my business to be like, and that is exactly what my business is today in 2017–2018.

In 2000, I went to Japan for a one-month training at a Japanese university, Yokohama Kenshu Center. There, I also learned a great deal in terms of different ways of thinking and modes of communication. This chemistry between what I saw in the United States and the meetings I had there and what I had learned in Japan is what actually helped me create the present-day M3 Communications Group, Inc.

We began as an advertising firm, but we ran away from advertising, although in small markets such as Bulgaria there are still many PR agencies today whose turnover is made up primarily of advertising revenue. That's true even in countries such as France and Germany, though not in the US and the UK.

I decided not to work in advertising for a number of reasons. One main one was that I could never be a strong competitor to the large advertising corporations—back in the 1990s, they were entering all emerging markets, including Bulgaria.

After my trip to the US and my meetings there, I got my famous email signed by Martin Sorrell, mentioned in the introduction of this book.

"Max, I've heard about your successful business in Bulgaria—if you want, it might be very helpful that you meet or contact Howard Paster, and we can see if we can cooperate." Howard Paster was the former President of Hill & Knowlton; he passed away in 2011.

We began working with Hill & Knowlton after I met Terence Billing, the most experienced, resourceful, and unconventional PR expert that I have ever met. My first teacher and mentor in the PR business, who later became my closest family friend.

He started at 9 a.m. in the morning with a bottle of white wine and a soda and could go on like that all day.

I went to our meeting in Frankfurt, Germany, in the Hessischer Hof Grand Hotel. Hill & Knowlton was the first American PR consultancy that went to Europe after World War II, and this was where their office was based at first. It occupied the entire first floor. Since then, everyone from Hill & Knowlton who's visiting Frankfurt stays there.

Unfortunately, Terence Billing passed away in 2012—I checked into the same hotel and went to the hospital to be with him during his last night on Planet Earth.

But back when I met Terence Billing on a dramatic Sunday in 2000, I was dressed as a Russian nouveau riche—a formal suit and a tie in the middle of a hot August afternoon, wearing a diplomatic bag, with a bottle of Mavrud red wine and a brochure of M3 Communications.

Then a man came in a Hawaiian shirt and shorts, with long hair like an old-school rock star, and asked at the reception for me. When they pointed at me, he said, "You are Max Behar? My name is Terence Billing. Go back to your room, put your jeans and T-shirt on, and come back please!"

I thought, "Is he some kind of an idiot?" I put on my jeans and went back downstairs. He had already finished half a bottle of wine. And he said, "You know, Max, I like you. We won't talk about business. Tomorrow morning you will come to my office, you will see the contract, next week I will come to Sofia, we will sign the contract. We won't talk about the contract. I like you, and I will work with you."

Terence Billing was one of the people who totally changed everything for me and made me part of the real business—the real PR business.

PR: DEFINING DEFINITIONS

From Wikipedia to Britannica, all the way to *PR for Dummies* and thousands of other online journalistic and academic articles, books, and encyclopedia entries—all of those sources feature some excessively long and horrendously convoluted definitions of PR.

Those definitions mean next to nothing in practical business terms.

Furthermore, the paradigm of the mainstream definitions of PR has barely shifted in decades. All the definitions you'll find have to do with creating corporate relations between the business and the media, regulating or managing the audiences, blah-blah-blah.

Having had my fair share of struggling with dry, tangled textbook definitions back when I entered the industry, one day I just said, "That's absurd! I can never make it in this business if I believe in such definitions only because they are given by academics. Those definitions are stiff and do not really say anything!"

My employees would keep pestering me, "What is PR? What is PR?" Back then, very few people knew what PR was.

My first definition of PR was that PR is the industry of news creation or good news-making.

Going back to the classic distinction between advertising and PR—namely, that advertising buys media, whereas PR earns media—we simply had to win media attention with something.

At that time media outlets were hungry for news, and we were supposed to create interesting news about the clients that we were representing in all sorts of industries.

The classic definition of PR that you will find in Wikipedia, Britannica, etc., does make one practical point: PR is about generating free coverage in the media.

Of course, the PR services are not free for the client. But, yes, you are not supposed to pay (i.e., bribe) the media to do your job.

In my work as a PR expert so far, there has never been a case in which we have paid even a single cent for that. Not on our behalf, and not on behalf of any of our clients.

As already noted, the only legitimate way for a PR representative to pay media would be if you purchase content that is clearly marked as paid or sponsored.

There are paid articles and pages in all large international newspapers, but they are clearly marked as such so the reader would be aware of that. They are sometimes called advertising surveys, industry surveys, or country surveys. Every newspaper, especially the most influential ones such as *The Wall Street Journal*, *The Sueddeutsche Zeitung*, and the *Financial Times*, makes its readers aware that specific content is advertorial and it has been paid to be published.

Since I had spent twenty years as a journalist, and I could never imagine taking even a single cent as a bribe in order to publish something, that has always been completely off the table. That was my starting point in contemplating how to win over the media as part of my PR business.

"What is the thing that will spark media interest? What will bring them to us? What do the media outlets want?" I wondered, answering myself immediately: "News, of course! What should we be doing, then? We should be producing news! We should be creating interesting news and writing press releases, sending out messages, and so on." Of course, back then there were barely any online media.

To this very day, we are trying to produce news. The difference between today and back then is gigantic, because today you have media in your own hands. You can do as you please with it, you can write anything you want. You can get paid by somebody to publish something. You can literally do as you please.

But back then, you really had to grab a reporter's interest, and to do that, you had to provide them with a real news story.

My vision of PR as news-making caused some major clashes with our clients back then—and still does in a certain way.

"Sorry, Max, but we have corporate PR materials that we send out everywhere in the world!" our clients would say.

"Your corporate PR materials are no good for Bulgaria!" I would reply. "They are dull, too general, and don't say anything, they don't communicate anything interesting."

Moreover, journalism has an entirely different approach to stories like that, which is why I have always told my clients, "If you want good PR, you should know it's like writing an interesting article, nothing more. However, that article needs to have an attention-grabbing title, a cool first sentence, etc."

"What is our definition of PR going to be? Our definition of PR will be: 'we make interesting news,'" I said.

If you produce interesting news stories, that means that all those "managing relations of the public and organizations, blah-blah-blah" that you find in formal definitions of PR can be forgotten.

Not to mention that if you meet someone in the street today, in 2019, and they ask you what PR is, and you answer with one of those definitions you'll find in a Google search, they will think that you've gone crazy. They will say, "OK, but what do you do? What is your job?"

It would have been like that back when Tatyana Vaksberg, a Bulgarian journalist who edited my first book, met her neighbor, an elderly lady. The neighbor asked her, "Where do you work now?"

"In 'Free Europe!'" she replied.

"Yes, but where do you work?" the neighbor kept asking.

The same would happen if you tell somebody one of those formal definitions of PR; they'd probably just reply, "OK, but what do you do?"

The 2017 Global Communications Report of the USC Annenberg School for Communication and Journalism concluded that "not-yet-jaded students are far more comfortable with the current terminology

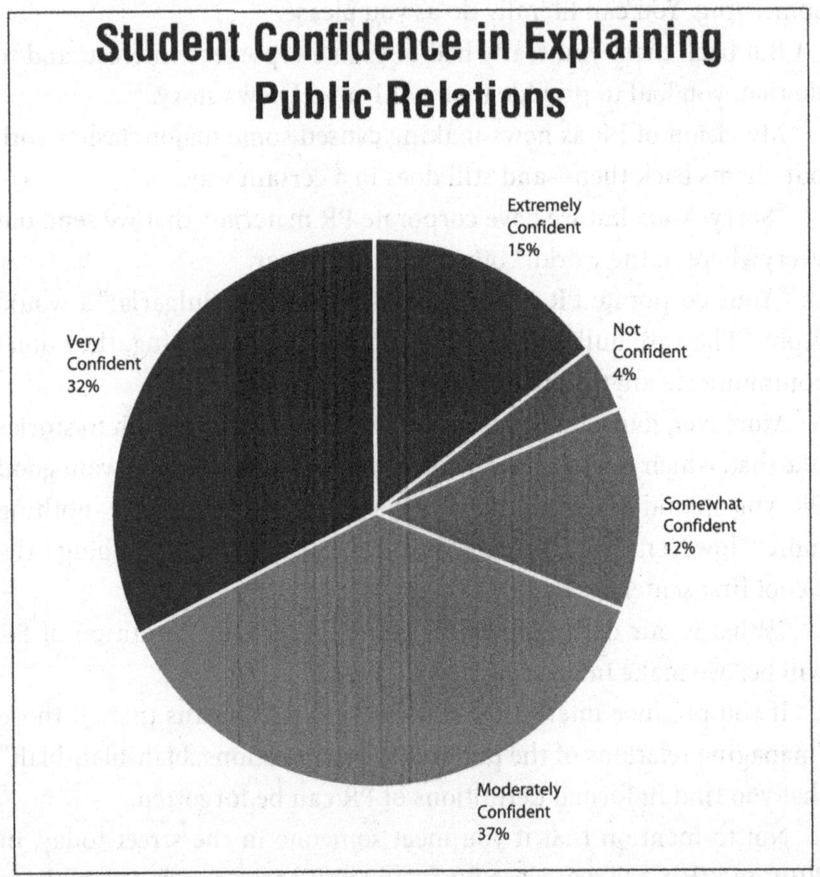

Source: 2017 Global Communications Report of the USC Annenberg School for Communication and Journalism.

than seasoned pros. Fewer than 20 percent think the name [of PR] needs to be changed and most are pretty comfortable explaining it."

Whether the self-perception of students reflects truthfully their ability to explain PR can hardly be determined.

To this day, I keep telling my colleagues that if they meet somebody in the street, they should be able to explain to people in a way they would be understood.

That's the way you should be writing a news release, a social media status, or any message anywhere. You should be able to create content in the language of your target audience.

That's why oftentimes when I discuss our work with my colleagues in the office, especially on Mondays, and I read some text, I ask, "What do you see on your laptop screen?"

You are forbidden from seeing the text, you cannot be seeing only the text. On your screen, you should be seeing the reader. The person you are writing to. The journalists? OK, you've got three friends who are journalists, you should be seeing their faces on the screen. Want to write to the buyers of watches, or smartphones, or yogurt? Then you should be seeing them. These people, these consumers, the people you want to be talking to must be visualized in some way inside your head.

That was how we began with news-making, since I was starting a new business in a country where people had no idea of the industry. Like everyone else who started fresh, everything we did was self-made. We are self-made today. We didn't have those traditions and that heritage many other countries have had, so we could creatively do what we believe is right, and we could discover new things.

It is my strong conviction that the rule that PR is good news production and good news writing is applicable absolutely anywhere.

Subsequently, of course, my definition of PR has evolved, first from just writing news to writing quality news, accompanied by the proper background information.

After that, it expanded to putting effort into maintaining good communication with the media, mainly print, because there was no social media back then—or at least in Bulgaria, it was not dominant at the time. Whatever one might have said on TV, that would come and go. The press reigned supreme.

We attracted more and more clients who became more and more demanding up until the point when I formulated my current definition of PR: Telling the truth in a way that people understand.

Ten years ago, my definition was more like "Telling the truth so that people would like it." But it isn't so much about liking anymore as it is about understanding, because we are all obliged to tell the truth.

Explaining things so that people would understand them. That's it. Because in social media, everybody nowadays is bombarded with information, not to mention all the fake news, all the different languages. Users are becoming very selective about the content they receive and pay attention to.

Sometimes even we, as PR experts, might get confused with the number of messages we wish to convey on behalf of our clients. Since we already own media, we should be presenting the news in such a way that people will understand.

Of course, the news has got to be interesting, but first and foremost, it has to be comprehensible.

STANDING OUT IN NEWS CREATION

If PR is the creation of news and telling the truth so that it can be understood, what makes the PR industry, revolutionized by social media, stand out among so many other sources of news—the lingering traditional media, mainstream news, alternative online media, and billions of social media users?

In my business, we are trying to produce news more creatively, directly, and as a third party—as though we are not involved in the news-making. We already have this opportunity.

PR also indisputably stands out among other communications businesses because it cannot afford to produce fake news.

Why? Because the moment we release even a single word of fake news, not even an entire article, our brand will be shattered, no journalist will ever pay attention again, and no client will come to work with us.

PR must be responsible for the accuracy and precision of the news it produces, while simultaneously being very creative and fast.

Speed is of the utmost essence; it is one of the crucial ten words in PR revolution that this book puts forth.

We have to be super-, even hyperfast. If a client stumbles upon a problem, we must be the one who communicates it, not end consumers.

Conversely, if our clients have some interesting or great news to share, that too needs to be communicated by us, not by other people who may have somehow learned about it.

What should truly be setting PR apart from everybody else in news-making—and it does so—is creativity and the diligence to make every news story comprehensible, detailed, and well explained.

PR's responsibility is enormous.

On the one hand, we are responsible for company and brand owners; and on the other hand, we are responsible for our clients and answer directly to them. Imagine sending out fake or inaccurate news about Microsoft, or BMW, or Mercedes—it is truly unimaginable, because the reputation costs for a client like that would be staggering.

MEDIA'S WOES AND PR'S "BLAME"

In the social media era, PR routinely gets blamed for hurting (traditional) journalism, marginalizing it, or even wrongly conquering it.

However, PR is hardly the culprit here. If one assumes it makes any sense to "blame" anybody about that, it should be social media and the profound changes it has caused in the overall communications industry. If PR had been the culprit, it would have been able to capture the media and journalism long ago. It wasn't able to do that, because it owned no media back before the advent of social media.

Today, citizen journalism really means something—journalism is everybody's job now, not just the job of the people who went to journalism school, have press cards, or show up on TV.

So if PR could be accused of destroying traditional journalism, the same should apply to the taxi driver with the secondhand laptop expressing his opinion on Facebook, or a lady who complains she was sold a faulty item at the mall, or some kid who witnessed a traffic accident and says that the police didn't come on time.

That is why social media is the source of a true revolution in PR and well beyond it—everything begins and ends with it.

Yes, we PR experts are making good use of social media platforms and will continue to do so—first, because we are the people who deal with content, and second, because we offer services through social media. We make money out of that. That is a legitimate way of putting it, and it all stems from the fact that out of the blue we ended up with media in our hands, just like everybody else.

The fourth or fifth employee I hired at M3 Communications Group back in the early days was a web developer.

"That is a different kind of business!" many people told me back then.

"How is it a different type of business?" I argued. "If you have a website, you have a platform to express yourself, you have a media outlet."

Back then, nobody believed that. During all my trips to the West, in the US, I would say that your own website is a medium.

"Well, it is a medium to the extent that it presents your company, nothing more," I would hear in return.

Nonetheless, websites evolved—they developed forums and blogs and ended up on social media platforms, which boast the power of interactivity, the overwhelming influence of citizen journalism, and the outstanding connectivity of the world.

PR hasn't hurt journalism. There have been many factors to that—and journalism itself, for that matter. Traditional media failed to respond to the change and adjust their language style to make it more understandable and closer to the language of online and social media.

Yes, there are still print media today. Of course, they are not going to last, that's more than obvious. But even if there are print media still lingering in the world, readers still spend 90 percent of their time reading online media. They get used to this language style of online media, and reading the surviving printed press becomes harder and harder for them.

It is hard to even read well-established newspapers and magazines such as the *Financial Times* or *The Economist,* because we are already used to consuming them differently—online. This is true of several generations already.

At the end of the day, print media have been doomed for a long time now, not because they are bad, but simply because they cannot survive competition in the market.

PR, NOT PROPAGANDA

Since before the advent of social media, PR has also been accused of being involved in corporate or political propaganda. The very term "PR" has sometimes been equated with propaganda and manipulation of the public.

Yet, actual professional PR was never conceived as a propaganda tool!

Delivering precise, interesting, real, and comprehensible news cannot be seen as propaganda. The goal of propaganda is completely different: to manipulate.

Propaganda means being able to lie in a way that deceives people to believe everything one says. Propaganda has always been closely linked to politics.

We don't engage in political PR. Nowadays, maybe politics is a kind of propaganda, with or without the PR.

Several years ago, my good friend, two-term Nevada governor Bob Miller, was a guest on Bulgaria's most popular talk show, where he was asked how he managed to win so many elections.

"I promised a lot," he replied. "In politics, there is no way around it. You promise, you win; you don't promise, you don't win," he said.

Politicians' promises are a type of propaganda in a certain sense. Political PR has always been dependent on the country itself—if you compare a country in North America with Eastern Europe, or in East Asia with Latin America, the differences are mind-boggling.

Corporate PR is different. It has much more in common around the world, because it presents a product or a service and, moreover, because there is a common and established business etiquette.

Sure, there are national and regional specifics, there are differences in how different cultures perceive certain products or services, but at the end of the day, consumers who use smartphones, for example, see them in the same way—like smartphones. It's not like left and right on the political spectrum, meaning different things in different places to different people.

One more reason why we do not get involved in political PR is that there are no politics anymore. Ideologies are gone, politics are gone.

PR is not propaganda and should have nothing to do with it—all the more so today, when people have access to hundreds of thousands of sources to verify what a politician is saying and form their own opinions.

You tell someone that a product is superb. They go to YouTube and find out that ninety out of a hundred comments about the product are negative. How can that product be superb then? What kind of "PR propaganda" can you use in order to convince them?

A few years ago, I was at the office of Hill+Knowlton Strategies in Brussels, and their manager told me, "Max, my colleagues have heard a lot about you; they want to meet up with you."

We met at a dining hall; about one hundred people showed up. I started talking about social media, how lobbyism is dead and that it is outdated.

People used to meet in lobbies of hotels when there were no valid arguments to be set on the "public" table and try to convince one another on matters concerning legislation and regulation.

However, today there is plenty of information—and all those people who meet in lobbies and restaurants and apartments are involved in corruption. That's not lobbying anymore—they meet in order to get some extra money.

In principle, lobbying has always been borderline, and you never know whether you are on the right or on the wrong side of the law. You always tread on the edge.

After that talk in Brussels, I had lunch with their manager.

"You colleagues seem rather depressed," I said.

"Max, in Brussels these people deal only with lobbying, and you talked to them for an hour about how lobbying was dying."

"God, he is totally right!" I thought. Because there are thousands of lobbying firms in Brussels, the capital of the EU, and each one is trying to overtake the others in terms of more efficient contacts and accomplishing results for their clients.

Thank God they're obliged to disclose their revenues and their clients. This should be the rule anywhere in the world when it comes to lobbyists.

PR emerged out of the necessity to explain a small part of backstage political and business relations to the public. Back then, all decisions were made behind closed doors. Everything happened in studies and lobbies. Those backstage-era politicians would think, "We have to say something to our voters. How should we go about doing that? Let's call James Taylor, a journalist from the *Pennsylvania Herald*, because we read his pieces and he knows how to write. Let's ask him to write an article for us, to explain that."

While initially everything revolved around the government relations, businesspeople gradually became aware of the necessity to be present in the public eye, not just through advertising. After all, America is the birthplace of advertising, and everything back then happened through advertising.

When the market got saturated with advertising, some businessman figured, "If that journalist writes an article about me, it will matter a lot more than advertising, plus I won't have to pay anything. But how can I get that journalist to write that article? I need an expert to advise me on that."

People who may have been involved in government propaganda may have advised such businesses one hundred years ago, but who knows?

What would be discrediting is if today somebody wrote something deceitful. That's hardly possible, though, because if anyone wrote something deceitful on behalf of a business or a PR company, he or she would be devastated.

Nowadays, it's just impossible not to react immediately. Otherwise, you risk an avalanche coming your way, as in the case of BP's *Deepwater Horizon* oil spill in the Gulf of Mexico, the United Airlines dragging incident, or the already discussed Bell Pottinger affair. Of course, those are extreme cases, but Facebook and YouTube are filled with examples in which companies do not respond on time, or do not respond at all, or are not prepared to react adequately. What are the results? They are simply destroyed.

That is why the social media revolution in PR is the time to put a definitive end to this perception of public relations as a potential propaganda tool, even if there is 1 percent of the public that still believes that.

The possibility that someone would give you false information is already almost in the past, due to the rise of the consumer power and the fact that companies, politicians, and public figures are constantly being "watched," and not only online.

If you claim that a type of pen is the best in the world because its ink can never be erased, some ten years ago people would have believed you. Reporters would tail you and then write, "Finally, a pen with completely impossible-to-erase ink has been invented." Now, the moment you pull something like that, someone somewhere will erase that ink and start writing . . . against you.

Another example is Volkswagen and their greenhouse gas emissions. Every single day, there are probably at least five companies in the world that go bankrupt because they have deceived their target audience and somebody exposed them.

This is why corporate propaganda is virtually impossible today. You can still use propaganda if you are a politician and promise things. Yet, once the current political system collapses—which won't be that far ahead into the future—then even politicians won't be able to lie, because they won't have four-year terms.

Why not hold direct elections of government officials on social media? Just an example: why not elect the secretary of energy in a competition of different candidates who lay out their platforms on social media? Sure, the prime minister or president is entitled to make their pick and choose the person they are most comfortable with, but why don't they pick the person who is assessed by the public on social media as having the best or most promising platform? Just as a board member is elected by shareholders, not by the chairperson of the board. The chairperson of the board is elected from among the board members. While critics would argue that nations are not corporations, the fact of the matter is that every nation's primary goal should be to generate profits so its citizens can lead better lives. The key word in politics in the near future is going to be "pragmatism"—every politician will seek to win elections with promises, and then to fulfill those promises. Theoretically, choosing officials could happen on social media: they promise five things, a public contract with the voters who support them, and if they fail to achieve them in six months, they are gone.

Such developments would, of course, make life far easier for the PR industry, because one of its difficulties has been to deal with old-school-type politicians. The changes would lead more businesspeople to the world of politics, and that would be very positive because they would need actual efficient PR experts, not just somebody to get paid and do nothing.

Politicians today have four years to find excuses and justifications, whereas a chairman of a board of directors in a large corporation listed on the stock exchange doesn't even have half a day to explain himself or herself. Not to mention any blunders such as sexual harassment claims, which would end you the second the information goes out to the public.

Take the famous Harvey Weinstein case. The widespread outburst of indignation over the Hollywood producer would have been impossible if there weren't a platform to express it, such as social media.

One angle that's barely been considered with respect to the Harvey Weinstein case and the entire #MeToo movement is that, among other things, it could also be seen as an act of revenge the US political elite took on Hollywood. Those two spheres of public influence seem like they never got along. And that's not even mentioning Trump, who in his own ironic way seems to have always despised Hollywood with its great, self-standing personalities who are used to being admired, being given awards, and bathing in the love of the people. Even the president of the United States didn't come out of the #MeToo movement unscathed.

While the cause of the #MeToo movement is certainly admirable and commendable, a more impassionate, neutral look at it could construe it as having actually generated a lot more negatives than positives, with its fixation on long-past events from twenty or thirty years ago and questionable circumstances. Even murderers sometimes get pardoned and get to walk free within the course of longer time periods. And in this case, there has been the sharing of numerous stories, such as, "Thirty years ago in high school, a classmate tried to kiss me, and I didn't let him, but I was the subject of sexual harassment."

A critical look would require drawing the line, and asking what #MeToo has actually achieved. Scaring a corporate employee out of considering whether to approach another? There have been broad updates to sexual harassment laws and corporate rules across companies in an attempt to ensure that, whenever they are breached, the perpetrators get what they deserve. There has been a rather intriguing reaction in France, in which 100 prominent women, including actress Catherine Deneuve, signed an open letter warning that the movement was only going to make men more timid and inept. It would also be fair to point out that the movement made its own cause vulnerable to attack by leaving a lot of doubts that, under the guise of a noble campaign, questionable circumstances from a distant past might be used now for personal revenge, to tarnish somebody, or just to bring them down by people with ulterior motives.

The myriad possible angles and viewpoints aside about its essence and cause and effect, the most prominent conclusion from the Harvey Weinstein case and the #MeToo movement is once again underscoring how social media have entirely reshaped PR and public communications.

In the era of traditional media, if a woman had gone to some newspaper with such accusations, the journalists might not even believe her and might refuse to publish her story. The increased opportunity for publicity thanks to social media, however, makes such cases impossible to ignore.

WHAT'S LEFT OF OLD-SCHOOL PR?

In this age of the social media revolution in PR, what's left of old-school public relations is the foundation, which boils down to morality, ethics, accuracy, and responsibility. My understanding of PR—old, modern, future, whatever—is that it would be absurd to lie about something.

This is a constant hot topic in my office. We don't sell services, we sell trust. The same way an insurance company sells trust.

You use an insurance company because you trust them. That's 90 percent of the reason to go to that particular company. The rest, 10 percent, is based on their professionalism and good products. Technology is so advanced these days that there isn't a big difference between two different insurance companies, and so they compete on who will provide the best offer to clients. The main difference is the trust you have for them.

It's the same with PR. If the clients don't have trust in a certain PR expert, in their integrity, honesty, professionalism, quick reactions—that PR expert will never have clients again.

The main things that PR was based on a century ago—being accurate and ethical with integrity—are the same today. You can build on top of those prerequisites with new media, reaction speed, and business dynamics. It is an extremely dynamic business now, because every day social media brings new surprises, new opportunities, new channels, and new communication options.

However, if we don't have a stable foundation of integrity, our business will be broken.

FOR HEALTH AND DIGNITY

It is my strong conviction that compromises can be made with everything except for two things—*your health and your dignity.*

These are the two things that should never be compromised in your business and personal life. We must work in a way that protects our health and allows time to rest, recharge, and gain inspiration for creative moments.

Social media and online communications have truly made life easier for us. Things that used to take hours can now be done in minutes or seconds.

Think about how we used to send out press releases. It was done the same way all over the world up until 2000—by fax. You have thirty journalists on your list, and you start faxing them. You send out thirty faxes, one by one. That thing takes hours.

Back in those days, my colleagues from one of the dailies in Sofia would call me and say, "Max, you are doing an interesting project. When you start faxing, can you please send it to us first?" Otherwise, you would have to wait for an hour, for instance. Now, you can send your message to 5,000 journalists in a second.

With all these opportunities to save time, it is worth thinking about how to spare your health and rest more.

The same goes for your dignity. A client who thinks that PR companies are slaves, or some type of spare tire, or a mindless transmission between them and the media is a client with no future. A PR company cannot work with such clients. You can maybe do one or two projects with them, but nothing long-term.

We have clients with whom we have been working for many years: fifteen years with Dannon, twenty years with TNT, while the global average period that a client stays with a certain PR firm is between two and four years. They usually go through a procurement process and change the PR company in order to have fresh ideas and people.

Staying with a certain client for a long time means that you have a very high level of understanding with them—you help them develop their business to such a degree that they appreciate you.

At first glance, there might be a discrepancy between requiring that a modern-day PR expert should be online nonstop and the absolutist rule to never compromise one's health and dignity. But if you think about it, that's not really the case.

As in so many other fields, time management is key in PR, and being online nonstop isn't really that bad for your health. It is a lot more dangerous for your dignity.

Being constantly online isn't unhealthy. It's not like in the old days when we were small children and were warned to keep a safe distance from the TV to protect our eyes. New technologies are nothing like that.

Of course, you must protect your health, you must not make any compromises with it—if it's gone, you won't be able to do anything, either business or personal.

It is true that being online nonstop might lead to exhaustion and complete loss of privacy.

But this is the cost of doing business!

If you want to be in the business, there is always a price to pay.

If you manage your time well enough, and if you perceive this activity as business, not entertainment, then things will work out well.

Even in the age of the social media revolution, PR's essence remains the same as always: honesty, integrity, and preparedness to react.

CHAPTER 3

THE REVOLUTION: THE FALLEN

THE DEATH OF THE PRESS RELEASE

RIP, Press Release!
1906–2007

"The Press Release Passes Away at 101"
—*The Global Enquirer Tribune*

"The Press Release (1906–2007) Led Full Life"
—Panoramika.Net

October 30, 1906—The *New York Times* prints in full the first-ever press release.[1]
November 6, 2007—Facebook launches Facebook Pages.

1 Written by consultant Ivy Lee on behalf of the Pennsylvania Railroad following an Atlantic City train wreck that killed fifty-three people.

The one-time ubiquitous emblem of classic PR, the press release, has technically been dead for a while now. To be a bit more precise, His Majesty the Press Release has been dying—a relatively slow death, but a death, nonetheless. And there is no coming back. Now we are in the afterlife, thanks to the social media revolution.

An admittedly arbitrary but still plausibly precise date pinpointing the death of the press release might be November 6, 2007—the day when Facebook launched its then vastly obscure, and today vastly dominant, Facebook Pages.

At first glance, it might seem as though the death of the press release was slightly exaggerated. After all, press releases are still in circulation. Our company, for instance, still sends out press releases on some occasions for many of our clients.

Yet the death of the press release has been a foretold death for one simple reason: it should have become clear to everybody years ago that with the social media tsunami hurtling toward the shorelines of public communication, news will be absorbed faster than ever and almost exclusively through social media, rather than the formal messages of PR agencies.

A further factor driving another nail in the press release's coffin is that whatever is left of traditional journalism has begun to use social media as their primary source for news stories. Unless it is a television channel that needs TV footage, or unless some personal presence is extremely necessary, traditional media simply do not dispatch reporters to check out the situation on the ground anymore.

What traditional media have been doing for several years now has been logging onto social media and monitoring the news feeds of profiles and pages of key public figures, politicians, CEOs, and celebrities.

There's an earthquake? You get on Twitter and Facebook and learn the latest. It doesn't matter if you are the end reader or reporting major news for tomorrow's newspaper.

With that in mind, when it comes to the press release, a PR professional cannot help but think, "What's the most efficient method for me? To send out a boring press release to the (traditional and classic online news) media, or to post a few updates on social media—a Facebook post and a couple of tweets?"

You may have noticed that with the advent of Web 1.0, and the rise of news sites on the World Wide Web, the "press release" got a bit of a makeover as a "news release." This happened simultaneously with the shift from "the press" to digital media (plus the electronic media that had already been around for more than a decade).

"News release" did sound good ten or fifteen years ago, but this is not the case any more. This is no more than a nickname of the good old press release. It didn't really signify any meaningful changes.

Then there is Twitter.

There is no way to send out a press release in 140 characters, but the fact is that a 140-character tweet is oftentimes capable of saying much more than a full-fledged old-school press release.

My advice: if you know how to write it, tweet it. Your tweet will likely be more comprehensible, and when a press release is more to the point, more down-to-earth, then the media will snap it up immediately.

In my company, we strive to convince the numerous clients we work with that all news should appear on their social media profiles and pages first. Only if their social media channels don't achieve sufficient coverage, which would be an exception, would we back up their posts with a press release.

Alternatively, when we do have to send out a press release, it often specifically takes the form of a Facebook status, or ten photos on Pinterest, or that 140-character tweet. It doesn't show up as a formal press release—there is simply no need for that anymore. It's not just inexpedient, it might even be counterproductive.

Wondering why the press release is dying off is like wondering why horse carts are disappearing. Because we've got automobiles now!

We in the PR industry now hold in our hands new tools for announcing news—and those tools are beyond exciting! These new tools are faster, more reliable, and—what probably matters most—they are interactive.

The last part is the truly good news for the public. The fact that social media platforms provide the opportunity to have a dialogue can be used to rectify all sorts of communication mistakes, manipulations, and injustices. This is also a huge part of the social media revolution era and goes back to strengthen further my point made above about the dissociation between PR and propaganda.

For instance, Samsung launched their new Galaxy Note 7 phone in August 2016. Soon after, Note 7 batteries started to explode (a manufacturing defect caused some of them to overheat).

In a case like that, regardless of the kind of "propaganda" one might have tried, no matter what press releases you might send out, whatever you do, the consequences are permanent.

Only a few dozen Samsung Galaxy Note 7 phone batteries "exploded," a tiny fraction of the total number of those produced, but many airlines still prohibit the phones on board.

Whatever Samsung may have done, thanks to social media, in just thirty seconds, the entire world knew that their Galaxy Note 7 batteries were "exploding." This is just one example.

The press release was an old-school instrument for communication with our clients' target audience.

There are other classic PR instruments—press conferences, media meetings, business brunches, business conferences, etc.

All those are now replaced by posts on social media, and occasionally still by personal meetings with journalists.

The press release has been suffering a slow death that will take a while yet, because such a development is a function of the maturity of the market. There are still countries where social media platforms haven't achieved such enormous penetration yet. There are also countries in which social media are very country-specific and probably not that popular with the general public.

In such markets, it might make sense for businesses to keep using press releases to communicate their messages to the media and the public and also, where possible, to use the most relevant social media platform for the specific country.

The beauty of truly global social media is that while your press release might go to 100, 500, even 1,000 media outlets (there probably isn't a country in the world with that many), news on social media could theoretically reach 2–3 billion people—that is, potentially, if your news story is super attractive and you know how, where, and when to post it.

Everybody knows how many "likes" celebrity Instagram posts get, usually without amounting to anything meaningful—just some music or film star takes a selfie on the plane, for example.

Quite recently, someone took a photo of Madonna in the economy class of a short European flight, posted it on Instagram, and got 10–15 million "likes" in hours, even minutes.

The power of "likes" is another big thing in this social media revolution, not only in PR.

If you "like" a certain social media post (a status, a photo, etc.), that doesn't necessarily mean that you really like that post. It means two things: first, your "liking" something means that you have seen it, i.e., you register the fact that you have seen it; and second, which is first, really, you demonstrate that you exist and you express an opinion.

In my view, this is the first and foremost reason people "like" on social media—to show others that they exist and make a statement: "I like, therefore I am."

You make it clear to everybody that you "like" something somebody else posted.

"She or he likes that, so they exist on social media. She or he is not just anybody, but 'likes' stuff," other users would think of you any time you "like" something.

In a nutshell, the potential of social media is unlimited, endless, unrestricted, while the potential of a press release is limited regardless of how many (traditional) media publish it.

What's more, if a press release is in English but has to go to Germany, it has to be translated into German; in the Netherlands, into Dutch. Perhaps it will be understood in English in most places, but you still have to translate it into the local language because of corporate rules.

At the same time, a post on Facebook can be translated with a mouse click. So here and there we still work with a press release, but in the US, that is increasingly rare.

THE DEATH OF THE PRESS CONFERENCE

While the death of the press release could be construed as more symbolic, the death of the press conference has actually been even more evident and overwhelming for the PR industry in the social media revolution era.

The simple fact is that going to a press conference nowadays is nonsense.

In most cases, it wouldn't make sense—unless it is a White House–type press conference, where you can hope to ask a question and get a comment by some key official or catch a sound bite. (Or unless you go to some military base, and someone throws a shoe at the president.)

Nowadays, something major must be expected to happen at that press conference for it to be worth going to.

Otherwise, crossing New York City, for instance, by car or subway in order to hear some boring CEO at some corporate press conference, and then to lose another hour to go back, and then to write a news article—is nonsense, which is why it is becoming increasingly rare nowadays.

The classic corporate press conference (or "news conference") is being replaced by presentations of new products or some innovative technology, because typically it's worth photographing the person who's doing the presentation.

However, these types of events still get 300 selected journalists as visitors, while 5 million people simultaneously watch them online in real time.

For example, the launch of the new iPhone X in September 2017. A hundred million people were watching it live around the world. There were no more than 300 people in the hall. That meant that they would be able to touch it, write about it, and you could present each one of them with an iPhone. But that right there is a whole other type of a corporate event that is remarkably different from a classic press conference.

Nobody cares anymore about those standard press conferences in which a corporation might make some boring announcement about what it intends to launch when this can be done a lot more effectively through a tweet or a Facebook status.

The press release and the press conference were (and arguably still are) just tools of the PR industry.

Very often, I compare this social media revolution and what it has done to the PR industry with that of Henry Ford with his gas-fueled carriage that revolutionized transportation, mobility, and the way people perceived the future.

It's the same way with social media. There are no horse carts; we have cars instead. We don't need the press release and the press conference, because we've got all the marvels of social media.

If the cars hadn't been invented, however, there would still be horse carts, since we would have no other option but to keep using them. We would be figuring out what to do to achieve some progress: whether to use ten horses harnessed one after the other, or to rotate them, or to improve the cart wheels—it is a question of imagination.

So if there had been no social media, there would still be press releases and press conferences, because the information would have flown at the same speed as before social media.

It is worth noting, however, that the tsunami of the social media revolution has more likely caused all those changes for the PR industry, rather than the arrival of the internet.

Web 1.0 did not offer what social media has given us: combination of the main existing online communication tools into one, the sort that Facebook offers, for example.

In social media, you have messaging, live chat, interactivity; you can post comments and share; you have all unrestricted communication opportunities.

Lathes are a case in point. Old lathes still exist in machine-building plants around the world, but now there are new lathes that make details faster and much more accurately. That's what social media has done to our business.

At the same time, it has made the PR industry infinitely more measurable, and much more transparent.

I myself could reveal to anybody who is interested what has been going on in my PR company, from A to Z, without any preconditions.

Today, even in the US, there are still companies, especially in the lobbyist industry, that say, "No, that's our corporate secret, our corporate affair."

But it's not like that in PR—social media has increased our industry's measurability and transparency beyond recognition.

WHEN SOCIAL MEDIA TRUMPED THE INTERNET

Social media *trumped* the internet before the rise of Trump.

Interestingly, the emergence of the internet did not cause a revolution in the PR industry the way the rise of social media did.

It might seem counterintuitive, but the internet of Web 1.0 was not a new tool for PR experts.

It was a faster way to communicate, and a way of gaining knowledge and doing research—but it was not an active tool that a PR professional could use to reach a target audience.

Here is what our industry was like up until the domination of social media, including in the times of Web 1.0.

You have a product or a service. You have to make news out of it, you need to make it interesting, and that news needs to be brought to consumers in a way they would understand and accept.

For example, you produce a new type of pen. You want to generate news that the pen has a special design and give that to the media, i.e., the consumers—because there used to be media between us and the consumers—so that the media might say, "This new pen is genius. Let's write something about it. Why? Because people will be buying more issues of our newspaper. We write only about cool, genius, new things, and when people see that it will give our sales a boost."

When consumers were simply on the internet of Web 1.0, they weren't organized. There was no way they could be targeted the way they can be now on social media. They were just users of the internet.

Whereas today, the consumers are organized in groups—on Facebook, LinkedIn, Instagram, etc. They are much easier to find and target.

So it was social media that caused the revolution in PR—the internet by itself couldn't do it.

This whole situation, in which the internet is not revolutionary but social media is, is very specific to the PR industry.

Take someone who makes cheese. The internet might have helped them research how to make better cheese, how to preserve it, who their competitors are, etc.

However, in PR, we communicate messages. Going back to one of my original points, if we produce anything, it's news stories.

Regardless of what you call your message, it is news. If it doesn't contain news, then you probably aren't doing a very good job.

Twenty or thirty years ago, we used to say, "There is nothing older than yesterday's newspaper."

Now, there is nothing older than news from five minutes ago.

GOING VIRAL: CONTAGION—EPIDEMICS—PANDEMICS

The main feature and top advantage of social media, which has made it such a powerful instrument in the hands of PR experts, is the ability to share—and especially the intriguing possibility of seeing your post go "viral." In that case, your post is so catchy and "contagious" that it spreads like an epidemic and can consequently become a pandemic.

If we use the term "viral" for social media, we should also be able to speak of "epidemics" and "pandemics."

"Virality" poses one of the great ethical issues in the era of the social media PR revolution, since, unfortunately, social media epidemics or pandemics very often emerge over fake or sensational news.

The 2017 Global Communications Report of the USC Annenberg School for Communication and Journalism points out that at the time when their survey was conducted, "only about 1/3 of the respondents thought Fake News would be an important trend." It notes further that their number has definitely increased by now. The number of professionals who thought Donald Trump would have "much impact on our industry" is also likely to have grown.

The 2018 report of these same organizations, which dwelled extensively on the topic of ethics in PR and global public communications, found that fake news tops the list of ethical issues, according to a whopping 92 percent of the surveyed PR executives. "Purposeful distortion of the truth" was ranked second with 91 percent.

While these concerns are beyond justified, fake news could be just part of how social media works. Everything has its glitches. If we go back to the example of the first gasoline car and the revolution it brought—it can nowadays get a flat tire or go off the road and crash in a ditch.

By definition, however, PR should be trying to achieve "virality" for its stories—that's one of its goals.

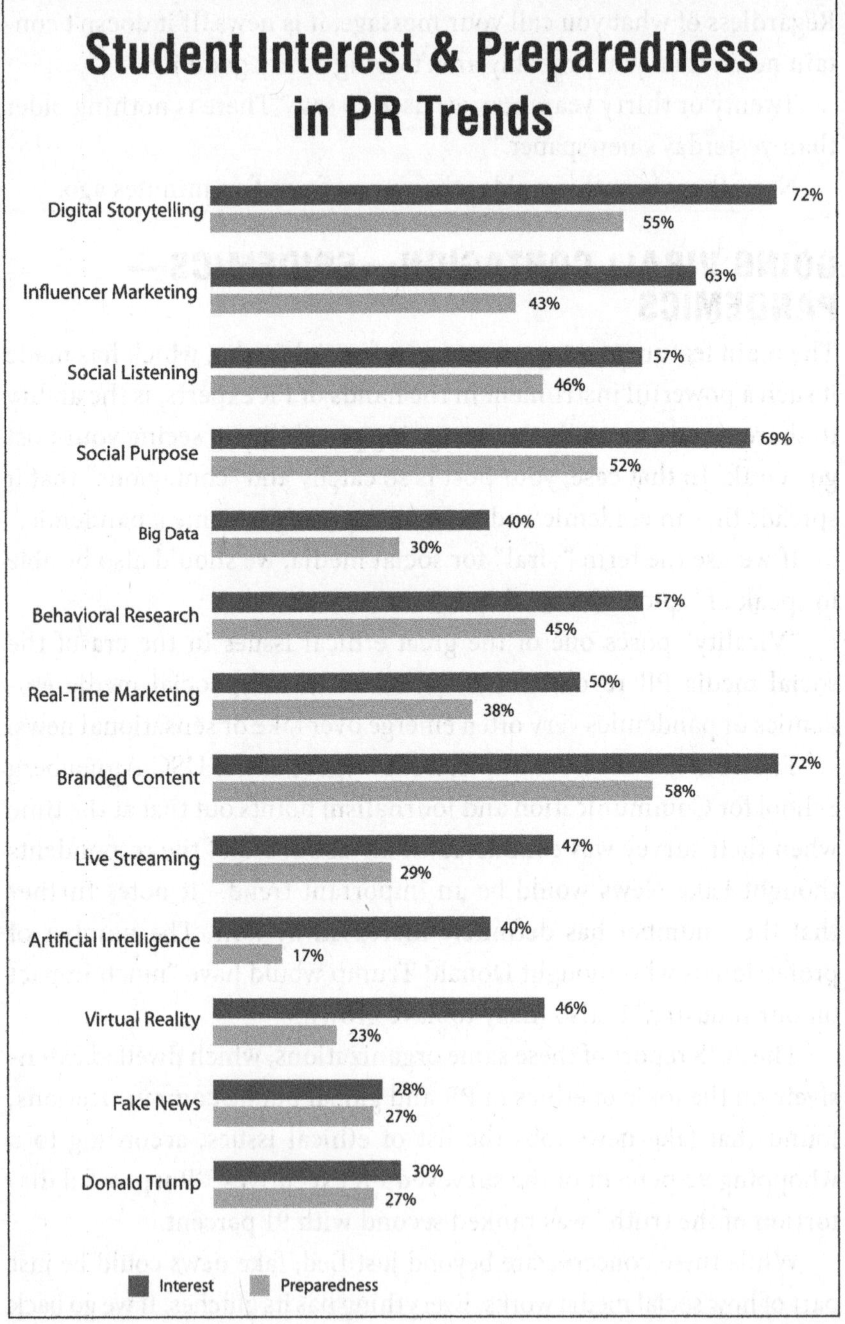

Source: 2017 Global Communications Report of the USC Annenberg School for Communication and Journalism.

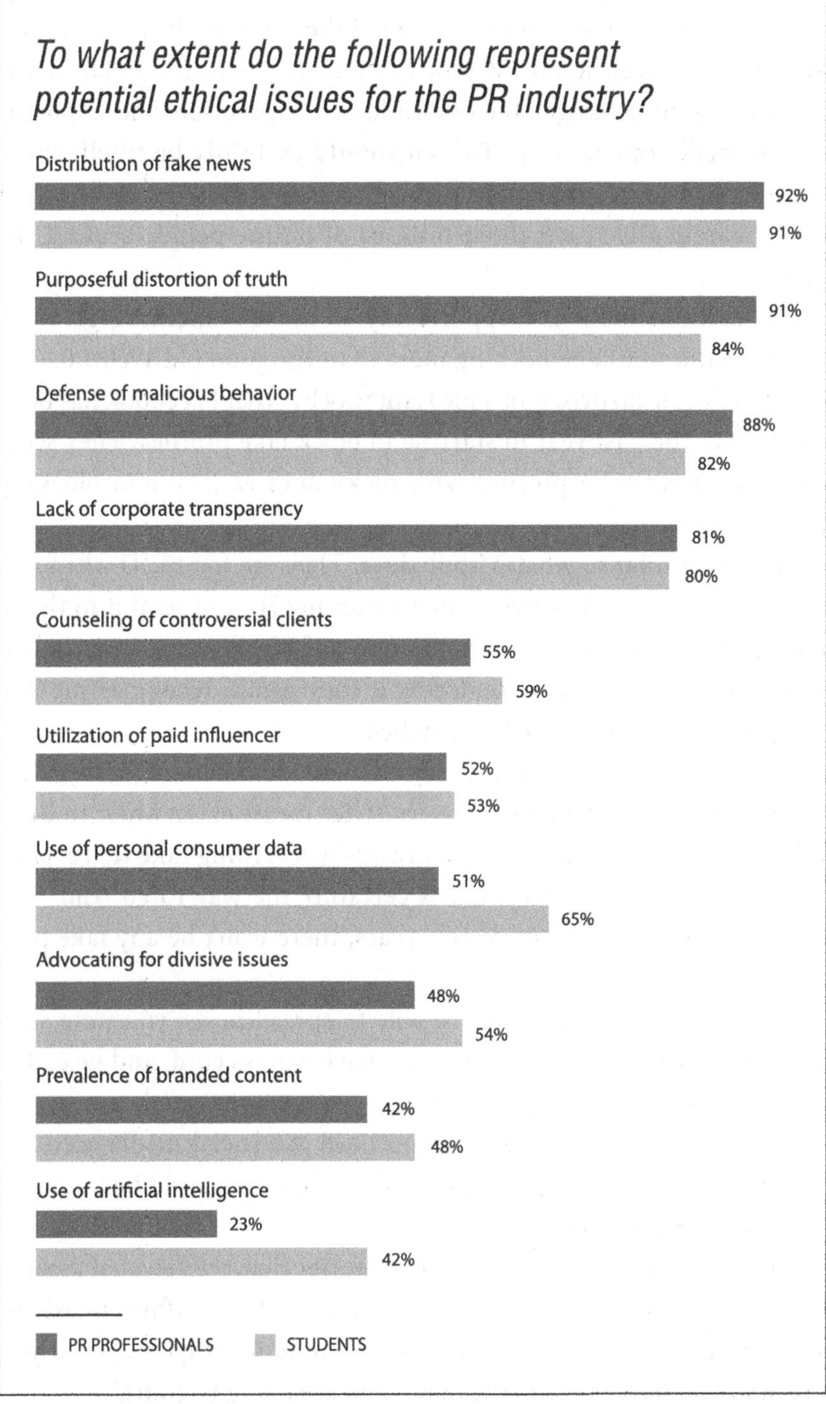

Source: 2018 Global Communications Report of the USC Annenberg School for Communication and Journalism.

As we have said in our discussion of the death of the press release and other conventional PR tools, one of the reasons social media is such a game changer for our industry is precisely the opportunity to make our message (which should certainly be intelligently written and trustworthy) go viral, because that is the only way it can theoretically reach those billions of online people around the globe.

Actually, without the opportunity to make something go viral, social media would be nothing more than the good old Web 1.0.

I have been surprised in a pleasant way by what Facebook has been doing over the past year in starting to block fake profiles. They seem to be deeming even profiles with nicknames as fake and blocking them, as well.

This is similar to what Airbnb does. They ask for an ID when you register as a user. They asked me to scan my ID and send it to them, and to send them a current photo of myself. At the time, I was in bed in my pajamas and was wondering if they would recognize me like that, but they said the photos matched.

All those operators of online social media services are finally, after all these years, starting to take very strict measures in order to limit fake news, fake profiles, fake identities—everything fake that's associated with social media. That is certainly the way to go, and very soon, perhaps in just four or five years, there won't be any fake profiles on Facebook.

Ten years ago, in order to be able to spread news, you were supposed to have a major in journalism, have a press card, and be called a journalist. Otherwise, you couldn't.

Now, to spread the news, all you need is a social media account. Nonetheless, you should at least be identified—it should be known if that user really is you.

If you share one or two fake news stories that get detected as such by Facebook or Twitter, it is perfectly valid for the platform to ask for your ID and say, "Let's see if you really are James Taylor. And if you are, and you have spread fake news, you are going to court."

We recently had a discussion at the ICCO summit in Helsinki about fake news. There was a Finnish expert who had spoken on the topic two days prior at a meeting of government leaders of the EU in Tallinn during Estonia's EU presidency.

He was not overly concerned in that regard, and not willing to espouse extreme measures against fake news. The Finns are very liberal and open-minded when it comes to technology, which is probably why they are so far ahead. But I think that the spread of fake news must be outlawed.

One shouldn't be allowed to spread false information on social media. If that information is false and it hurts people's businesses, for example, if you do so-called "black PR," targeting certain people and destroying certain companies and their reputations, then you should be held accountable.

There is no way around it, because posting on social media is a public activity that influences people's thoughts, acts, and decisions.

Perhaps the spreading of fake news shouldn't be criminalized as a felony, but it must be penalized in some way, and there should at least be court trials for that. There have been such court cases already, but the crackdown against fake news is yet to be taken to the next level. This is because there are still millions of people who spread fake news about others but cannot be brought to court because they hide behind fake names and fake profiles.

THE WAR WITH ADVERTISING

I have been aware of the undeclared war between PR and advertising ever since I entered this industry more than twenty years ago.

Neither side admits openly that they are, and have been, at war.

This war has been escalating gradually, and it will probably be in full swing by 2020–2025.

Why is it being waged at all, and why has it been so intensive recently? Because we in the PR industry have been conquering some of the territories that have traditionally been reserved for the advertising business.

One such territory is graphic design. Clients would come to us and say, "We have a million dollars in our advertising budget for this year. We want to spend half of that on social media because social media efforts are measurable and easily visible, viral, and easy to share."

That's when advertising agencies would step in: "Wait a minute! We understand social media, too. We know what Facebook is. We can do that for you."

And so the fight rages on. They are fighting to keep their clients, and we are fighting to protect our territory, which is called "content." That's it: they are "visuals," and we are "content," although content now also contains visuals to a great extent.

In all those years, we in the PR industry have worked with visuals a lot, whereas the advertising industry hasn't really worked with textual content. Or if they have, they have worked with advertising messages only.

This is the main reason the advertising industry is categorically losing ground. They will lose even more, since social media budgets go to PR agencies.

Going back to my original point: at the end of the day, if a client has some kind of crisis, they cannot solve it with an advertising agency.

They can solve it only through social media, but again, that cannot be done by the advertising agency.

If the client has a problem connected with reputation or credibility or trust, they cannot solve it through an advertising agency. It is we, the PR experts, who know their customers, and we know the techniques for managing the news stream.

These recent developments have incredibly boosted the role of media-monitoring agencies.

The fact that fifteen years ago I decided to establish a media-monitoring company as part of M3, which is not typical at all for PR businesses anywhere in the world, now makes me really happy. In our field, you cannot afford to delay reaction to any crisis situation.

There is no print media that's still fully alive today—all of its exclusive news stories get published online first. We know about it long before it shows up in print.

The fact that we have an in-house media-monitoring and media-analysis agency gives us the opportunity to respond to a crisis for any of our clients as soon as it has broken out.

There are probably other PR companies out there that have their own media-monitoring agencies or departments, but we are definitely a minority.

PR firms usually use subcontractors for media monitoring. This means that the subcontractor may or may not tell you about a crisis in time—or at all—because they are not responsible for your client. They are responsible for you. You are the one responsible for the client.

Advertising doesn't really have any media monitoring at all—it has never crossed their minds.

The advertising business has been using media research to figure out the best messaging, or the best time slots for broadcasting ads, or the best ad space in the newspapers, or banner spots in online media.

We in PR don't care if an article about our client is one column or ten pages. We are interested in what it says.

If our client's reputation can be hurt by that one column, that article is more important to us than ten newspaper pages about our client.

Therefore, it makes no sense for advertising to even compete with PR, because advertising is not competitive anymore. PR's edge clearly rests on creative and strategic services.

"Creative thinking and strategic insight are top reasons for clients to hire PR agencies, while research and analysis are last," states the 2017 Global Communications Report of the USC Annenberg School for Communication and Journalism.

The 2017 report on "The Evolution of Public Relations" conducted among in-house marketers by the US Association of National Advertisers (ANA) and the USC Center for Public Relations at the Annenberg School for Communication and Journalism discovered that 75 percent of the respondents plan to increase overall spending on PR over the next five years, and 62 percent are planning to increase internal public relations staffing over the same period.

Yes, it is true that many companies claim to offer PR services as part of their portfolio. For example, accounting and real estate firms.

Because of this omnivorousness, where everybody claims to understand PR and marketing and offer those services, it has been logical for advertising agencies to declare that they can do PR, as well.

However, advertising can never be our competitor—it simply doesn't have the tools and experience that we have.

Nevertheless, even though our industries are at war at the moment, the merger of PR, advertising, and digital companies, as already

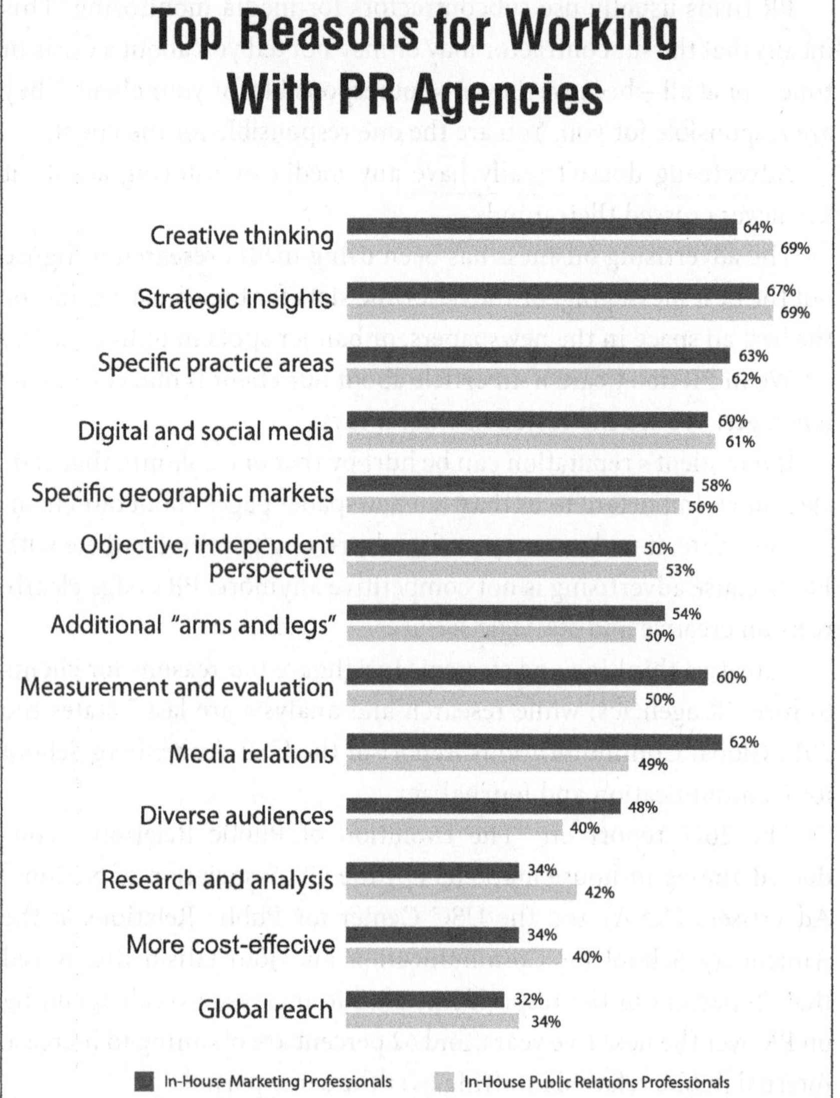

Source: 2017 Global Communications Report of the USC Annenberg School for Communication and Journalism.

noted, is absolutely inevitable, because clients need full-service communications consultancies.

First of all, clients will find this merger to be of great convenience, because they will be in contact with only one company, who will be responsible for the overall communications.

Internal Staffing and Spending to Support Public Relations

	Internal Staffing		Spending	
	In Next Year	In Five Yeras	In Next Year	In Five Yeras
Significantly Increase	3%	8%	4%	8%
Moderately Increase	13%	54%	21%	67%
Stay About the Same	79%	31%	69%	15%
Moderately Decrease	5%	8%	3%	8%
Significantly Decrease	0%	0%	3%	1%

Q. Will your company's internal staffing to support public relations increase, decrease, or remain about the same in the next year? Five years?

Q. Will your company's spending to support public relations increase, decrease, or remain about the same in the next year? Five years?
Consider spending to be categories including, but not limited to: agency fees, internal and external communication, product public relations, and brand reputation.
Percentages may not add up to 100 percent due to rounding.

Source: 2017 Report on the Evolution of PR by the US Association of National Advertisers (ANA) and the USC Center for Public Relations at the Annenberg School for Communication and Journalism.

Second, there is no way for advertising to avoid suffering the PR industry's foray into graphic design and visuals, because today, clients tend to come to PR agencies regardless of what happens to them, as a fix-all station of sorts.

A client goes to a PR agency not just for reputation management and crisis management, but also increasingly for advertising and digital services, such as website development.

For years now, PR has been developing services in the era of social media that cover more and more communication needs. That's part of the reason why PR will be on top of the future merger of the three industries.

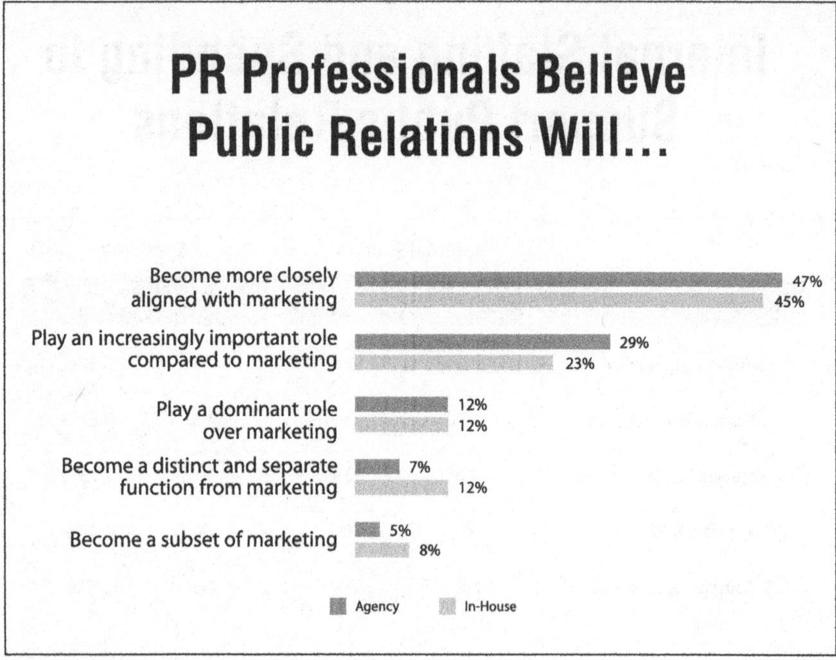

Source: 2017 Global Communications Report of the USC Annenberg School for Communication and Journalism.

We solve things that nobody else can solve for our clients, starting first and foremost with reputation management and brand issues.

We solve them with our ability to speak to various audiences in social media, with our quick reactions, and, most important, with our expertise and experience with content. Content is our strength, and that's our main advantage.

"Recently, two major holding companies 'bundled' their PR agencies with their advertising agencies to provide clients with a more integrated solution. Internally, some companies are restructuring their marketing functions to include public relations," pointed out the 2017 Global Communications Report of the USC Annenberg School for Communication and Journalism.

The report also noted that "almost half of the PR professionals and more than 60 percent of marketing executives believe that the two disciplines will become more closely aligned in the next five years. Some think PR will dominate. Others think it will be dominated."

The 2018 Report of the USC Annenberg School for Communication and Journalism contained further evidence of this pattern's continuity.

Source: 2017 Global Communications Report of the USC Annenberg School for Communication and Journalism.

"Last year, 47 percent of agency and 45 percent of in-house professionals predicted that PR would become more integrated with marketing in the next five years. This year, that number jumped to 90 percent for agency and 82 percent for in-house professionals, with half of all PR professionals stating that this integration will be driven by senior management," the 2018 report said.

The 2017 report on "The Evolution of Public Relations," in which the ANA and the USC Center for Public Relations at the Annenberg School for Communication and Journalism surveyed client-side marketers, indicates a perception that PR and marketing will become increasingly intertwined over the next five years.

This book actually goes further to argue that marketing has essentially already been dissolved in this merger. As Paul Holmes, the founder and CEO of the Holmes Report proclaimed several years ago at the Communication on Top forum in Davos, Switzerland: "That's the end of marketing."

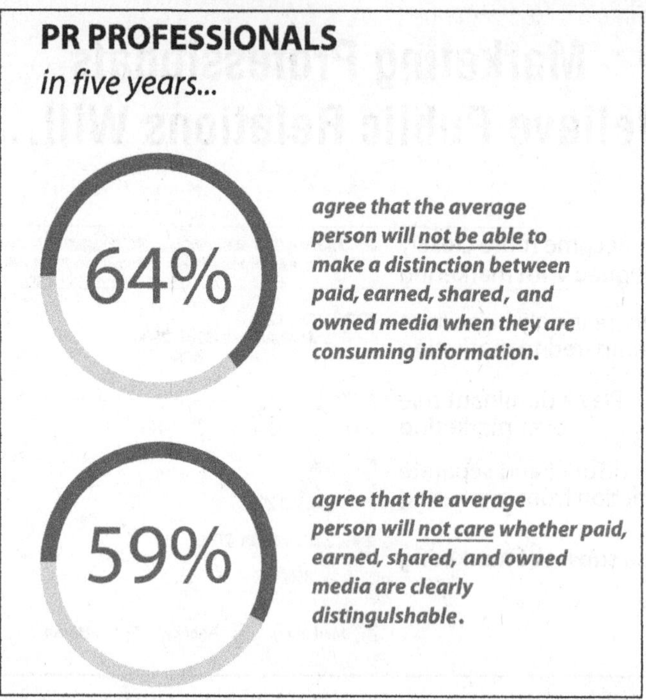
PR PROFESSIONALS
in five years...
64%
agree that the average person will not be able to make a distinction between paid, earned, shared, and owned media when they are consuming information.
59%
agree that the average person will not care whether paid, earned, shared, and owned media are clearly distingulshable.

Source: 2018 Global Communications Report of the USC Annenberg School for Communication and Journalism.

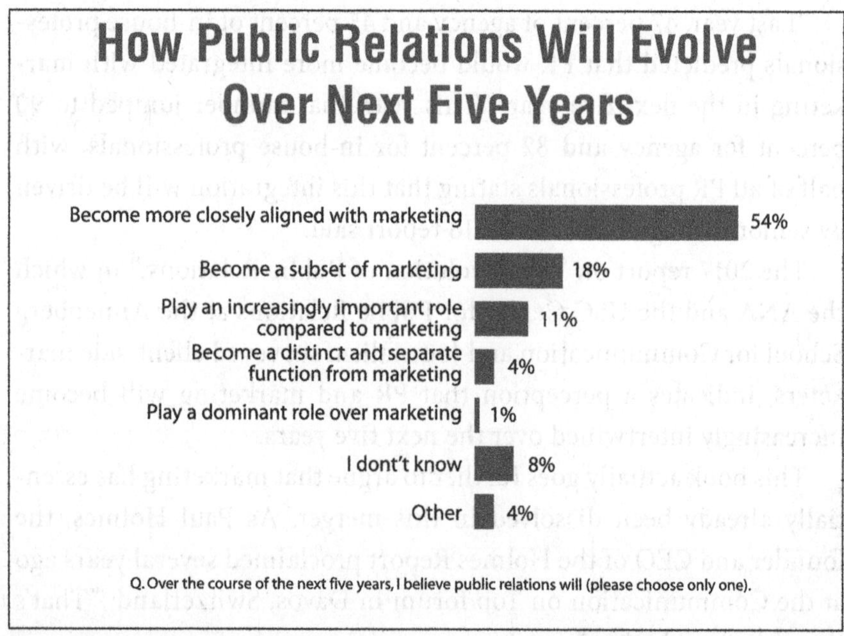
How Public Relations Will Evolve Over Next Five Years
Become more closely aligned with marketing 54%
Become a subset of marketing 18%
Play an increasingly important role compared to marketing 11%
Become a distinct and separate function from marketing 4%
Play a dominant role over marketing 1%
I dont't know 8%
Other 4%
Q. Over the course of the next five years, I believe public relations will (please choose only one).

Source: 2017 Report of the Evolution of PR by the US Association of National Advertisers (ANA) and the USC Center for Public Relations at the Annenberg School for Communication and Journalism.

Social media today gives the best, most in-depth picture for any marketing expert. Classical marketing, with its analysis and research tools, can barely develop itself further given that at a client's request, a PR company can do the same research in social media in Google Analytics, Facebook, etc.

You pay, and you get all the relevant data to understand the big picture. Data are online, and you can modify your data request settings at any time.

No marketing agency can match the information that can be gained through social media, which can easily be used by any PR agency anywhere in the world. This effect on the marketing industry is just one of the far-reaching ramifications of the social media revolution.

One million-dollar question regarding the future merger of PR, advertising, and digital industries into one full-service communications industry is what will be preserved from each field, and which parts will fall into oblivion.

Quite naturally, each industry will have to say good-bye to some of its subfields, forced by the global market that has been altered by the social media revolution.

Some things will have to be deleted from each one, so they can be merged into a new industry.

My forecast is that what will drop out of PR will be what is called media relations. There simply isn't a need for media relations anymore, because we own media.

The advertising business will probably suffer more losses—only the creative departments will remain, and to some extent the copywriting departments.

But media buying is going to die in maybe three to eight years, because advertising agencies won't have anything to buy anymore, since media outlets will be managing that on their own.

Think of what Google does with AdSense/AdWords, and what Facebook does with its Facebook ads—this is exactly the thing.

What is the point of hiring an advertising agency to plan social media presence, given that social media itself does that much more successfully and you are just setting the parameters for that?

Here is the conclusion of the 2017 Global Communications Report of the USC Annenberg School for Communication and Journalism with respect to PR's encroachments into media buying, a domain traditionally reserved for advertising. The conclusion is drawn in light of the shifting revenue balance between earned media (E) on one hand, and paid, shared, and owned media (P-SO) on the other.

The finding that most PR professionals believe that future consumers will not be able to differentiate between earned and paid media content also underscores the ongoing shift in the PESO (paid-earned-shared-owned) media mix. There is no doubt that this PESO shift has been brought about by the advent of social media.

From the report:

> The number of revenue agencies generated from earned media will decline over the next five years, while revenue from paid, shared and owned will increase. Corporate media budgets are moving even faster towards owned and paid.
>
> Supporting that direction, 60 percent of all PR executives believe that branded content and influencer marketing, which are both primarily paid, will be important trends in the next five years. This changing media mix creates an opportunity and a challenge.
>
> The opportunity is to move aggressively into paid content, an arena long dominated by advert-teasing. This will require PR professionals to master media buying, which currently ranks last on the list of skills they think are important to the future.
>
> The challenge is more than half of PR executives believe the consumer of the future will not make a distinction between paid and earned media. Another one-third disagree. The answer to that debate has profound ramifications for everyone.

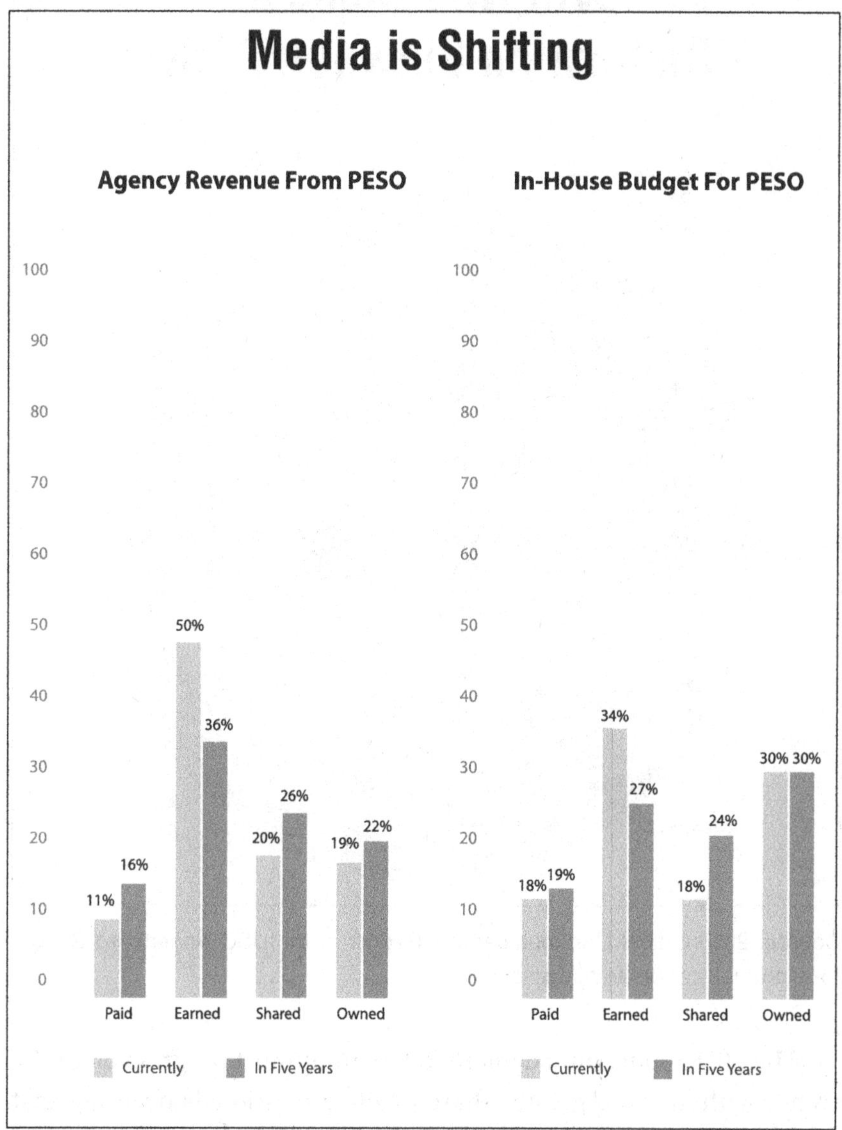

Source: 2017 Global Communications Report of the USC Annenberg School for Communication and Journalism.

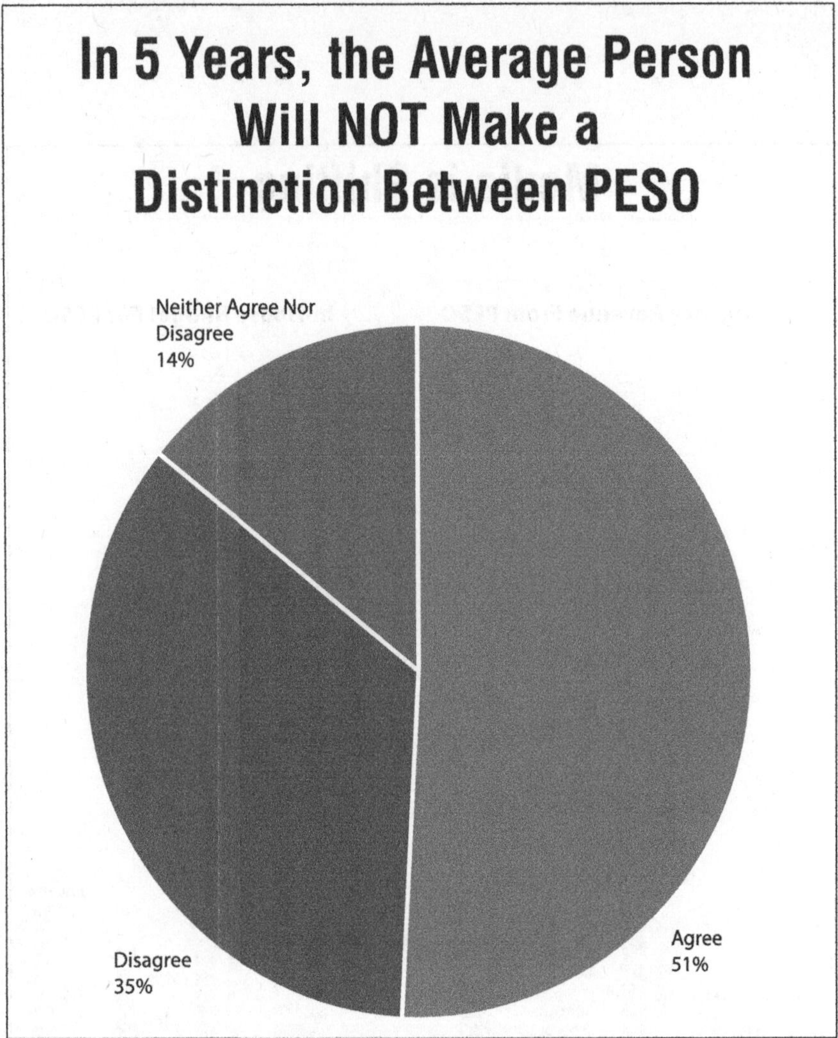

Source: 2017 Global Communications Report of the USC Annenberg School for Communication and Journalism.

The 2018 report only demonstrated an upward progression of the trend, with an even greater share of PR professionals deeming that the distinction between PESO is bound to disappear.

Many things will disappear from each of the three main communications industries so that a new industry can be born. I don't know what it will be called. It could be named "social relations."

PR PROFESSIONALS
in five years...

agree that the average person will not be able to make a distinction between paid, earned, shared, and owned media when they are consuming information

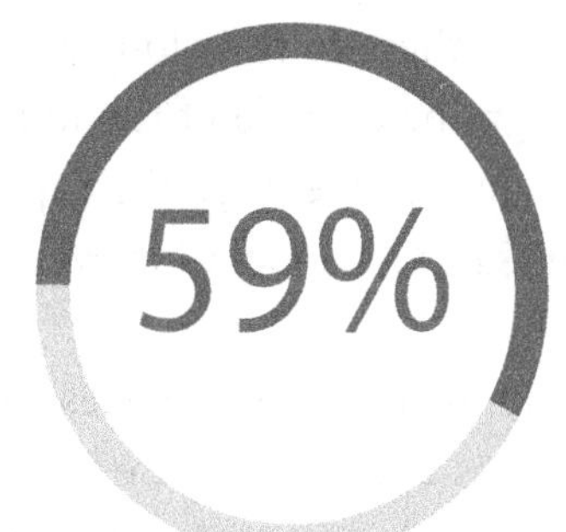

agree that the average person will not care whether paid, earned, shared, and owned media are clearly distinguishable

Source: 2018 Global Communications Report of the USC Annenberg School for Communication and Journalism.

TURNING PUBLIC COMMUNICATIONS UPSIDE DOWN AGAIN: SIR MARTIN SORRELL

Sir Martin Sorrell—featured a number of times in this book—is an emblematic figure in public communications. That is precisely why his decision to depart his position as CEO of WPP was expected to rattle both the public relations and advertising businesses on a global scale.

He has started a new project, and by the time this book is released, it will probably be well under way. No doubt, it will be successful, as all of his past projects have been. He managed to establish certain rules in the communications industry over the past two decades, with WPP becoming the largest business group in public communications.

It is my opinion that the model that Sir Martin Sorrell stood for was actually a lot more beneficial for advertising, as this was prioritized in his work. For him, the PR companies in WPP were more of a side industry; the main thing was media buying and advertising—most likely a reflection of the times.

The people who will follow after him in managing this gigantic mastodon worth billions of dollars will probably be a lot more pragmatic. They will probably focus a lot more on PR and new media. Sir Martin Sorrell was focused on advertising, and he didn't hide it—he would tell everybody that advertising would change the world.

I stood my ground with my view that there is no way public relations wouldn't become the leading business in the modern-day communications industry, if only for two simple reasons: that it is impossible for advertising and media-buying companies to solve clients' crisis situations, and it is impossible for them to fully look after their clients' image and branding. You might be capable of the most genius advertising in the world, but that doesn't mean you're capable of solving a public relations crisis for, say, Coca-Cola (or even a smaller company).

Every time I've heard Sorrell speak at forums, conferences, or on television in recent years, he always talks about social media as viewed through the eyes of advertising. Advertising barely has anything in common with social media. For advertising, social media is just another channel for ads and nothing more, whereas for the PR industry, social media is an opportunity to create new content and influence its audiences in a novel way.

I've always liked Sorrell—no doubt, he is a genius—but his views emphasize advertising as the highest priority, which can no longer be the dominant view in the public communications business. I think his departure is turning the public communications industry upside down simply because the people after him will be more pragmatic with respect to the PR business.

SOCIAL MEDIA TIMELINE

1997	SixDegrees.com becomes the first-ever social media website. It was bought by YouthStream Media Networks for $125 million and closed down in 2001. Release of AOL Instant Messenger.
1998	AOL acquires ICQ.
1999	Yahoo! Messenger is launched. MSN Messenger is launched. Blogging platform LiveJournal is launched.
2002	Social networking site Friendster is launched. LinkedIn is launched.
2003	Social networking site Hi5 is launched. MySpace is launched. Skype is launched.
2004	Facebook is launched as a college social network called thefacebook.com Flickr is launched.
2005	Bebo is launched News Corporation buys MySpace for $580 million.
2006	Reddit is launched. YouTube is launched. Yahoo! acquires Flickr. Facebook launches photo feature. Twitter is launched. VK (VKontakte.com), Russian social network mimicking Facebook, is launched. Facebook launches News Feed. Google buys YouTube for $1.65 billion. Facebook is opened to everyone over thirteen.
2007	Tumblr is launched. FriendFeed is launched. Live-streaming site Justin.tv is launched. Facebook launches Pages.
2008	AOL buys Bebo for $850 million; sells it in 2010 to Criterion Capital Partners. Facebook reaches 100 million users. Facebook overtakes MySpace in visitor numbers.
2009	Facebook buys FriendFeed for $47.5 million. Chinese microblogging site Sina Weibo (sometimes called the Chinese Twitter) is launched.

2010	Pinterest is launched. Instagram is launched. Quora is launched. Facebook reaches 500 million users.
2011	Snapchat is launched. Microsoft acquires Skype for $8.5 billion. Google launches Google+. News Corporation sells MySpace to Specific Media for $35 million. LinkedIn goes public. Twitch.tv, a spinoff of Justin.tv, is launched. Twitter adopts the Fly design.
2012	Facebook goes public, generating the largest valuation of a newly listed company with an IPO of $104 billion. Snapchat launches video sharing. Tinder is launched. Facebook buys Instagram for $1 billion. Facebook reaches 1 billion users.
2013	Vine is launched after being bought by Twitter for $30 million. Twitter goes public, reaching a valuation of $31 billion. Instagram launches video sharing. Bebo's founders buy it from Criterion Capitol Partners for $1 million. MySpace is relaunched with a new design and a mobile app.
2014	Amazon buys Twitch.tv for $970 million.
2015	Friendster is shut down. Twitter launches Periscope, a live video-sharing app. Bebo is relaunched.
2016	Time Inc. buys MySpace. Facebook launches Marketplace.
2017	Facebook reaches 2 billion users.

CHAPTER 4

THE GLOBAL PR REVOLUTION: SO FAR THE ONE AND ONLY!

PR'S "PREVIOUS LIFE"

Why is social media revolutionary? What caused a revolution in PR?

Here's the recap:

First, because social media has tremendously shortened both the time for communication and the deadlines for decision-making.

Second, because social media users own their accounts and have the freedom to express themselves (almost) without any restrictions.

Third, because this ownership of social media by their consumers is public, clear, and known. It is usually known who owns page ABC and profile XYZ.

Fourth, because social media now possesses a gigantic power of influence. A message posted on social media could theoretically be seen by the entire world in seconds, a thing that we couldn't even imagine twenty years ago.

Finally, because social media provides opportunity for interaction.

What can only be described as our "previous life," life before social media, truly feels like it was ages ago.

Back in that previous life, if some media outlet had published something against you or a client of yours, maybe even a lie, the road toward rectifying that might have been too long or even impossible.

Even if it had been possible, it would have taken days. Today, in social media, it takes seconds.

Social media has truly turned our industry upside down. Because of the social media revolution in PR (and elsewhere), we have been transformed into professional intermediaries, epitomizing the symbiosis of reporters, editors, and publishers.

We, the PR consultants, have in essence turned from consultants into decision-makers, because now decisions have to be made instantaneously. Just because of that one change, the PR business is totally different from what it used to be.

It is one thing being a consultant and telling your client, employer, or boss what your opinion is, so they can make an informed decision.

It is a whole other thing for you to be forced to make a decision *instead* of them because by the time you get in touch with that client, exchange thoughts, and agree on a course of action, a crisis situation might have become a hundred times worse.

That is why we, the PR experts, are now the people who have to make decisions.

The abovementioned five points are the gist of why PR has seen a revolution brought by social media.

Of course, at the end of the day, every revolution is made by people.

In our case, the transformation of the PR industry is also brought by people—but, more important, by thought leaders. Our industry is one of leadership, futuristic visionaries, and believers.

Those who drive the PR industry ahead keep themselves always in the public eye—yes, this may bring some negativity, but it brings a lot of positives, as well. This keeps us in the public mind, and of course, we bear the responsibility for being public figures. That really sets us apart as leaders.

We were in those shoes before the social media revolution, but now we own media, and the image that we present there is what we really are, and not what was portrayed before in traditional media.

PR'S FIRST TRUE REVOLUTION

Is there something else in the history of the PR industry that could be deemed comparable to the current revolution caused by social media?

Absolutely not. Today's revolution is the first true revolution in the PR business ever since its inception. That is indisputably so.

PR used to always be dependent on traditional media, as well as being dependable.

The media in its classical form—already long known as traditional media, which continues to linger on today—existed long before PR, print media in particular.

Radio and television, the electronic media that came after the press, were constituted in the same fashion as print media—they had different channels for delivering their messages, their messages might have even been different, but they were all one-way. No dialogue.

This has changed completely with social media, which has uplifted the quality of Web 1.0 to a whole new level, a whole new dimension, that of the interactive Web.

Dozens of leading global PR experts have contributed to this book by agreeing to be interviewed on the topic of social media revolution. Below you will find the most pertinent quotes from CEOs of top-notch PR companies around the globe.

Every single one seems to agree that the PR industry has been experiencing something huge and completely new.

Some agree with me that social media has brought about a true revolution in the PR business. Others deem it a fast evolution. Yet others say it's just a moderately paced evolution that is hugely important nonetheless.

The most skeptical of them even argue that the field and practice of public relations have remained the same—it's just stumbled upon some new channels of communication.

The PR professionals interviewed for this book have offered a marvelous palette of opinions as to what has been happening in the industry. It is an invaluable snapshot of a vastly tumultuous time for our business.

Overall, the revolution vs. evolution divide is roughly half and half.

There are those who believe that what the industry has undergone in the last few "social media years" is simply an evolution with revolutionary traits. This is probably because they do not take into account one of the most important factors: media ownership.

Yes, we can still write press releases, and we still use channels for communication for sending our messages.

However, those channels are of an entirely different type. And all of us, not just the PR companies, but all of us, the users, have ownership over the media platforms and can manage them as we please.

That was not the case just some ten years ago when we were fully dependent, the traditional media and online news media.

Everything used to revolve around that moment when the client would come in and say, "Could you present my product to the media?"

There wasn't even a discussion of the end consumers, because the main target audience was the media, the journalists, the reporters, and the editors: how to win them over, how to present this product as a great one, how to explain all of that to them.

Today, we are right there with the social media and hold it in our hands.

In my opinion, such change of ownership always means revolution, regardless of its direction.

The fall of Communism in Eastern Europe, for example. It is questionable whether that was a true political revolution (because many members of the former Communist elite still stick around), but it did bring up another revolution property-wise—privatization. Privatization was an absolute change of ownership and an absolute—at least mental—revolution.

That's the case not just with Eastern Europe, but in many other countries around the world.

Given that we have seen a change of ownership of the media, it is more than clear that we now have a wholly different PR industry—a revolutionized one.

In many countries where I went as ICCO president, I encountered the following when I went to PR companies. I would be told, "We do traditional PR!"

I would say, "What is traditional PR?" They said, "Well, it is this: we send out press releases, the clients come, we provide consultation, and we get paid for that . . ."

These times are long gone now. The times of the traditional image of the PR experts—in white shirts, red ties, and red suspenders with their legs up on the desk, with the client coming over and paying them $250 per hour for the consultation—has been long forgotten.

In my view, the image of the modern PR (human), *homo PR-icus*—that's the person who is nonstop plugged into social media—communicates and debates all the time and thinks creatively about how to reach the right people, the right target readers.

To a great extent, the PR experts need to know the target consumer, their traits, media consumption habits, preferences, everything.

The social media revolution has even changed the way PR experts dress. The far more casual dress code generally used to be the business card of the advertising industry. This style of dressing has now become dominant in the PR industry as well, because the power of the PR expert no longer lies in consultation. The expertise is now behind the keyboard, scrolling and posting in social media—this is how we communicate with clients and achieve their objectives.

Knowing social media to the tiniest detail is an absolute must for every single PR expert—from the CEO of the large PR corporation to the regular assistant or intern who sits behind a desk and does something on behalf of a client.

Multinational corporations use external PR companies to communicate with their clients via Facebook, Twitter, Instagram, etc. The responsibility is huge, because we have media in our hands—if one makes a blunder, this will not just discredit the business of his or her employer, it will also make a fool of the client and their reputation.

Even the business of giants such as IBM, Microsoft, Sony, Samsung, and BMW could literally be demolished with a single inappropriate tweet or a Facebook post. That is the beauty—and horror—of the social media revolution in PR and beyond!

Of the 100 PR experts from a total of 62 countries all around the world who contributed their opinions and observations to this book, roughly two-thirds are of the view that the PR industry has indeed experienced a true revolution as a result of the advent of social media.

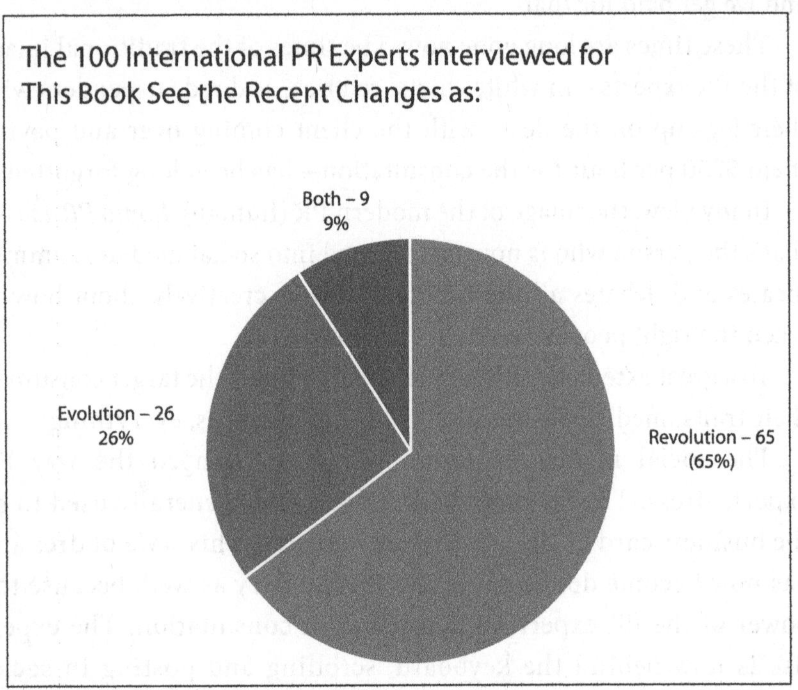

Following are the opinions and beliefs of some of the world's top PR experts as to whether they see social media as a revolution or an evolution in the industry and why.

Question: Do you consider the changes as revolutionary? Please explain why.

AARON KWITTKEN, CEO and Chairman, KWT Global (New York City, USA)

Yes! In fact, I don't believe specialized agencies will exist in five years. I think specialties will become practice areas of agencies and vertical practice areas will go away.

ADAM BENSON, Managing Director, Recognition PR (Brisbane, Australia)

The changes that successful firms have had to make to their business model, skill set, marketing, and sales are revolutionary. Apart from certain specialist PR firms, many across Australia have been pivoting for the past five years and now compete directly with social agencies, advertising agencies, content writers, design studios, marketing consultancies, and others.

ADRIANA VIEIRA, CEO, InterMídia Comunicação Integrada (São Paulo, Brazil)
Yes, these changes are super revolutionary because they force the brands/companies to find a new way to communicate with the public, no longer to "show what they sell," but to focus on creating value and social proposal. I do believe in social activism as the new great work of PRs. Creating projects to protect minorities and the environment, to empower women and teens, to invest in global education, and so on are the new challenges for global PRs.

AGNIESZKA DZIEDZIC, Managing Partner, Weber Shandwick (Warsaw, Poland)
Yes, because they require that PR agencies hire people who have different skills than the traditional PR consultant would have, or that traditional PR consultants develop these new skills (which is more difficult). Some PR agencies and consultants fail to recognize this and still see their job as limited to traditional media relations. And even though there is still a demand for media relations, for good knowledge of the media landscape, and good personal relations with journalists consultants must also live up to their primary role: being communication consultant to the client in these new times. This means they must understand how social media works, recognize the role and be able to identify the proper influencers as well as other stakeholders who affect the client's reputation.

AHMED JANABI, CEO, Harf Promotions (Baghdad, Iraq)
Yes. Revolution, in essence, is the word of the public overtaking any regime. I live and work in Iraq, and we have witnessed the effect of the Arab Spring and the new media's major influence on politics, society, religion, and everyday life. What the governments had built classically through traditional media for years was broken by social pressure through new media in a few hours.

AIVE HIIEPUU, President, Estonian PR Association (Tallinn, Estonia)

Of course! Because PR professionals need to be like multitalented journalists, ad experts, media experts, and behavioral psychologists.

AKI KUBO, Managing Director, North Asia, Williams Lea Tag (Tokyo, Japan)

The communications themselves have been/are/will be revolutionary changes.

ALAN OGDEN, Former Deputy Chairman, Hill+Knowlton Strategies (London, UK)

The changes in PR over the last decade have been primarily driven by technology as has the globalization of trade. In this context, they are of an evolutionary nature rather than revolutionary and follow previous twentieth-century technological inventions such as cinema, radio, and TV. However, like the invention of the mechanical clock and the printing press, which destroyed the stranglehold of the medieval church over time and information, the impact of affordable mobile digital platforms and advanced 4G communications that empower the individual as well as corporations and governments will have revolutionary applications in how societies govern themselves and, more worrisome, how vested political interests defend their power bases. Activism in the age of the internet is here to stay. For PR practitioners, the challenge to stay on top of these ongoing changes is a formidable one but not impossible, for evidence-based advocacy still remains the fundamental tenet of good communications.

ALISON CLARKE, Founder, Alison Clarke Consulting (London, UK)

Are these changes revolutionary—yes, because they place even greater emphasis on the importance of thoughtful, creatively relevant, and well-targeted content at the heart of effective campaigns . . . That is what our profession has always mastered, so this presents a real opportunity for the PR industry.

ALMA GERXHANI, CEO, Manderina Promotions (Tirana, Albania)

Yes, they are. They require use of technology to measure the sentiment about the brand and to deliver the right message to most of an audience at a given time. They require resources to monitor and respond with a tailored message that follows brand guidelines and satisfies the public and consumers.

ALTHAF JALALDEEN, General Manager, Phoenix Ogilvy—PR & Influence (Colombo, Sri Lanka)
Yes. Our approach to PR has shifted due to the recent changes. For example, more and more brand crises start from the social media platforms. It functions around the clock, and PR professionals now need to be more vigilant. Hence, our PR/influencer landscape has now expanded. Our PR strategies now have transformed from traditional approaches.

AMIR RASTEGAR, Director of International Affairs, Arman Public Relations Institute (Tehran, Iran)
Although technology has changed the way of PR performance due to digital and social media, changes are occurring with difficulty regarding the PR business in Iran. We must keep up with the times, so revolution is about to happen.

ANDRAS SZTANISZLAV, Senior Consultant and Managing Director, PersonaR (Budapest, Hungary)
No, I do not really see it as revolutionary. The markets have always been in constant change, and the rise of social media influence is not shockingly fast.

Yes, the communication channels have changed significantly in the last couple of years—more targeted campaigns, more results can be measured. But I do not see the market (especially the Hungarian market) adapting very fast. I look at this from a very optimistic perspective, because the new channels and tools mean new opportunities for PR professionals to get more jobs, more control over content.

ANDREW BONE, Chief Strategy Officer, Middle East and Africa, Hill+Knowlton Strategies (Riyadh, Saudi Arabia)
Yes, it's revolutionary in the way in which content publishing has shaken up the market, but it is not surprising. Everyone has a story to tell, and there are so many different ways to tell those stories through different channels. The result is we have much richer, more informative and more entertaining stories to read, watch, and listen to.

ANDREY BARANNIKOV, CEO, SPN Communications (Moscow, Russia)

Absolutely! Communication has reached a new level. Now we're working directly with our target audience though the social media. Communications have become personalized. New technical base makes this interaction very well targeted.

ARUN SUDHAMAN, CEO and Editor in Chief, The Holmes Report (Hong Kong/China)

For good PR people, no—these changes are evolutionary. But for too many in this business, the changes are revolutionary, because they represent a radical shift from business as usual, toward an environment where the customer is king and has the power to destabilize your brand like never before.

ASSEL KARAULOVA, President, Kazakhstan Press Club and National PR Association (Nur-Sultan, Kazakhstan)

It might not feel revolutionary, because it was incremental and we take it for granted. However, I think it is, because it completely changed the communications business. You don't need intermediaries anymore—it is direct communications. No boundaries, you can speak globally. No time constraints—viral might go to millions in minutes. Influencers, opinion leaders, bloggers with a huge audience—we have to understand how to work with these new trends and what it means for your business. Fake news is also a huge challenge. Technologies, especially AI in our industry—all is revolutionary and impacting every aspect of the PR industry.

BASHAR ALKADHI, CEO, Middle East, North Africa, and Turkey, Hill+Knowlton Strategies (Dubai, United Arab Emirates)

Clearly, the impact of social has been absolutely huge. YouTube and Twitter, for instance, have the largest penetration per capita in the world in countries such as Saudi Arabia and Kuwait. Facebook is massive in Egypt. These media have also had a significant impact on the sociopolitical environment in these countries, giving a direct voice to populations that did not have a voice and allowing much more peer-to-peer communications.

BOŽIDAR NOVAK, Owner, SPEM Communications (Ljubljana, Slovenia)
Yes. With social media, everybody is The Media.

BRIDGET VON HOLDT, Business Director, Burson Cohn & Wolfe (Johannesburg, South Africa)
Public relations is a dynamic profession and needs to constantly evolve. We have moved from the teletext to printed press releases delivered by hand, then to emailed media statements, now we can intervene with our own news channels—sometimes more effective and impactful than the conventional. Don't get me wrong—there is a place for all—just now, we have expanded channels.

Our audiences want information now! They are not prepared to go searching or hunting. It needs to be convenient, succinct, and entertaining. There is so much information out in the cyber world, the trick and strategy are to make sure we catch the customer in the moment.

CATALINA ROUSSEAU, President and CEO, BDR Associates (Bucharest, Romania)
Yes. It is revolutionary, as the future is already here! The new PR successfully combines strategic thinking, fast-changing technologies, and creativity.

These represent the intelligent ingredients for the most sophisticated communication era, in response to volatile environments that keep exposing clients to uncontrolled factors of influence, impacting businesses and damaging reputations.

CESARE VALLI, Former Managing Director, SEC (Milan, Italy)
This is an evolution, not a revolution; and it is not the first time this has happened. It happened "mutatis mutandis" with the diffusion of the radio and then television. Along with scientific and technological developments, communication has always been impacted and required adaptation. But the "essence" of communication is always "content." And this is the jewel that remains in place. Specially for Public Relations, being the most holistic communications discipline.

CHRISTOPHE GINISTY, Head of Digital Engagement, OECD (Paris, France/Brussels, Belgium)
Yes, of course, it is a revolution and a total game changer for PR professionals all over the world. It is a revolution for at least three reasons: (1) We've moved from a world of mastery to a world of humble collaboration; (2) corporations can invest millions of dollars to convince their audience, but that will not overcome any bad experience the public might have had with them; and (3) the target group that PR professionals were relying on (journalists, traditional opinion leaders) to perform their tasks have lost their influence to the benefit of newcomers who do not behave the same way and do not share the same ethical codes.

CIRO DIAS REIS, CEO, Imagem Corporativa (São Paulo, Brazil)
These changes are disruptive, because they stress the capacity (or not) of PR agencies to compete in a completely new business environment. In this new scenario, the competition comes from different places (ad agencies, marketing companies, consultancies, even law firms), not anymore exclusively from the traditional PR firms.

CLARA LY-LE, Managing Director, EloQ Communications (Ho Chi Minh, Vietnam)
Social media is a relatively new concept in Vietnam, but it has been adopted rapidly and changed everything. Crisis communication focuses more on brand health online monitoring. Brand communication digs more to shareable content instead of strictly brand-oriented content. Influencer marketing's impact is more measurable with the social media metrics and online fan analysis.

CLAUDINE MOORE, CEO, C. Moore Media International Public Relations (New York City, USA)
Not revolutionary. That would be too strong a word. But certainly, the way we do business has changed to mirror our environment.

DANIJEL KOLETIC, CEO, Apriori World (Zagreb, Croatia)
Yes, I think that these changes are definitely revolutionary. New generations bring new insights, new standards, new sources of information, new occupations, new dynamics, and that's simply part of a new communication age that is no longer just innovation, but a need. The digital revolution will not stop so quickly; it will only change its form.

DAPHNA TRIWAKS, CEO, Triwaks PR (Tel Aviv, Israel)
Yes and no, but in general yes. The PR industry will have to talk a new language that is suitable for mobile. Sharp, quick, short, and very visual.

DAVID GALLAGHER, President, International Growth and Development, Omnicom PR Group (London, UK)
This is part of what organizations like the World Economic Forum call the Fourth Industrial Revolution, and the PR business—like all others—will be transformed.

DAVID GORDON, Managing Partner, Cohn & Wolfe Canada (Toronto, Canada)
Yes. While "revolutionary" may not be the best term, these changes are nonetheless significant. However, at the same time, they may be temporal. As the pushback against "fake news" (often created to satisfy consumer demand) increases, and so does demand for integrity among news sources, a rebalancing may emerge.

DIMITRIS ROULIAS, Managing Partner, Out of the Box PR (Athens, Greece)
The technology available is revolutionary, and this forced all of us PR practitioners to revisit the fundamentals of our discipline. At the end of the day, though, we have to tell a story, which has to be relevant to a specific audience. Indeed, the tools we use to do it are evolving at an unprecedented pace.

EITAN HERSHCO, Chairman, Israeli PR Association (Tel Aviv, Israel)
This is without a doubt a revolutionary change in the approach and the PR actions that are focused on leading to the optimal and maximum exposure.

ELISE MITCHELL, Founder and CEO, Mitchell Communications Group (Fayetteville, Arkansas, USA)
No, it's not revolutionary. I would consider it evolutionary, as it's the next iteration of our agency business model. But its impact has been significant. We are constantly searching for better ways to serve our clients and deliver business-impacting ideas, and sometimes the most powerful impact can come from innovation to the way you do business.

ELIZABETH GOENAWAN ANANTO, Founding Director, International Public Relations Summit (Jakarta, Indonesia)
The interest outbreaks thus change people's attitude and behavior. As a professional in public relations, I don't think these changes happen in all of a sudden. We could predict what will happen in the era of digital technology.

ERIK CORNELIUS, Cofounder and COO, G3 Partners (Seoul, South Korea)
In Korea, the PR landscape has undergone more of a steady evolution than a revolution. Korea has long been on an accelerated digital adoption trajectory. The government also has a long history of taking regulatory actions that attempt to even the playing field. Korea's media and culture in general are conservative, which means change is slow and steady.

FABIÁN MOTTA, Director, Smart PR (Bogota, Colombia)
Without any doubt, digitalization is an aspect that has revolutionized the industry to the extent that we need to create stories for another type of consumer. For them, we must create stories that not only are easy to read, but also offer additional value. We also must use other types of tools such as infographics, videos, and podcasts that differentiate us from the competition and that give us the possibility of sending our message more bluntly. Right now, we are in a decade of opportunity for journalists and public relations, and so we must become great storytellers.

FILOMENA ROSATO, CEO, FiloComunicazione (Milan, Italy)
It depends on the perspective. Changes happen slowly, gradually making the right adjustments in all the pieces of the puzzle. "Revolutionary" is something able to deeply and definitively change a situation. The internet is just a tool, and the changes can only be superficial. It has made everything quicker, it has increased the applications of our job, it has created new skills. Yet it hasn't changed the DNA of PR.

GABRIEL PASLARU, General Manager, Perfect Co. (Bucharest, Romania)
A revolution? For sure, yes! The great loser, however, is credibility, while popularity at all cost tends to steal the show. Vast amounts of

information are traded on an ever-growing number of communication channels.

Former journalists are now on their own, freelancing in the way of blogging. They have old-school training and ethical and professional standards. But a new breed of news-makers is gaining ground: the self-made bloggers who do not necessarily care about the virtues of truth, timeliness, or morals.

GERMAN SAA, Group Director, Kyodo PR (Tokyo, Japan)
Just as when radio replaced the telegraph and TV replaced radios, yes, I guess we could consider these changes "revolutionary," because they oblige everyone in the industry to readjust the way we work from planning to execution. Also, KPIs have changed completly, and clients are no longer satisfied with good coverage on traditional media. They also need and ask for Integrated PR programs that cover all areas of commmunication, reaching their audiences on all platforms available.

GUNTRAM KAISER, Managing Partner, Kaiser Communication (Berlin, Germany)
If you interpret a revolution as a drastic and far-reaching change in ways of thinking and behaving, then I entirely agree. The role of PR is becoming bigger and more relevant as such values as trust, ethics, credibility, sustainability, reliability are becoming more important. Dramatic changes in the instruments of PR, although not as radical as the social media and the internet now, also occurred in the past if you consider the rise of radio and TV, for example.

HALIM WALID ABOU SEIF, Senior PR Consultant, Rada Research & PR (Cairo, Egypt)
Yes, of course, the digital revolution, the use of the web, the domination of social networks have made PR take different approaches. Not only different tools, but also different strategies and more focused, personalized approaches.

ILARIJA BAŠIĆ, PR Director, MITA Group (Sarajevo, Bosnia and Herzegovina)
Unfortunately, despite the changes, we are still facing many difficulties, such as the lack of understanding of PR's role in companies (in

many, PR is still part of the marketing department), small budgets, and doing jobs that a PR expert should not do. Our profession is interesting to young colleagues who have their place in the PR field, but they have to understand that this is a profession that requires daily work on yourself, learning, and training.

JACK MARTIN, Former Global Chairman and CEO, Hill+Knowlton Strategies (Austin, Texas, USA)
The world is progressing rapidly, making every day different from the one before it. Public relations as an industry is no longer just about communicating most effectively, but it is also about understanding new channels of communication that often appear unexpectedly and become rapidly prevalent. In today's world, if you blink, you'll miss it.

JAFAR MANSIMI, Cofounder, PRoloq Magazine (Baku, Azerbaijan)
PR standards have changed, and this affects us. Being more creative, being accountable, experiencing experimentation, and making better observations require us to be deeper in this field, to be more careful. So there is always a need for improvement in these issues. The PR experts these days do things that they never did before. And this is a good sign that we live in a different and much more interesting time for business.

JAROSLAV MAJOR, Senior Consultant, Hill+Knowlton Strategies (Prague, Czech Republic)
No! So far, these changes are not revolutionary and (until now) have been quite predictable. We can speak about revolutionary changes only when angry Czech citizens mobilized on social networks (following the example of the Arab Spring) perform the third Prague defenestration.

JOAN RAMON VILAMITJANA, CEO, Hill+Knowlton Strategies (Madrid, Spain)
No. We're not seeing a revolution. We're seeing a tremendous acceleration in the speed of change. This is an incremental change, and the essence of our job has remained the same since I joined the industry, believe it or not, in the late twentieth century: influence, persuade, convince, and, above all, be authentic. Be true.

JOHN SAUNDERS, CEO and President, FleishmanHillard, (Dublin, Ireland/St. Louis, USA)
We're seeing these changes more like a "natural progression" rather than a "revolution." PR has had front-row seats to the rapid advancement of technology and—since technology continues to play an enormous role in how people communicate and perceive information—our industry is very closely attuned to these trends.

JÜRGEN H. GANGOLY, Managing Partner and CEO, The Skills Group (Vienna, Austria)
Yes, it's a revolution. Social media don't only change our own industry sector in PR and communications, they change societies, companies, and how free speech and democracy, in general, will look like in the future.

JUSTIN GREEN, Director, Wide Awake Communications (Dublin, Ireland)
Yes, revolutionary, as even though many have been aware of the upcoming changes, nobody thought their impact would be so quick. Departments that have existed for over twenty years have died over the past three years and have now been replaced by new digital lead departments.

KAMAL TAIBI, Founder and CEO, Stratëus Group (Casablanca, Morocco)
These changes are revolutionary in the sense that the C-Suite is more and more engaging with high-level consultants with a clear understanding of public behavior. That was not the case when communications was a one-to-many channel only. That's why many PSFs (Professional Services Firms) are offering services in communications and eating up market share from PRFs (Public Relations Firms).

KARA ALAIMO, Assistant Professor of Public Relations, Hofstra University, and CNN contributor (New York City, USA)
Yes. Never before have chief executives played the role of activists. Nor have they ever been worried about their own endorsers publicly attacking them. Previously, public relations practitioners felt that when reporters made mistakes, they could pick up the phone and get them corrected. But, with fake news sites, that's no longer the case.

KHALID BADDOU, President, Moroccan Association of Marketing and Communication (Casablanca, Morocco)
The clients' attitude is game-changing, especially in markets like Morocco and the rest of Africa. For the past two decades, the communication industry was moving toward specialization (advertising, digital, events, PR), obliging the client to speak to different partners, while losing precious time, effort, and money. Today, agencies are asked to offer a one-stop shop to clients, with the right understanding of business problematic, customer needs, and how to address them.

KHRISTO AYAD, Senior Director, BLJ Worldwide (Doha, Qatar)
Yes, the rise of digital communication constitutes a revolutionary change. The fact that everybody now has become a media owner in their own right, easily, without significant cost, globally and without delay, is opening a myriad of possibilities for PR practitioners and audiences alike. This in principle unfiltered two-way exchange should result in better, more tailored content, greater productivity, better understanding, better products, better services, and better governance.

KIM NYBERG, Chairman, M-Brain, and Special Adviser, Hill+Knowlton Strategies (Helsinki, Finland)
The technology revolution means both good and bad for communications. Never before has it been possible to communicate as effectively and rapidly with a large number of people, being able to measure their reactions, understanding drivers, and drawing conclusions based on so many facts. All this is great, but at the same time, therein lies the risk that we are losing our focus, forgetting creative planning and execution, and, above all, understanding human thinking what it is that makes us tick).

KRESTEN SCHULTZ-JØRGENSEN, CEO, Oxymoron (Copenhagen, Denmark)
The entire consulting market is changing due to global and technological megatrends—and as an industry, we have to stay ahead of the curve.

LARS ERIK GRØNNTUN, Global President, Hill+Knowlton Strategies (Oslo, Norway)
It's more of an evolution. This is a change taking place over some time, so it is not a revolution. But the effects from it change a lot of what we do, so in that sense, you might say they are revolutionary.

LORENA CARREÑO, President, Confederation of Communication Marketing Industry (Mexico City, Mexico)
Yes, they are definitely revolutionary changes; we need to be faster, more reliable, more precise; the key messages charge more life than ever.

LOULA ZAKLAMA, President, Rada Research & PR (Cairo, Egypt)
Of course these changes are revolutionary; the digital revolution, the use of the web, the domination of social networks made PR take different approaches, not only different tools, but also different strategies and more focus, more personalized approaches. Segmentation of stakeholders has totally changed: now stakeholders are categorized by the way they act, more than the socioeconomic class they belong to. And that is much more traceable by the new digital arena. Now we can target certain stakeholders better and with more focus on their attitude.

MARTIN PETERSON, President and CEO, H&H Group (Stockholm, Sweden)
It is revolutionary in the sense that it represents a new level of opportunity for our industry to make a real difference.

MARTIN SLATER, CEO, Noesis PR (Milan, Italy)
Yes, the changes are revolutionary. But there are always successive revolutionary changes—the printing press, daily broadsheets, radio, TV, etc. Traditional media has had to make painful readjustments in the past few years. Anyone can be a journalist, commenting the news, so there are many more sources of information.

SIR MARTIN SORRELL, Founder, WPP and S4Capital PLC (London, UK)
Technology, in particular, has revolutionized many aspects of the way in which we conduct our business, but the fundamental value of what we do is unchanged. Investment in marketing services such as public relations is just as vital for the long-term health of a brand as it was five years ago, and indeed as it was more than thirty years ago, when we started WPP.

MASSIMO MORICONI, General Manager and CEO, Omnicom Public Relations Group (Milan, Italy)
Not really. I think this is what we somehow expected. The point is that it is happening faster than expected.

MICHAEL THOMAS SCHRÖDER, CEO, ORCA Affairs (Berlin, Germany)
Yes, because the interlinking of disciplines and know-how is growing. The combination of know-how and the interlinking of the various disciplines is more than ever the key to a successful corporate communication online. Today's PR professionals should be flexible and open to new forms of communication and web technologies. Even some basic search engine knowledge is no longer enough for a PR professional. Only those who manage to develop PR texts for people and machines can optimize visibility and reach in the search engines.

MICHAELA BENEDIGOVÁ, Managing Director and Partner, Seesame (Bratislava, Slovakia)
The rise of social media brought with it situations where brands lost control of communication. They had to deal with public pressure while maintaining values. It was this public control that brought a huge transformation. The development of technology substantially influenced the communications industry as a whole.

MINA NAZARI, Public Relations Expert, Tabriz Electric Power Distribution Company (Tehran, Iran)
There has been no revolution in my country over the last five years, but in the world in the field of propaganda, there has been a tremendous transformation that has proven the importance of public relations more than ever for all people.

MYKOLAS KATKUS, Chairman of the Board, FABULA (Vilnius, Lithuania)
I would not call it a revolution, as everything was in place five years ago, as well. It is the continuation of the evolution, and, if you ask me, I thought everything would change at a much faster pace than it has.

MYRON WASYLYK, CEO, PBN Hill+Knowlton Strategies (Moscow, Russia)
Of course, I consider these changes revolutionary, because they are changing the behavior patterns from what we were accustomed to when PR agencies were started in the 1930s and 1940s. Now we have the Internet of Things and mobile devices, which have revolutionized the way we receive information, who and where we receive it from,

and the speed with which we receive it. That's why I think revolutionary is the right way of putting it.

NITIN MANTRI, Group CEO, AvianWE (New Delhi, India)
Yes, I think the changes are revolutionary. Till some years back, the PR industry was seen as a bunch of order takers at the end of the value chain, while strategy and creative programming were led by advertising and other marketing functions. Today, we are sitting at the high table with clients and helping clients navigate their business environment. These are exciting times for an industry that has been struggling with meager budgets for years. We have come a long way from the days when we were just expected to communicate to the media what the brand has done to the present day, when we are looked upon as trusted advisers to brands.

NURUL SHAMSURI, Project Director, Yayasan Juwita (Kuala Lumpur, Malaysia)
Definitely. The fragmentation of media due to the proliferation of online platforms means that the reputations of companies are now more vulnerable than ever before. Companies and their PR units or appointed agencies have to be rather quick in their response. In order to survive and thrive, PR agencies—like media companies and advertising agencies—have to evolve. The old ways don't work anymore.

OKSANA MONASTYRSKA, Managing Director, PBN Hill+Knowlton Strategies (Kiev, Ukraine)
Yes, these changes are revolutionary; they are transforming the communications industry. The growing demand of consumers for social responsibility and transparency of brands is changing the way businesses operate. The role of employees as brand advocates is growing by the day, while building trust has become the #1 task for company leaders, placing CEO activism ahead of products and services.

PATRIK SCHOBER, CEO, PRAM Consulting (Prague, Czech Republic)
I do not think these changes are revolutionary. I see them instead as an evolution, and from the historical point of view, it will be just minor changes or the beginning of a complete change of work and communication behaviors.

PELIN KOCAALP, General Manager, Hill+Knowlton Strategies (Istanbul, Turkey)
Yes, of course; technology is now the most important communication tool for organizations. The rapid development of new technology has changed the way of doing communications through traditional media. Social media has made public relations more challenging, but it has also helped the corporate's accessibility to their audiences. In the early years, communications managers weren't able to engage with their audiences as easily as they can today. Now you can interact with your stakeholders and target audiences immediately through real-time channels.

PETER MUTIE, CEO, Peterson Integrated Communications (Nairobi, Kenya)
The changes are revolutionary, because they have shifted the way we do business. For instance, we are doing more advertisements online than in daily newspapers. Second, the young population has shifted in terms of taste.

PHILIPPE BORREMANS, Independent PR Consultant, Reputation & Co. (Casablanca, Morocco)
No, these changes have been under way for more than ten years. The whole "social media revolution" started with blogs in the early 2000s, and we're now almost twenty years later. Rather, I would call it a very slow evolution on the part of the PR industry and its clients. The general public is adapting much faster than the industry.

RANA NEJEM, Founding Director, Yarnu: The Art of Social Intelligence (Amman, Jordan)
I find it more evolutionary than revolutionary. It is the natural progression of communications and the way that everything seems to be heading toward less mass and more personalization—more power to the individual.

RETO WILHELM, Managing Director, Panta Rhei PR (Zurich, Switzerland)
Yes, as technology is the driving force—no new business idea with knowledge and even ownership of own specific technology tools—a huge investment for midsize agencies.

Yes, as the classical split of owned and paid content disappears.

Yes, as the influence of fake news—distributed by so-called user-generated content distributors and other media—is challenging the credibility of classical PR consultancies.

RHINGO MUTAMBO, Chief PR Officer, Prime Minister's Bureau (Windhoek, Namibia)

The public relations profession has evolved so much in the last thirteen years, particularly in terms of scope of work and recognition, especially in the public service, as the largest employer.

For instance, the role of public relations in the public sector in terms of media and public engagement and information dissemination has notably improved over the years.

In general, the industry is at a growth level as characterized by an increasing number of PR professionals, high competition for available jobs, specialized disciplines at tertiary institutions, increasing demand for accredited professionals, and an increasing number of specialized niche markets within the industry.

RICHARD MILLAR, Global President, Hill+Knowlton Strategies (London, UK)

I (we) have seen more change in the past five years than in any preceding period of my more than thirty years in the profession. A fundamental shift in power and influence away from the institutions of the state, from business, and from a once objective and impartial media into the hands of the public. The public now has the power to make and break reputations and at a speed once unimaginable in the days before the internet.

For this reason, I see the changes as "accelerated evolution" rather than revolution. Accelerated evolution that now demands higher-than-ever levels of transparency, and truth.

SARI-LIIA TONTTILA, Founder, Ahjo Communications Oy (Helsinki, Finland)

Paul Gauguin once said, "There are only two kinds of artists—revolutionaries and plagiarists." They are revolutionary because if we accept that purpose is a universal force, then we must begin to see its positive presence everywhere. We are just starting to acknowledge that business can save the world. Like all revolutions, the movement toward values captures more minds and hearts. Social issues are business issues.

SAURABH UBOWEJA, CEO, Brands of Desire (New Delhi, India)
I see these changes are evolutionary and necessary rather than revolutionary. The current media environment creates many versions of the same story.

While none of them may represent the whole truth, at least the reader gets to see multiple perspectives and is able to form her own unique perspective out of it. This is only possible, as everyone is now becoming a journalist and a storyteller of sorts. The traditional role of journalism is now under threat!

SCOTT E. FAHLMAN, Research Professor, Carnegie Mellon University, and inventor of the "Smiley" emoticon (Pittsburgh, USA)
Over the past five years, the growing success of Facebook, Twitter, Instagram, and all the others has surprised us all. When I first heard about Twitter, I thought that the idea of communicating by spewing 140-character snippets to all your "followers" was the worst idea I had ever heard and that Twitter could never catch on. Now I only believe half of that. :-)

This too is revolutionary, I think, and mostly in a good way.

SERGE BECKERS, Managing Partner, Wisse Kommunkatie (Arnhem, Netherlands)
Yes, these changes were a real game changer. Digital and social have really entered the battlefield, forcing us—old-school PR people—to adapt. And in the meantime giving us the possibility to develop new ways to deploy PR activities.

SERGEY ZVEREV, CEO, Cross Communications (Moscow, Russia)
Sure they are. Every PR specialist is now in a position when tomorrow he may be replaced by a bot or AI. So we have to develop constantly and integrate more deeply and densely into our clients' businesses.

SHAMIL TUMISANG AGOSI, Director, Square Gate Holdings (Gaborone, Botswana)
Definitely yes. With digital PR, big data, technology, and social media guaranteeing audiences' interaction, this raises the need for a real-time response. Big data in this regard affords a way to predict

audience behavior and preferences that PR professionals would have to embrace. This in itself is revolutionary.

SHELLEY SPECTOR, Founder, Museum of Public Relations (New York City, USA)
In my view there is no revolution, but an evolution of technologies that allow us to communicate faster and faster and with potentially greater numbers of people. Social media provides another set of channels—albeit very powerful ones—in a long list of other channels and is considered as powerful as TV in the 60s, radio in the 20s, and photography in the early 19th century.

SOLLY MOENG, Convenor, SA Brand Summit & Awards (Cape Town, South Africa)
Definitely yes. The implications are that PR professionals have to do more, master more platforms, know how to create content and work with huge data.

SOPHYA BALAKINA, Cofounder and CEO, Bureau of Communications TAGS (Bishkek, Kyrgyzstan)
Unfortunately, I can't call them revolutionary. They are logical and inert, and, rather, they did not allow the market to fall behind. But I strongly believe that the mentality of the Central Asian people, peculiarities of communications in local communities are worthy of separate interest and research. The results and conclusion made can be scaled not only for a particular region, but also applied in other parts of the globe.

STUART BRUCE, Managing Consultant, Stuart Bruce Associates (Leeds, UK)
Revolutionary or evolutionary. Change has happened rapidly, but still over a period of time, so it must be evolutionary? But the Industrial Revolution happened over a period of time, so perhaps this is a digital revolution. But if we think what we've been through is a revolution, then we ain't seen nothing yet. An even bigger revolution will be artificial intelligence, which within the next twenty years—the rest of my working life—will displace millions of jobs. Politicians, governments, companies, nobody really understands how society and the economy will change as a result.

SVETLANA JAPALĂU, Managing Director, BDR Associates—Strategic Communication (Kishinev, Moldova)

Step by step, PR & Strategic Communication gains position as an industry in the market. Here I'd go back in the history of PR in our country: this industry is quite young, as it started when BDR Associates Communication Group entered the market back in 2002 following a successful pitch.

As any other young industry, it needs to be regulated by national laws and industry ethics. In this respect, yes, all the changes mentioned above are revolutionary for our market, as step by step all of them will lead to the regulation and consolidation of the industry.

TAMARA BEKČIĆ, Managing Director, Chapter 4 Communications (Belgrade, Serbia)

The way we do our work and reach stakeholders now, and the way we have fifteen, ten, or five years ago, has changed a lot. The changes are revolutionary, and my work day does not even resemble the one from, let's say, 2010, let alone 2005.

The greatest challenge is to keep up with what the modern world represents, through new channels and opportunities, and get the message across in a timely and attractive manner, because the needs, likes, and dislikes of our audiences have changed dramatically.

TATEVIK PIRUMYAN, Communication Key Expert, EU Assistance to Armenia Project (Yerevan, Armenia)

Maybe to some extent. However, all changes are in line with the technological developments and are pretty proportionate. To me, the changes are more evolutionary than revolutionary. One thing that can be considered as revolutionary is the availability of big data and the opportunities it brings in all stages of PR strategy—from the identification and analysis of the target groups to the measurement of the effectiveness of its implementation.

TATJANA LOPARSKI, CEO, Element PR (Skopje, Macedonia)

The changes are revolutionary, and it changes the rules and setup of the communications strategies. People read fewer newspapers, and they are spending more time online, reading news from social media and commenting. Now everyone became a sort of "journalist."

THIERRY WELLHOFF, President and CEO, Wellcom (Paris, France)
With the advent of digital and social media, the credibility of companies is in free fall, hence an increasing role to play for PR. This is a revolution!

THOMAS TINDEMANS, Chairman, Hill+Knowlton Strategies (Brussels, Belgium)
This generalized skepticism in the public mind destroys traditional PR impact. Truthful narratives that restore confidence in the intentions and the purpose of organizations combined with absolute honesty and transparency could help to overcome this skepticism.

VIVIAN LINES, Global Vice Chairman, Hill+Knowlton Strategies (Singapore)
These changes are evolutionary, not revolutionary, but it is an evolution that has jumped from dinosaurs to humans in a matter of months and years, driven by the immediacy of communications. That is an impact that is being felt globally.

YASEMIN EDIGE ÖZTUNC, Group Coordinator, Lobby PR (Istanbul, Turkey)
Yes, I do. Because it transformed (and is still transforming) business, commerce, and society. It also changed how we do our business, public relations. Of course, the basic principles remain the same, but the mechanisms by which we apply those principles in practice—that has changed. For example, building trust was always important. Ten years ago, you would start by placing ads on newspapers or organizing a press meeting. Today you cannot afford not having social media in your plan.

Today, reputation can be leveraged for strategic advantage through insights gained from the scientific application of real-time big data analytics and multidisciplinary approaches. This is revolutionary.

YOMI BADEJO-OKUSANYA, CEO, CMC Connect Burson Cohn & Wolfe (Lagos, Nigeria)
Most definitely yes. As the global space evolves constantly, PR must ride with the tide. Why? Failure to do so will consign our practice to the dustbin like the typewriter. Every practitioner must reinvent

him- or herself. Our jobs are at risk of being taken over by management consultants.

ZDENEK LOKAJ, Former Managing Director, Hill+Knowlton Strategies (Prague, Czech Republic)
No. Revolutionary would be too strong a word. Technology always brings some changes, from the time that writing on parchments came about and then the printing press was developed. These changes are important factors for societies and their development, but they rarely changed social orders.

ZHAO DALI, Secretary General, China International PR Association (Beijing, China)
Yes. The changes reflect the promotion of China's soft power. What's more, the changes make the PR people in China have a long-term view of development in the future.

ZSOFIA LAKATOS, CEO, Emerald Communications (Budapest, Hungary)
Yes, our whole profession is changing, and only those who are able to adapt will survive.

THE GLOBAL PR REVOLUTION THESIS AND ITS DISCONTENTS

As demonstrated by the opinions provided by my colleagues from many different countries, there are various viewpoints on whether what's been happening in the PR industry is a revolution, or evolution, or nothing much at all.

Nevertheless, I don't believe that my thesis about the global PR revolution has any weak links that can be attacked—save, perhaps, for the simplistically basic fact that we all use language as the means to influence our audiences.

Yet before the revolutionary changes in the past few years, this language content was conveyed in a different way, first and foremost. Because of those changes, content now reaches our target audiences almost immediately, within a matter of seconds.

Second, for the first time, this content is interactive—that is, it can be influenced itself, as communication is now two-way.

Third, which I emphasize many times throughout this book, is that everybody is media. Everybody has access to media and could therefore theoretically try to influence you, send messages your way, even manipulate you.

This entire revolutionary transformation, in which everybody now has access to their own media, could be likened to Eastern Europe's revolutionary transition from a centralized, state-owned economy under Communism back to private property and free enterprise.

Before the global revolution of online media and social media, whose ramifications certainly go way beyond the PR industry, traditional media were owned by a handful of people, and only they had access to their content. The average Joe couldn't send any public messages through what we now refer to as traditional media in any meaningfully independent way.

Similarly, under Communism, only a handful of people, the top party functionaries and intelligence operatives, had access to the levers of power and economic activity. The regular people were entirely disenfranchised in that regard. That is largely why the collapse of the Communist regimes and the restoration of private property and free economic and political will is seen as a revolution.

All of a sudden, all had free will and the means of economic production back in their own hands.

I am sorry for the politically charged analogy, but the global PR revolution is quite similar: all of a sudden, you hand three or four billion people media of their own, enabling them to spread whatever information they like or write and publish what they please, be it fake news, truths, personal stories, curse words, useful information, etc.

Actually, when I delve deeper into this notion, I can't help but think that it's something even greater than a plain old revolution.

Because of the sweeping and overwhelming changes in the past few years, I see no weaknesses in my concept and thesis about the global PR revolution.

Of course, in the PR industry, in addition to other spheres, there are many who have perceived this transition so gradually and smoothly that they don't even deem it a revolution.

However, I am certain that if those people had to go back in time ten years, and were forced to work the way they did back then, it is far from guaranteed that they would even manage to do it. That goes for both those of us who specialize in the PR business, and for our clients.

One of the mightiest features of this revolution that I personally feel every single day is that back in the old days, we used to change over years; today, we change within a matter of hours.

One has got to be constantly alert and follow everything that has changed. On Tuesday, there might be one type of media; on Wednesday, there might be an entirely different type that has much greater features, which might enable you to bring far more tangible benefits to your clients and your own business.

My global PR revolution thesis will certainly not go down without criticism. The most severe criticism should be expected from the people who don't know the PR industry. They might say, "Revolution? What revolution? Facebook is just out there anyway!"

The revolution is actually so profound that even civil servants, the people who are literally paid their salaries by the taxpayer, feel their influence. Civil servants are actually the most vulnerable now, because they generally used to live as if in a sanatorium: nobody could bother them in the age of the newspapers!

Even in the most developed markets, even in the United States, where public communications are probably more advanced than anywhere else, the civil servants used to be under some kind of government protection. Hundreds of movies and a huge load of books have been written on these topics.

Today, that is just not possible. Nobody is safe, nobody's peace and quiet are guaranteed if they do something stupid or illegal or corrupt. With this global revolution, we are witnessing the (re)surfacing of things from thirty years ago, which should have become nullified by the sheer amount of time that has passed since they occurred. Within a matter of thirty years, there could be legal amnesties, even for murderers.

In order to tackle such extremes, we need to have values, moral receptors, because not everybody who tried to kiss a woman thirty years ago is a criminal. Many of those who did it are by now happily married with twenty-nine-year-old children.

This book certainly goes beyond the PR industry to mention advertising, marketing, and politics. Nevertheless, there is hardly going to be criticism on the part of our colleagues from the public communications industries who don't deal with public relations. Rather, there might be some envy there because of how rapidly we're developing and changing.

The advertising industry, for example, has not seen that many changes. Even though budgets for online advertising are beginning to catch up with those for traditional media, the advertising industry still relies on classic media.

While millions of digital companies have sprung up, and have started to develop vast online advertising niches, the large budgets concentrated in the hands of media shops still keep going to traditional media.

Of course, the most important platform, which is destroying this type of concentration of huge money in the hands of media shops, is Facebook. Again, there is no point in paying a media shop $1 or 2 million for advertising when you can give that money to Facebook, who will provide you with more targeted and effective advertising than any media shop.

Many of us in the PR business, however, feel the change in a very tangible way, because this industry now requires a whole other type of quality, a different way of focusing on things, a different language and way of expression, and an array of other tools, advance preparation being first and foremost. You just have to be hyperprepared for all kinds of situations.

Which is great news for myself and my own business, because now, after twenty-five years in the industry, I know how pleasant it is to be very well prepared, to know a lot of things, and to have been through a lot of different situations, especially in the online business. Thanks to that, whenever a client walks in or contacts us, we are immediately able to offer them a solution. Because my colleagues know as well as I do that we must read a lot and change a lot every single day.

That wasn't the case before! A market used to have, say, fifteen newspapers you would know very well, and you had ten tools that you knew very well, and there was no point in any kind of change. Sure, you would edit some headlines here and there occasionally, but that was part of the business.

Every single critic of the global PR revolution thesis can be refuted extremely easily using several arguments. Here are the two strongest ones.

First, everybody has access to the media, and everybody is media, and everybody can operate media. This is a cataclysmic revolution in itself, not just in PR, but in all public life and social relations, not to even speak of politics, governance, corporate management, etc. The very fact that everybody has access to media of their own doesn't just concern PR, it concerns our very existence.

Second, these media and their messages are interactive, they are not one-way, and they can be used to hold debates and discussions that could, in turn, produce a lot of truths. In my view, this is helping societies make gigantic strides forward.

CHAPTER 5

THE AGE OF TOTAL TRANSPARENCY (TT)

A BRAVE NEW TRANSPARENT WORLD

The tsunami of social media that has conquered global communications within a few years has swept away privacy, once predominant, and has laid the groundwork for a new world where everything is public—or is rapidly becoming so—and where everything is transparent—or is about to be.

Welcome to the World of Total Transparency!

It might seem scary, but it will certainly be a better world.

Though, nobody is really obliged to be transparent in such an era.

Transparency remains a selectable feature, a matter of choice for the individual.

However, when it comes to the corporate world, there isn't a choice anymore—there are no opt-outs from TT. A corporation's sustainability depends on transparency in this competitive world.

Modern-day consumer awareness has reached such staggering levels that consumers get to know everything about a certain product and the corporation producing it. If consumers are not informed the same minute about any changes or alterations, they may never purchase your product again.

Brands are no longer the property of the companies, but of the consumers, and consumer power over brands is enormous.

As Paul Holmes has put it, and as I firmly believe: "A brand is what people say about you when you are not in the room."

There is no way to avoid total transparency anymore, at least when it comes to doing business. It is absolutely necessary and mandatory.

TT BASICS

The two main traits of the world of total transparency are its hyper-dynamics (because everything is shifting at a mind-blowing speed) and an immeasurably higher dose of ethics.

Back in 2001, as part of Bulgaria's Business Leaders' Forum, I wrote the first business ethics code in Bulgaria. Then I visited each of our twenty-eight provinces to talk business ethics to the local business communities.

Usually they asked what business ethics actually was, and as a result, I formulated the most concise definition of business ethics: *making a profit in a transparent way.*

That is precisely what the world of total transparency is all about. We are in business to make a profit, and if we do that transparently, this means we do it ethically.

If you try any dishonest tricks, that will become obvious immediately.

Sensing the advent of the world of total transparency, it seems as though people have become a little bit more apprehensive, more cautious, more distrustful, fearing that something they say will end up online because of hidden cameras, data leaks, stolen flash drives.

It used to be that news of whatever happened to an individual would spread to fifty or a hundred people, no more. Someone told someone else, there was a rumor, and that was it. Now, the entire world may easily learn about anything the moment it happens.

The march of total transparency is aided by a powerful snowball effect. Once transparency kicks in, there is no going back.

Regardless of many people's perceived need to be extracautious in this new age, the rise of transparency caused by the social media revolution is rapidly building a far better world.

For the PR industry, the No. 1 consequence is that PR experts need to be trained much, much better in order to be well prepared for any eventuality.

Creativity, honesty, and accuracy remain as essential as ever, but brilliant preliminary preparation for crisis situations, which may strike at any time, is of the utmost importance for the PR expert in the social media revolution.

At first glance, total transparency, fast communication, and the unrestricted use of media presuppose a fertile ground for manipulation, which may be one reason the world is becoming so cautious. But transparency doesn't have that much to do directly and specifically with manipulation.

Manipulation can be exercised through traditional media even if the audience is very restricted and exclusive. It is just that now there is a much greater possibility for manipulation to spread faster and wider, with greater coverage and influence.

On the other hand, the opportunities for thwarting, exposing, and disproving manipulation stories are also invariably greater because of social media platforms' interactive quality, which sets them apart from any other means of public communication to date.

We all come across fake news, but the moment five people post comments declaring it as such, readers should be able to realize that themselves.

PR: LESS ELITIST THAN EVER

When it comes to social media, a PR professional needs to be literally all over the place and on top of everything. Public relations was never truly an elitist industry, and today it is less so than ever.

A very small portion of PR is designed to serve the CEOs and the senior management of corporations. If you work with grocery products, or mass consumer goods such as consumer electronics, or other types of goods that are used by various groups of people, you have to use their language to communicate effectively. That is largely linked with the individual social experience of a PR professional, which is a necessity.

Political marketing and PR could be described as elitist to some extent, although again, you have to express and verbalize your messages in the language of the people who are not part of this elite. Messages such as "America First" or "Make America Great Again" tickle both the elite and the common folk.

PR is not an elitist industry. Rather, it is an industry for the people it is supposed to reach. If it needs to reach a working-class demographic, then PR experts would have to speak their language and know how to speak to them in the most effective manner. This means that we, the PR people, should be able to explain one and the same thing to various audiences in ways that they understand—whether it's the president of the United States or someone fixing cars in their own garage in the Bronx.

Yet, at the same time, language changes so much and so quickly—especially in English—that there is a barely noticeable difference anymore between elitist language and conversational language.

The public landscape is actually dominated by the language of online communication, and of social media in particular. Elitism is the last thing to feature prominently in social media, because such platforms are for mass consumption. However, social media does provide an opportunity to create certain societies that might not necessarily stand out but are valued for their qualities (i.e., elitist members).

There is some criticism that many people around the world might be unable to take advantage of the abundance of opportunities presented by the social media revolution because of insufficient comprehension and underdeveloped critical thinking skills.

Yet when it comes to our industry, that might not be very relevant, given that the average citizen of Tucson, Arizona, for example, does not need PR services. And if such a person *does* happen to need PR services, thanks to social media, he can now handle it on his own.

The owner of a small shop in Tucson doesn't need media reporters at his door—he just needs to tell his story on social media and attract the people in the neighborhood. He can do that on his own, or some local journalist can do that for him for a small amount of money, or his teenage kid can do it for free.

Solving a PR crisis, reputation management, or building and developing a corporate image, for example, when there is a merger between companies, especially in the financial sector, is a whole other story. These are activities that need to be done proactively and by a professional.

When it comes to PR, everybody benefits from social media platforms—from the large corporations to the "little people."

Along with everything else, social media has given a gigantic boost to business, something that has never been seen before.

That person with the small store in Tucson would have never even thought of being able to promote his business in a medium of his own, and instead, he would have been saving money in order to run an ad in the local newspaper or on local radio, or he would have been trying to befriend some local journalist and chug a couple of tequila shots with him in the bar in order to get him to write something about his business.

Now, every single person has the terrific opportunity to promote their business on social media and to develop, boost, and grow it with minimum funds, perhaps even without any funds at all.

All it takes to make it at this basic business level is perseverance, persistence, tenacity, and ambition.

This is especially true of online businesses and online stores, which have turned the very notion of doing business upside down. Social media is taking over online trade, as well. There are already online stores with no specific websites that sell products solely on social media—the so-called Facebook stores.

But players such as eBay, Amazon, and Alibaba have truly transformed the world from a business standpoint.

Even though it started much earlier, the bulk of this transformation of social media and the social web occurred in 2007–2008. What has changed since then is that social media has completely conquered the world.

Even though Twitter and Facebook already existed in 2008, Facebook had "only" 100 million users. Now it has over 2 billion, plus a great variety of new functions and options.

Additionally, visuals and imagery are on the rise, becoming more important than ever in any kind of communication. Live communication has also become an invaluable option for social media.

ABUSING TT

Can PR abuse or misuse the opportunities offered by the world of total transparency?

Sure it can! There certainly are PR companies out there that still succumb to their clients' demands to slander their competitors or somebody else.

The notion of "black PR" hasn't died yet. It is the holy grail for unethical and dishonest people who would do all in their power to harm their competitor and clear the market for themselves or their clients.

Conversely, they can try to whitewash the reputation of a dishonest company, which is another form of manipulation.

This is the reason there are codes of ethics and guidelines for good practice, fair competition, and transparency that are increasingly gaining traction in our industry, as well as in media, especially with respect to issues such as media ownership.

What ICCO and the other global organizations have been tirelessly working toward is to try to guarantee that PR companies among their members strictly comply with all codes of conduct and not misuse the power given by social media platforms.

There have been codes of ethics all around the globe for a while now—perhaps for the past twenty or thirty years. They are particularly crucial now, since PR experts need to be more aware than ever that they have a powerful weapon in their hands.

Some twenty years ago, as we were adopting the ethics standards at my company, M3 Communications Group, Inc., I was explaining to my colleagues about the tremendous responsibility that we bear, using the "potato" example: You go to the marketplace and get yourself a sack of potatoes. You go home and discover that most of the potatoes you've just bought are rotten. So you go back to the marketplace, start shouting at the seller, and they either replace the rotten potatoes with good ones or give you your money back.

Whatever the outcome, the whole scandal stays between you and the seller. It should be like that in any case with any kind of service and any seller.

Nowadays, in the PR business, the moment we decide to try to fool somebody, it usually blows up in our faces.

In the old days before social media, we would have fooled the (then-traditional) media, who would, in turn, delude the readers/buyers/customers—the general public.

Now, the situation is much more dangerous, because we are capable of fooling everybody without even going through traditional media. That's why every single PR expert must be perfectly aware of their enormous responsibility.

This is one aspect of total transparency. There is a risk that social media can be turned into a loose cannon. A profile or a page on some social media platform can be used against opponents, critics, anybody you dislike, in a way that has nothing to do with ethical use of media. Not to mention that such a practice is usually done through fake profiles.

The world of TT does create opportunities for abuse and unfair play, but on the other hand, since everything is public, and because of the interactivity of social media, thousands of other opinions are also allowed.

In any case, those who have been targeted or otherwise affected by malicious activity have the opportunity to react—which is a major part of our industry, public relations.

This reaction needs to be very well calibrated and very professional. Very often the reaction is either inadequate or simply botched.

Part of the danger of failing to react appropriately is demonstrated by the old joke about a guy who invited a friend over to lunch. The next day, he called his friend and asked, "John, did you take a gold teaspoon from our house, because we're missing one?"

"No, Bill, I didn't take anything!"

"John, it must have been you; nobody else has been here since yesterday. Nobody else could've taken it!"

"No, I didn't take it!"

Two weeks later, John calls back and asks, "Bill, what happened with that golden teaspoon you were missing?"

"Ah, we found it. But you know, the bad feeling somehow remained..."

Every single public figure has been attacked by ill-wishers, including by people who specialize in PR and know how to manipulate public opinion professionally.

When you or your company are slandered or targeted by a "black PR" campaign, every response is very uncertain because it's impossible to know whether your response will ever reach the same number of people as the original attack.

This is why, when we work with big companies, our main recommendation is to always, always, *always* be extremely proactive, even hyperproactive, with news about the company, so that whenever somebody decides to libel you, your news stories will still be dominant. That way, all of the corporation's positive achievements can stay in front of the general public, so that even if someone spills some dirt, it will dissolve in that sea of positive stories.

Being permanently proactive on social media, in particular, is one of the most important things that the PR industry must always do in the current revolution.

Because we handle media on our own now, we will be held accountable for using this tremendous opportunity to share a huge number of news stories, which should be both intelligently written and interesting.

If we fail to do so, we will have only ourselves to blame for any missed opportunities—and our clients will blame us, too.

Nevertheless, between ethics and manipulation, there is simply no question as to which trend will prevail. It is impossible for the rise of ethics not to emerge triumphant eventually. Even at the present moment, in my view, global manipulation attempts make up no more than 15–20 percent of the entire ocean of communication.

People are increasingly cautious and selective with respect to the information they share and the way they read, which is also a prerequisite for the ultimate triumph of ethics. Moreover, consumer power is increasing with every minute.

It is a matter of the development of *Homo sapiens* and the way in which we harmonize ourselves with social media—ethics is destined to prevail.

In a world where consumers have the power, there is no way for an immoral and unethical business to stay operational for long.

Because—going back to the Bell Pottinger case—everything becomes public knowledge sooner or later, and nowadays, that's increasingly happening sooner rather than later.

Here is one golden rule for the world of total transparency: whatever happens, and whatever you might do, there is no way it won't become public one day.

My categorical forecast is that as transparency takes off, and social media becomes ever more dominant as the main means of communication in the PR industry and everywhere else, PR experts will have to become ever more professional and attentive and will increasingly adhere to a robust set of ethical norms.

A MUCH BETTER INDUSTRY

This rise of ethics, which is still in progress but is unequivocal progress in itself, is not the only reason the PR industry has already become a much better business field.

PR evolved and is now a much better industry in 2018 than it was in 2013 or 2008, because we finally have the opportunity to send out our messages directly—without the need of mediators.

Of course, we are still using media, but not traditional outlets and not even online news media. Instead, we have our own outlets now in social media that we can use to tell our clients' stories to the target audience.

So, first, the intermediaries we had to deal with just some ten, even five, years ago are gone.

And second, our industry has finally become measurable: everything we do can be perfectly evaluated, and PR practitioners are now able to account for their work.

The measurability, the disappearance of the intermediaries, and the rise of ethics all make the PR industry a much better business to be in today.

In PR now, decisions are made much faster.

"The worst decision is better than no decision."

That's Rule Number One in my 2009 book, *111 Rules on Facebook*, a collection of rules, or aphorisms, that I published as statuses back then on the world's most ubiquitous social media platform.

Today, nine years later, I can reaffirm that rule ten times as passionately.

The greatest problem in PR—in any industry, for that matter—remains decision-making, because not everyone is able to live up to the rule of the three S's (speed—simplicity—self-confidence), which is tackled in another chapter of this book.

In today's world, if you don't make that decision right now, it will be outdated in fifteen minutes. There will be no point in making that decision anymore—you will be facing the necessity of making another decision, bearing the consequences of not making the first decision.

Why is it better to make a bad decision than to make no decision at all?

First, you carry out a reaction. Second, you make a demonstration. Third, no decision is irreversible.

However, if you remain without any decision whatsoever, you lose for sure.

Of course, nobody claims that bad decisions should be made. Yet when you make a decision swiftly, you are in your head, you're thinking, you're making a move. You're not just showing a reaction—you're showing a point of view. You demonstrate a position.

In today's world, one can realize much faster if a decision is bad, because oftentimes it is noticed by people who will comment on it. That way you are able to rectify it immediately.

It is far worse to make no decision at all.

THE POWER OF STORYTELLING

One of social media's greatest changes to modern-day PR is the rising importance of storytelling.

This book has already pointed out that the job of today's PR professional is now invariably connected with the creation of news and interesting stories.

Yet we cannot tell or "announce" a news story the way a journalist would. It would be boring, formal, or unnecessary to "report" a story about a client of ours as a reporter would.

We can't just say, "This pen is great, and consumers should buy it!" We ought to wrap up this message and create not only a convincing, but an interesting story around it.

Here I am, improvising on the spot:

A lady dropped her pen in the street, it was raining heavily, and a gentleman picked it up and said, "May I have your number?"

She was flattered, gave her number, he wrote it on his hand, and despite the torrential rain, the ink lasted because it lasts forever, etc.,

etc. This story could be about a phone number or anything else that would make sense, keeping the target audience in mind.

We should be able to tell some kind of a news story in such a way that the reader wouldn't think, "Ha, it's so obvious that this is a paid ad!" That would be too direct, and it would be repulsive.

Whereas when the story has added value for the readers, it will be perceived in a totally different way. Achieving that feeling is a huge part of our business nowadays.

Stories today are getting more and more visual. They will probably become short videos soon. A lot of people are doing that already, the so-called vloggers, but these are mostly amateur attempts. They are yet to become top-notch video stories.

Indeed, one day not too far ahead into the future, all things will be wrapped inside visuals and audio, not so much in written word, to such a degree that everything will be real time.

My long-term forecast has been that two industries are going to experience a giant boost as a result of these developments—the fashion industry and the optical lenses industry.

Why the fashion industry? Because people are going to care a whole lot more about how they look, how they are dressed, and their overall appearance. There will be no voice calls anymore, since phones will offer video instead. I'm sure that if you do a video call early in the morning, you will get up earlier to shower and get dressed.

Technology is developing so rapidly ahead that in just a few years, there probably won't be even a video button on your phone—you will have a video call by default. Someone calls, you pick up, and they can see you immediately.

The second industry that will experience a giant boom because of these developments, in my view, will be optical lenses. Because sooner or later all devices that we use today—laptops, smartphones, tablets—will be incorporated into smart glasses (lenses).

At that point, every single person will be wearing glasses, because that's where their computer display will be.

Google already attempted it with Google Glass. I tested it for a while; it wasn't the best. But that is going to happen someday soon.

This is why the power of storytelling—today in text, and already in visuals—will be the defining feature of PR following the social media revolution.

Storytelling was never an essential part of PR before social media, because it was the bailiwick of journalists.

We used to feed material to the journalists, but classic PR never dealt with all that: writing an article, sending it to a journalist, and telling them, "Publish this!" because that was beyond any ethical and professional norms.

Now that we have media, it is very different—going back once again to the definition that today's PR expert is the perfect mix of a publisher, editor, and reporter.

We already have the opportunity to write and publish stories about the products and services of our clients. That's one more revolutionary development in the PR industry today.

It wasn't typical for a PR expert to draft stories. They were supposed to convey news and put forth the advantages or qualities of the products they represented.

That's why it is fair to say that storytelling is new, uncharted territory for the PR industry.

"When public relations executives were asked which communications trends will be the most important in the next five years, digital storytelling ranked above the rest, followed by social listening, social purpose, and big data. That's a dynamic combination and a striking example of how the industry has changed. Fortuitously, these happen to be the same topics students are interested in," according to the findings of the 2017 Global Communications Report of the USC Annenberg School for Communication and Journalism. "Emerging technologies, like Virtual Reality and Artificial Intelligence, fall further down the list," it adds.

"To adapt to the[se] changes, PR professionals say they are going to need new expertise in social media (83 percent), multimedia content development (79 percent) and data and analytics (78 percent). They also perceive they will need to be strong in traditional skills such as written (84 percent) and verbal (75 percent) communications," the 2018 report found.

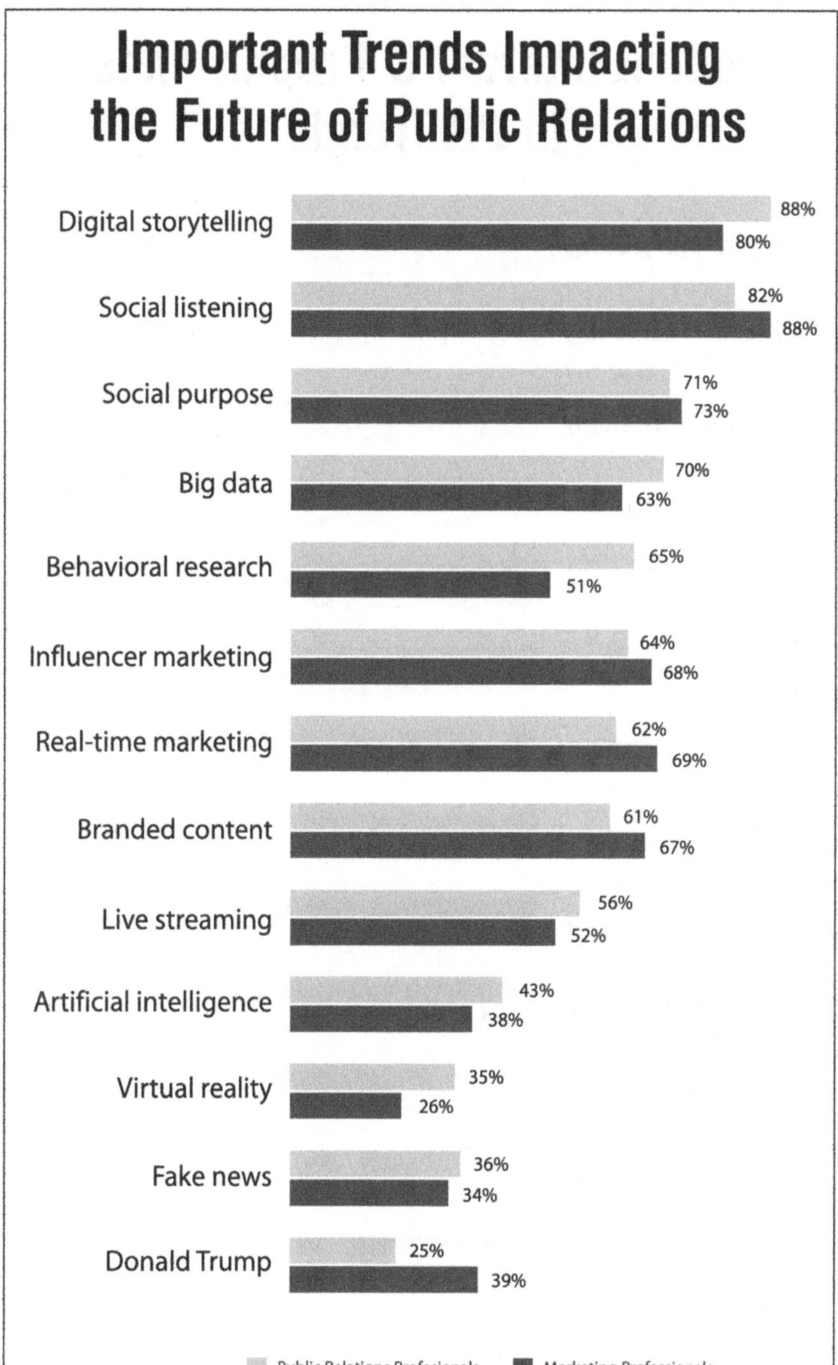

Source: 2017 Global Communications Report of the USC Annenberg School for Communication and Journalism.

Student Interest & Preparedness in PR Trends

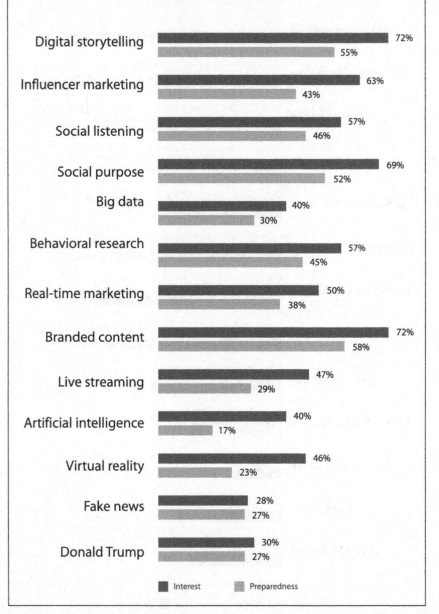

	Interest	Preparedness
Digital storytelling	72%	55%
Influencer marketing	63%	43%
Social listening	57%	46%
Social purpose	69%	52%
Big data	40%	30%
Behavioral research	57%	45%
Real-time marketing	50%	38%
Branded content	72%	58%
Live streaming	47%	29%
Artificial intelligence	40%	17%
Virtual reality	46%	23%
Fake news	28%	27%
Donald Trump	30%	27%

Source: 2017 Global Communications Report of the USC Annenberg School for Communication and Journalism.

A 2017 report on "The Evolution of Public Relations" conducted by the US Association of National Advertisers (ANA) and the USC Center for Public Relations at the Annenberg School for Communication and Journalism ranked digital storytelling second, right after social listening, among the "trends important to the future of the PR profession."

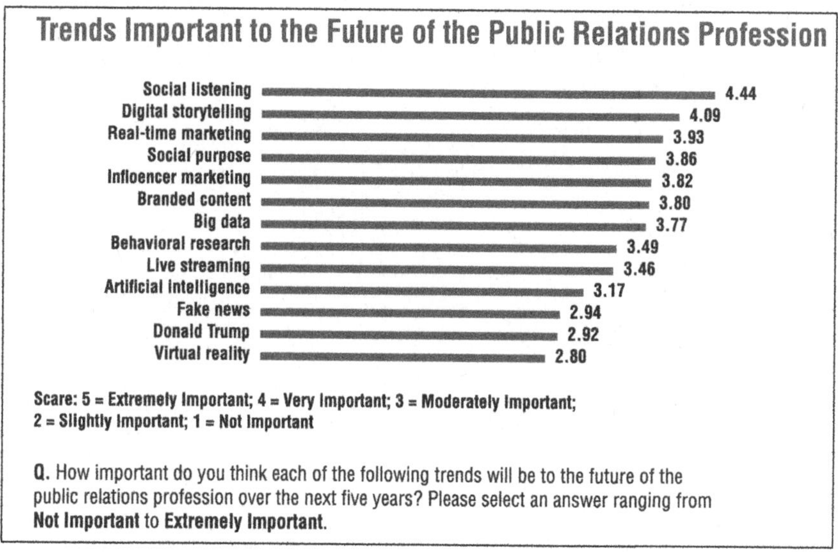

Source: 2017 Report of the Evolution of PR by the US Association of National Advertisers (ANA) and the USC Center for Public Relations at the Annenberg School for Communication and Journalism.

The data demonstrate some growing awareness of the power of storytelling. Yet it is still not certain to what extent the vast majority of PR professions comprehend how important storytelling has become to our profession (both in writing and in visuals). The next step would be realizing the various benefits this could bring to our clients.

Is the power of storytelling here to stay as a defining feature of the PR industry?

Yes, certainly! What is more, it will be developing increasingly on the visual side.

And if today we can tell the best stories in writing, tomorrow that will no longer be the case—visuals will prevail. In my opinion, images, short videos, interviews, brief documentaries even, or maybe entirely new formats are coming in the near future.

CHAPTER 6

MEDIA BEYOND THE MEDIA

OBJECTIFIED BY THE NEWS

As the social media revolution is rapidly progressing in PR and a myriad of other fields, the media of this new world are well above and beyond the old media (including online media from Web 1.0).

One of the most notable features of this new world is that it's no longer the people who seek out news. Rather, it's the other way around.

It's not the human users of social media who are out there searching for news; it's the news that's looking for an audience. For the PR industry, this is a crucial change happening as part of the social media revolution. Indeed, it's a key paradigm shift.

This shift means that all users, in addition to being able to write the news themselves, being empowered as subjects in social media, have also become the objects of social media, i.e., the passive party. Therefore, we as PR experts are supposed to be the much more active party.

If there are fifty comments or opinions posted under a news article, and they mostly dispute its content, readers are increasingly more likely to have higher confidence in the trustworthiness of those opinions, rather than trusting the news article itself.

That is why in the PR industry, we are, or at least we should be, focusing primarily on two indicators that are very important for our clients.

The first is whether and when any news stories or other media articles about a client are published.

The second is the comments posted under or about those stories or articles. We should be reading the comments with even greater interest and attention than the original story.

We cannot influence the news story, but we can influence the comments. We do that by joining in the discussion in the comments section, which technically amounts to supplementing the original news article.

Of course, the most important change of all in the social media revolution is ownership—the fact that the readers can themselves not just write news, but also run actual media stories on their pages, profiles, and channels. Billions are now actually doing that.

But the significance of this additional shift, in which the user is targeted by the news stories, ought not to be underestimated.

Because while traditional media and the online media of Web 1.0 presumed that the user would be interested in finding news and therefore actively seeking it, now, even without being interested, users get bombarded with information on social media, including news.

The Facebook example is the most powerful one, because when you are logged in, you get shown news that artificial intelligence—the algorithm—deems interesting for you.

So the media and news become the active party, as well; they are no longer simply objects. In this case, the reader's role boils down to being available to consume this product or service. The readers just pick preferences and get what they need.

This might seem like a questionable development, but though it might generate some immediate concerns, the fact that the user/reader is becoming the passive party doesn't really hurt the interactive nature of social media.

On the contrary, it makes it even more interactive, since the reader can participate, or interact, even more easily and quickly. Seeing news stories that pop in their feed, they can agree or disagree, or they can write a comment or simply react to it.

Unless the news is proactive with respect to readers, it would be very difficult to provoke most readers to participate, i.e., to be active.

WHO OWNS THE MEDIA?

One of the overarching—and overwhelming, really—traits of the social media revolution is the fact that billions of media owners have emerged thanks to the opportunity to run a social media page, profile, channel, whatever. PR companies must be absolutely aware of who those people are.

Of course, this development has occurred against the backdrop of another intriguing merger that has already materialized—that of traditional media with "traditional online media," a.k.a. their own websites.

Traditional media have been dependent on their websites for a long time now. Even the largest international newspaper has been relying for its survival much more on its website than on its print edition.

A large number of the surviving press outlets exist solely thanks to their websites, because a print medium is not a dynamic media platform updated by the minute. Plus, it is a lot more susceptible to bankruptcy for purely economic reasons.

Of course, this first merger of traditional media with their own websites has hardly gone smoothly. One of the gravest mistakes has been the failure to adapt identical content to the different environments.

Even today, as they are struggling for survival, many of the traditional media, regardless of the merger with their online divisions, still do copy-pastes of their print stories, instead of adapting them for online (not to mention the need to adapt to the social platforms!). Luckily, if the merger with their online outlet has materialized, when they hire experts, they can adapt their writing and publishing style pretty fast.

It's not limited to newspapers—it's the same with TV and radio. There is hardly a decent radio station that doesn't have a proper website that's updated regularly.

And what is the effect? The emergence of billions of social media users, owning media. However, this has not eclipsed concerns over the ownership of the traditional media gone digital—in both the developed countries where media is bought or already owned by major corporations and in the developing world, including fledging new democracies, where media often gets snatched up by ruthless oligarchs.

Yet in the new media realm, regardless of their buyouts, even large corporations or hefty oligarchs can hardly boast 100 percent control over the media content of the outlets they own, simply because access to that media's online platform cannot be limited only to them.

Because if a present-day media outlet isn't interactive, if it doesn't give people the opportunity to debate on any topic, or readers the ability to express opinions differing from the position of the publisher, that medium is going downhill, at least from a purely financial point of view. Nobody is going to read it anymore.

Even in post-Communist Eastern Europe, which has become notorious for its oligarchs, one can hardly think of a media outlet banning differing opinions as supplements (comments) to the main news stories that outlet publishes. A media outlet like that simply has no future.

Of course, on the other hand, the evident downside is that the ownership of media is influencing the editorial policies more and more.

The First Amendment of the US Constitution that ensures freedom of speech was adopted a little over two centuries ago, yet it seems as if that happened light years away—because today's media doesn't have much in common with the media that existed back then in America and Britain.

Regardless of how ruthless of a media owner you might be, the more staunchly your outlet focuses on defending and promoting the owner's business or political interests, the more insignificant that outlet will become, and the less readership it will have.

A media outlet like that could actually still have many readers, clicks, likes, etc., but it will not be trustworthy. And the main thing media are supposed to sell is trust.

With solely traditional media, there is still an opportunity to do that, to propagate your interests and nothing else. Say, a multimillionaire buys a couple of newspapers or a TV channel somewhere in the world and starts promoting his or her actions or products in those papers or channels.

OK, good job. However, the reader and viewer of today have other channels for information and usually prefer them. The reader is not going to rely solely on those papers and TV channels to stay properly informed about a topic.

Even if a corporate or oligarchy owner of a media outlet isn't interested in making a profit from it, they are still interested in their outlet being perceived as trustworthy.

The point is that in the online environment, and especially now in the social media environment, there is no way for a media outlet to solely feature the agenda of its owner.

The social media environment is bound to force that owner to give an opportunity for people to react and interact, share their views and opinions, whether commenting on the media website itself, or on Facebook.

That's one great advantage of the social media era.

AN ARMY OF AMATEURS

With all that said, an army of amateurs has taken over the media realm as a result of the social media revolution.

In this particular sense, the "amateurs" are all those billions of users who don't know how to handle the written word. They simply aren't used to using it, yet all of them are on social media, which for the most part remains a textual environment.

A virtually unlimited number of people who had never communicated by the means of the written word before have emerged everywhere, and this is a great source of stress for professional communicators as well as for the amateurs themselves.

An amateur in written communication who has been let into the social media realm is like a person who drives a car but doesn't have a driving license. They get in the car, and in the best-case scenario, they might barely stay on the road without hitting anybody. In the worst-case scenario, they might cause an accident, they could hit and kill somebody, they could kill themselves, etc.

In exactly the same way, a person who has never dealt with the written word for communication all of a sudden logs into Facebook and starts engaging with others. If their writing skills are poor, their posts will be filled with typos, poor grammar, and odd word choices. Other social media users who view these posts will be skeptical of the poster's intelligence and competence—and if this amateur is writing content for an organization, this will all reflect poorly on their employer as the audience questions their credibility and professionalism. All of this erodes public opinion of the poster and/or the company they represent.

Another obvious sign of an amateur is poor social etiquette. Many behaviors are unacceptable in face-to-face interactions, yet so many people fail to observe basic manners online, often resulting in badmouthing, slurring, even harassing their fellow social media users. The amateurs on social media don't have the tactfulness, desire, habit, or instinct to hear the opinions of others and to debate and discuss them. This situation often leads to conflicts, even personal or professional disasters.

The upside is that, nonetheless, a growing number of people from all around the world are learning how to communicate thanks to social media. The emergence of social media is a powerful, enormous educational process.

Billions of people are now learning how to write—not just in terms of actual writing, but in terms of communicating, discussing, debating, and presenting their arguments in writing.

The amateurs are all those social media users who aren't professional writers or professional communicators.

Those who fail to learn how to write and communicate properly in the new environment will fall behind on social media.

A CRISIS INDEED

A crisis has been unfolding against this all-out transformation of communications brought about by social media.

In fact, it has been causing millions of crises every single day: in communications, in professional relations, in personal attitudes, in the interaction between our clients and the users, i.e., the clients of our clients.

We, the PR professionals, must be in the middle of all that to keep helping them communicate with one another.

Every single misunderstanding between a client of ours and a client of theirs presents a crisis for us at that moment.

Back in the good old days before social media, a crisis was when something really huge had happened: a front-page newspaper headline, or when some actual disaster had occurred.

In contrast, now even the smallest misunderstanding presents a crisis, as in the classic example of United Airlines and the passenger who was forcefully dragged out of his seat and off the plane in April 2017.

One of our large clients is an enormous chain of supermarkets. Even the slightest disgruntlement of a customer of this chain presents a crisis for us.

"That's a petty occurrence, nothing has happened, really, let it go," many people would say.

For example, a customer finds an expired box of yogurt or an expired sausage or something like that.

To me, that is a supreme crisis, because something this small can destroy customer trust in the entire supermarket chain. A minor case like that can now go viral and become so huge within a matter of minutes that none of us would be able to find the way out as fast as needed.

That is why I reckon even the smallest matter as a potential major crisis.

Next time a client tells you, "That's not a crisis!" you tell them, "Shut up! It's a crisis! Because you don't know what you're talking about, and we do!"

We have such discussions and even arguments with our clients every single day. They would say, "Let it go, that will pass, don't pay any attention to it!"

"No, I cannot let it go. Because if your position or view of the situation is not posted online, that for sure means a crisis."

So since the arrival of social media, for all practical purposes, all people are in a permanent state of crisis.

All that it takes is for someone to log in and read the statuses of ten Facebook profiles in order to see that whatever happened during their day, and thousands of things happen to us every day, people's dissatisfaction eventually pours out on social media—from the guy who is now the forty-fifth resident of the White House to the least known janitor somewhere in Bangkok.

Every single person who has experienced something negative and wants to dish it out goes on social media and does exactly that. And by doing that, they instantly cause a crisis, because fifteen other people see that and either are against or support them.

As a result, a spiral of tedious, heated, ultimately torturous discussions is set off, which almost invariably ends with hard feelings for everybody.

This kind of thing always generates a tremendous amount of negativity.

Unfortunately, collecting precise data is probably impossible when it comes to human feelings, but it can safely be assumed that the "hating" on social media is probably equal to or greater than the positive stories and messages that are shared out there. This is definitely a crisis.

We ponder the things that happen to us throughout the day, and the reasons why they happen. Why someone said what they said or did what they did. We should just be prepared to face these crises and get through them.

Therefore, from a business standpoint, we should be ready to view every single little scratch on our client's reputation, or our own reputation, for that matter, as something that very often can cause a lot of rust, and as a thing that should be taken care of right away!

REPUTATION: GONE IN FIFTEEN SECONDS!

In the age of social media, one's reputation may literally be destroyed within a matter of fifteen seconds.

Theoretically, there is a way to restore one's badly damaged reputation, but of course that would require a lot of work, and if you've done something wrong, you will have to come out and openly admit it: what, how, when, and why you did it.

Nonetheless, perhaps in some extreme cases, it might be possible that there is no coming back from a scandal that has utterly devastated one's image. It all depends on the extent to which a person or a company's reputation has been killed.

Take the Harvey Weinstein scandal that shook Hollywood and focused global attention in the fall of 2017 and unleashed an avalanche of similar sexual harassment or rape allegations against celebrities, often referring to events from twenty or thirty years ago.

There probably isn't going to be a comeback for the reputation of a person in such a situation. A lot depends on the specifics of the crisis. There might be cases in which it is absolutely impossible to restore a reputation.

One has to be mindful of the fact that oftentimes accusations against celebrities seem to be popularity stunts, in addition to perceived attempts at achieving justice. Popularity stunts are part of the public relations business. Many people have become famous, and even rich, solely thanks to revealing things, or even just making claims about celebrities, whether substantiated or not.

If you are a company, it is possible that you have put a bad product or a flawed product on the market, and there might be news stories exposing you. Or there might be malicious rumors, attacking you for a perfectly fine product, that have nothing to do with the truth.

That's why you must monitor every single media platform, every single second, in order to be able to respond to whatever comes up in a timely fashion.

There is no universal formula for all that. The only golden rule about reputation management and damage control is that if you want to enjoy the possibility of sustaining smaller damages from an unexpected, unethical, and dishonest attack, you should become very proactive in social media long before anything like that happens. Very proactive!

MAJOR PR DISASTERS OF THE SOCIAL MEDIA AGE

This point cannot be emphasized too strongly: in the social media age, it is absolutely essential that brands, organizations, or personalities apologize immediately after making an offensive mistake.

That is the key takeaway from the top PR disasters of the past few years, since the advent of the social media revolution in PR and media.

As social media enables even minor missteps to snowball beyond anyone's expectations, refusing to recognize and apologize for an offensive mistake within seconds can be ruinous even for the biggest players out there. The longer an apology takes, the worse the fallout will be.

In the event of insulting follies, consumers, fans, admirers, and even the wider general public who might not be directly associated with the matter at hand deserve an apology, and a truly sincere, down-to-earth one at that, not slippery statements mired in corporate lingo.

Following are some of the top PR disasters of recent years in which mistakes spiraled out of control because of the power of social media coupled with the inadequate reactions of the protagonists, who failed to assume responsibility as quickly as they should have.

United Airlines Flight 3411: How NOT to Drag Out a Passenger

In April 2017, United Airlines stock plummeted and its consumer perception dropped to a ten-year low after videos of a passenger's violent removal by law enforcement from Flight 3411, bound for Louisville from O'Hare International Airport in Chicago, hit social media.

After the flight had been sold out, United announced it needed four seats for airline staff. In spite of being offered $800 vouchers, no passengers volunteered to give up their seats, so United staff selected four passengers to leave.

While three left voluntarily, David Dao, a doctor, refused to leave, arguing he had to see patients the next morning. He resisted when Chicago Department of Aviation officers started to pull him from his seat.

As a result of the confrontation, Dao suffered a number of injuries, including a broken nose, broken teeth, and a concussion. Smartphone videos taken by other passengers hit social media immediately, causing a furious public reaction.

Regardless of the obvious damage to United's image, the company initially stood by the forceful removal. CEO Oscar Munoz issued only a cold apology at first, expressing regret for having had to reaccommodate the four passengers, and describing Dao as "disruptive and belligerent."

Only after the backlash kept building up did Munoz assume "full responsibility" for the passenger-dragging incident. Extensive damage to United Airlines' image had already been done. Dao subsequently reached an undisclosed settlement with the company, while the incident prevented Munoz from assuming the position of chairman.

BP Gulf of Mexico Oil Spill: Wanting One's "Life Back"

BP's stock sank 26 percent, to an eighteen-year low, between April 2010 and April 2011, after an explosion of the *Deepwater Horizon* oil rig in the Gulf of Mexico caused the largest accidental marine oil spill in the history of the petroleum industry.

Eleven people died and unimaginable environmental damage was caused as a result of the disaster of April 20, 2010, with crude oil gushing from the sea floor for eighty-seven days, a spill of nearly five million barrels.

Among its other aspects, the *Deepwater Horizon* explosion was a major PR disaster for BP, not least because of the inadequate communications reaction of then-CEO Tony Hayward.

When trying to apologize to the residents of the Gulf Coast, Hayward infamously uttered, "I'd like my life back!"

This quote quickly made global headlines, cost him his job, and remains the epitome of one of the worst PR catastrophes in the history of the corporate world.

The revelation that Hayward took a day off to go sailing in the Solent during the height of the crisis did not help, nor did his stiff apology via YouTube, which only gave more food for further criticism and ridicule.

The environmental, corporate, and even PR ramifications from the 2010 Gulf of Mexico oil spill have lingered on.

As late as 2012, there were reports the well was still leaking, even though it had been declared sealed in September 2010. Marine life in the Gulf continued to die out at a much faster rate.

By February 2013, BP had lost over $42 billion in criminal and civil settlements and payments to a trust fund. In July 2015, BP agreed to pay the largest corporate settlement in US history, $18.7 billion, in fines, bring its total loss estimate to $61.6 billion.

In 2016, a Hollywood film called *Deepwater Horizon* starring Mark Wahlberg, Kurt Russell, and John Malkovich further immortalized the disaster in popular culture.

Volkswagen's Dieselgate: The Emissions Cheat Software Scandal

September 2015 saw the biggest scandal and PR bust ever in the car industry when German manufacturer Volkswagen admitted having to deploy cheat software in VW and Audi diesel cars to falsify exhaust emission level readings.

The Volkswagen emissions scandal began on September 18, 2015, when the US Environmental Protection Agency found that Volkswagen had manipulated the nitrogen oxide readings of turbo-charged direct injection diesel engines in order to meet US standards during regulatory testing.

In real-world driving, however, the engines emitted forty times more nitrogen oxide (NOx). The cheat software programming was used by Volkswagen on eleven million cars between 2009 and 2015, including 500,000 vehicles in the US.

The admission hammered Volkswagen's stock immediately, with a 40 percent drop three days after the scandal went public. CEO Martin Winterkorn was forced to resign, alongside several other top executives, and sales fell by 5 percent in 2015 and 8 percent in 2016.

VW had to spend some $25 billion in the US on claims from owners, dealers, and regulators over Dieselgate.

VW's subsequent image response was to change its worldwide ad slogan "Das Auto," meaning "The Car," to just "Volkswagen," an apparent show of humility.

It is safe to say that the emissions scandal incurred PR damages to the entire auto industry as it brought about greater awareness of car makers' tendency to exceed legal emission limits.

Samsung's "Exploding Batteries" Smartphone

What was supposed to be one of the best smartphones of 2016 ended up a major flop and PR disaster for manufacturer Samsung when social media exploded with posts about their new Galaxy Note 7's tendency to catch fire.

As discussed in Chapter 3, the Samsung Galaxy Note 7 was officially released on August 19, 2016. Two weeks later, on September 2, Samsung suspended its sales and announced a recall due to a manufacturing defect in the phone's batteries, which caused them to generate excessive heat and catch fire, or what social media users termed "the exploding batteries."

After reports that replacement phones with batteries from a different supplier also caught fire, Samsung recalled the Galaxy Note 7 worldwide on October 11, 2016, and permanently stopped making it.

The recall dealt a blow to Samsung's business in the third quarter of 2016, with a 33 percent decline in operating profits compared with the previous quarter. Credit Suisse analysts estimated that Samsung would lose at least $17 billion in revenue from the Galaxy Note 7 fiasco, the worst launch of any smartphone in history.

Pepsi's YouTube Ad Controversy (Saved by United Airlines!)

On April 4, 2017, Pepsi posted a commercial titled "Live for Now" on YouTube, showing model Kendall Jenner leaving a photoshoot to join a street protest in progress.

The protest ends when Jenner hands a police officer a can of Pepsi, a gesture that has the effect of reuniting everybody.

Pepsi immediately came under attack on social media for being insensitive to protest movements such as Black Lives Matter, and the Kardashian half-sister was mocked for participating in a commercial seen as trivializing important public causes.

At first, Pepsi defended the ad, arguing that it conveyed a "global message of unity, peace, and understanding." As the social media firestorm didn't let up, the next day, on April 5, Pepsi removed the controversial commercial from YouTube. It did issue an apology, but that has been criticized as having been directed toward Kendall, rather than the public.

Eventually, however, the fallout from the Pepsi ad fiasco was cut short by the erupting United Airlines Flight 3411 scandal, described above, which occurred several days later.

Domino's YouTube Embarrassment

Pizza chain Domino's also suffered a major PR disaster back in April 2009, when two Domino's employees made disgusting food pranks, filmed them, and posted the videos on YouTube.

In one clip, a male worker named Michael stuck cheese up his nose and added it to an Italian sandwich. In another, Michael sneezed into a cheese steak sandwich, which, according to the shooter and narrator named Kristy, was "to be served to some unlucky customer that's in need of some snot." In a third clip, Michael rubbed himself with a sponge, then used it to clean a pan.

The Domino's employees' pranks became a trending topic on Twitter, in an early demonstration of the viral power of social media to cause PR damage.

By the time Domino's responded two days later, some one million people had seen the videos on YouTube. It fired the two employees and issued an apology (also via YouTube), but its consumer perception was reported to have been massively damaged within a matter of hours. The videos ended up on other video sharing sites and were reedited and reposted long after the apology.

H&M and the "Coolest Monkey in the Jungle" Disaster

On January 8, 2018, Swedish clothing retailer H&M unveiled on their official UK website a photo of a black child wearing a green sweatshirt reading COOLEST MONKEY IN THE JUNGLE.

This sparked an outcry with accusations of racism, with crowds of protesters vandalizing the chain's stores in South Africa, leading the company to close them temporarily.

"This image has now been removed from all H&M channels and we apologize to anyone this may have offended," H&M said in its formal apology. However, it did not help that the mother of the model urged people to "stop crying wolf," calling the controversy "an unnecessary issue."

The damage to the brand was exacerbated by the fact that this was not the first time H&M had been accused of racism in South Africa.

When it opened its first store in the country back in the fall of 2015, it turned out that its photoshoots lacked black models. H&M responded that its ads were meant to convey "a positive image," which led to outrage among South Africans on social media.

In the wake of its second racism controversy in South Africa in two years, on January 17, 2018, H&M's global head office announced that retailer had appointed its first diversity leader.

KKK in the UK: The Krispy Kreme Klub's PR Blunder

In February 2015, a franchise store of Krispy Kreme Donuts in Hull, UK, announced an event called "KKK Wednesday."

That was supposed to stand for Krispy Kreme Klub, an activities group meant to occupy kids while they were out of school on holiday.

However, the deliberate but unfortunate spelling of "club" with a "K," rather than a "C," quickly unraveled by reminding everybody of the white supremacist organization.

Krispy Kreme Donuts was quick to remove the promotion and apologize, saying the mistake was due to "a completely unintentional oversight on part of our longtime franchise partners in the UK," but it was too late to prevent the backlash on social media.

Cosmopolitan Magazine's Weight Loss Article Headline

In April 2017, *Cosmopolitan* magazine found itself in a PR crisis because of a tweet and an article headline reading, "How This Woman Lost 44 Pounds without *ANY* Exercise."

It turned out that the woman in question had lost weight because of a rare cancer. Disturbed readers attacked *Cosmo*, whose eventual reaction was to change the headline to "A Serious Health Scare Helped Me Love My Body More than Ever."

Neither the magazine nor its owner, Hearst Communications, offered a formal apology, which made it the target of further criticism on social media.

Adidas's Boston Marathon "Survival" Email

In April 2017, four years after the Boston Marathon bombing that killed three people and injured hundreds of others, Adidas made a sorry PR blunder.

It sent out an email to Boston Marathon participants with the subject line, "Congrats, you survived the Boston Marathon!"

Social media immediately picked up on the insensitive wording, prompting Adidas to issue a swift apology. While the wording was unfortunate, it is believed that the quick reaction did spare the company much more serious social media backlash.

Ed Miliband's Bacon Sandwich Fail

An attempt by former UK Labor Party leader Ed Miliband to consume a bacon sandwich during the 2014 local elections campaign is considered by some to be among the most iconic PR disasters in British history.

The act is said to have been a PR stunt designed to position Miliband "as one of the common people."

Instead, because of the apparent awkwardness, it backfired, leading to intense ridicule on social media and criticism for the then-Labor leader as being "out of touch with the working class."

Miliband, however, is deemed to have subsequently managed to mitigate the effects of the PR gaffe by demonstrating that he did not take himself too seriously.

US Department of Defense's Low-Flying Planes over Manhattan

In 2009, the US Department of Defense spurred a scare followed by outrage by organizing an Air Force One photo-op without notifying anyone in New York City.

The sight of a plane flying over Manhattan pursued by a fighter jet was quick to bring painful 9/11 memories among New York City's residents and tourists, resulting in a widespread panic all over lower Manhattan.

Then-US president Barack Obama is said to have been infuriated by the incident. "Poor judgment would have been a nice way to put it," then-NYC mayor Michael Bloomberg commented. The Department of Defense official responsible for the mistake resigned.

Syrian Leader Bashar al-Assad's First Political Unrest Speech

Syrian president Bashar al-Assad is believed by some to have committed a major PR mistake with his first speech after the start of the political Arab Spring unrest in Syria in March 2011, thus possibly contributing to the eruption of a full-blown civil war.

The rationale of this argument is that regardless of the disgruntlement among the population, Assad himself enjoyed a predominantly good reputation with the Syrian public. The demonstrations that began on March 15, 2011, initially asked for greater freedom of speech, investigation of violations, and social improvements, not the president's removal.

However, Assad's first and long-anticipated speech, which came two weeks after the start of the unrest, has been described by some as aggressive toward the protesters' agenda, and so has a follow-up media campaign of the government. What is seen is an "inadequate" speech is interpreted as a PR disaster, because it is said to have quickly shifted public opinion against Assad, a factor potentially exacerbating the domestic crisis.

WHAT A PR EXPERT SHOULD BE

The need to be hyperproactive on social media, mentioned previously, underscores the fact that in the age after the social media revolution, the PR expert must become an entirely different person.

The only thing the new PR expert has in common with the old PR one is that they are both *Homo sapiens* made of flesh and blood.

The PR expert of the new age needs to have entirely different reflexes. They are just a whole other type of person.

Several years ago, during the Communication on Top forum in Davos, I styled that person *Homo socialicus.*

Yet that wasn't very accurate, because *Homo socialicus* is just a person who is highly active on social media, whereas the PR expert should have many, many additional qualities.

For instance, in addition to being superproactive, which is the most important quality, the new PR expert must always be on top of everything and read constantly. The new PR expert must be a very erudite and intelligent person, online twenty-four hours per day.

Of course, there are the undying qualities from old-school PR that need to stay no matter what: honesty, transparency, accuracy, professionalism.

Back in the days before social media, I used to joke by saying that the office of M3 Communications Group was 3 x 24. At the time, we had twenty-four people on staff, we were online twenty-four hours per day, and our team's average age was twenty-four.

The second and the third things still stand—our average age is still twenty-four, and we are online nonstop. I think that after the social media revolution, this setup, or at least mindset, is applicable to every single PR company in the world.

MODERN PR TOOLS: AMEC'S INTERACTIVE TOOL

The new Interactive Tool recently developed by the International Association for the Measurement and Evaluation of Communication (AMEC) is a superb example of a user-friendly framework that really fits the modern-day PR environment.

Here is how key AMEC Chair Richard Bagnall explains the process for its development:

> Many of the evaluation methods and techniques that the industry took for granted for so many years are no longer enough. As traditional organizational structures are dismantled, PR professionals are being asked to work across all forms of media and to use, and most importantly measure, these new channels and tactics. Work must encompass paid, earned, shared, and owned media. To be effective at our jobs, we now need to plan and measure our communications in a truly integrated manner.
>
> To prove the value of communication in an age of accountability, it is vital to move beyond measuring just the content (or media) analysis that largely sufficed for the previous twenty years. Now communication professionals must show the effects of their work with regards to the initial communications objectives.
>
> The International Association for Measurement and Evaluation of Communication (AMEC)'s new Integrated Evaluation framework shows how to do this.

The interactive element of the Integrated Evaluation framework will guide you through the process from aligning objectives to establishing a plan, setting targets, and then measuring the outputs, outtakes, outcomes, and impact of your work.

At each step of the process, it provides additional information and suggests potential approaches and metrics that might be appropriate.

- It cannot be an exhaustive list and it doesn't provide the numbers for you.
- You will still need to source the data yourself to put into the tool.
- What it does is provide a consistent approach to allow you to plan and measure in an appropriate manner.

AMEC's Integrated Evaluation framework provides a consistent and credible approach that works for organizations of all sizes but which can be tailored to very specific cases and objectives. Anyone can use it—it is free and non-proprietary, allowing any organization, whether university, in-house department, PR agency, or measurement company, to benefit from it.

The Integrated Evaluation framework replaces both of AMEC's previous Valid Metrics and Social Media Measurement frameworks. The industry now has one integrated approach to respond to the challenge of measuring results.

This new framework shows how to "operationalize" the Barcelona Principles and demonstrates how to turn principles into action and to finally prove the value of our work.

For over six years, AMEC has been championing a better way of measuring communications with its education initiatives and measurement frameworks. These

> have helped many agencies and clients improve their measurement and evaluation systems.[1]

Giles Peddy, group managing director UK, LEWIS, further explains the benefits of AMEC's Interactive Tool as follows:

> A working group spanning agency, in-house, market research and academia designed and built the new Interactive Integrated Evaluation Framework.
>
> We wanted to make something that took users on a clear measurement journey from planning and setting SMART objectives, defining success and setting targets, through the implementation and the measurement and evaluation of the results. Importantly, we wanted to find a mechanism that would help credible and meaningful measurement pervade the industry.
>
> **The New Interactive Tool**
>
> We have built it in a tile format for a clear step-by-step process. Each tile is numbered so you know where you are in the process. The journey takes you from organization objectives and communication objectives all the way to business impact.
>
> When you click each tile, you get the space to fill in your work. To guide you, within each tile is an (i) icon, which when clicked provides a pop-up with additional information and an explanation of the section. Furthermore, inside the pop-up is a link to a measurement taxonomy—giving you even more information on what types of measures to include.
>
> Below we have provided some basic information on how to use it and also show how Lewis PR is using the framework to put our clients at the heart of the process.[2]

---

1 Richard Bagnall, "Integrated Evaluation Framework by AMEC," AMEC, accessed May 16, 2019, https://amecorg.com/amecframework/.

2 Giles Peddy, "Introduction to the New Interactive Tool," AMEC, accessed May 16, 2019, https://amecorg.com/amecframework/.

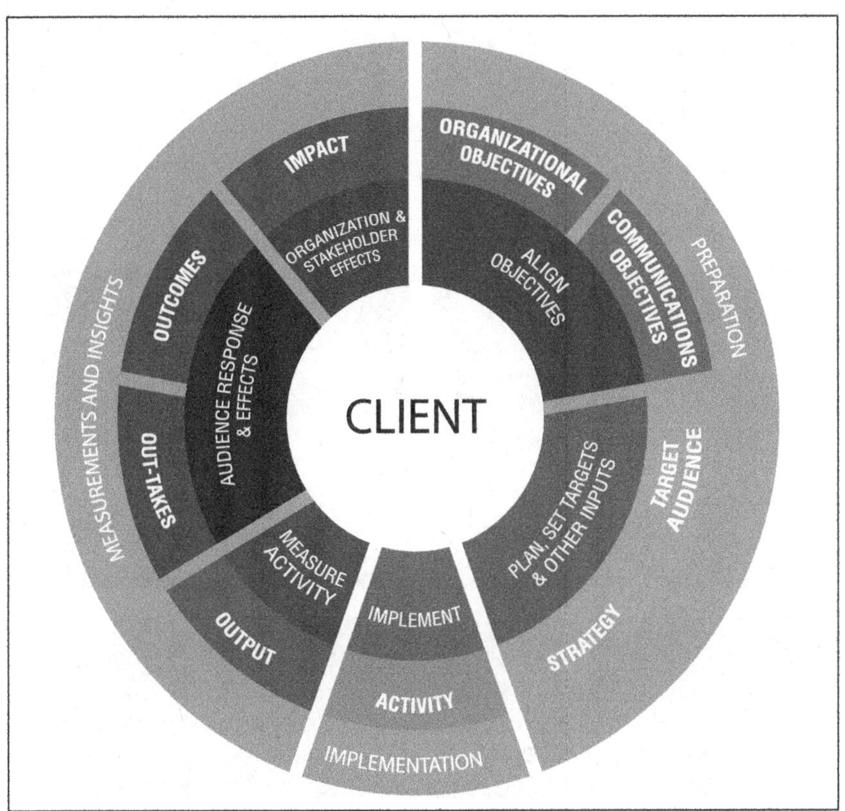

Source: International Association for Measurement and Evaluation of Communication (AMEC).

OBJECTIVES

Like all good measurement, it should start with clear organizational objectives. These can come in many different forms, whether they be awareness, advocacy, adoption or demand related. Following on from organizational objectives, is communication objectives. These should reflect and mirror the organizational objectives. Remember, the difference between an objective and a goal is that an objective has a measure of impact (e.g. 20% increase in brand awareness), compared to a goal that is an aspiration (e.g. increase brand awareness).

INPUTS

This section covers two important areas. Firstly, to deifne the target audiences of the campaign. Second, is the strateguic plan and other inputs such as describing some of the situational analysis, resources required and budgets.

ACTIVITIES

This section is outlining what activities were carried out, any testing or research, content production etc. Importantly, the tool recognizes the importance of paid, earned, shared and owned (PESO) and gives users the ability to tag accordingly.

OUT-TAKES

In out-takes, this refers to the response and reactions of your target audiences to the activity. How attentive were they to the content, what was their recall, how well understood is the topic, did the audience engage with the content or did the audience subscribe to more information.

OUTCOMES

In outcomes, this measures the effect of the communications on the target audience. Have the target audience increased understanding, has it changed their attitude to the topic, has it increased trust and/or preference, has it had an impact on the intention to do something (e.g. trial, subscribe, register) or increased online advocacy.

OUTPUTS

In outputs, this covers the core measures across PESO. So for example what was the reach of the paid advertising, how many visitors to the website, how many posts, tweets or retweets, how many people attended the event, and how many potential readers of the media coverage. This is quantitative and qualitative measures of outputs.

IMPACT

This final section is where impact on the organizational objectives is evaluated. So here the tool is looking to cover reputation improvement, relationships improved or established, increase in sales or donations, change in policy, or improved social change. This is a clear demonstration of business outcome and link to organizational objectives.

Now what? Once completed click the SUBMIT buttons and you can convert your work into PDF for sharing or using in meetings or presentations. If you want to go back and EDIT, then click the red button at the top to make changes. Then click SUBMIT again. Save the PDF to your computer.

Source: International Association for Measurement and Evaluation of Communication (AMEC).

BARCELONA PRINCIPLES 2.0

In 2010, AMEC adopted the Barcelona Principles, the first global standard to effectively measure public relations. It was much needed and came at "a powerful moment in time in the development of public relations," according to David Rockland, former chairman of AMEC. In the years since then, the organization has made some updates and released the revamped Barcelona Principles 2.0 in 2015. AMEC describes the shift in the following press release excerpt:

> London, 3 September 2015—A new look to the first international framework for measuring communications performance was unveiled today, reflecting the huge changes in the media landscape which have taken place.
>
> Barcelona Principles 2.0 was launched by the International Association for Measurement and Evaluation of Communication (AMEC) in London and streamed to PR professionals around the world.
>
> The new framework was developed by AMEC in conjunction with the original partners involved in the original Barcelona Principles of 2010—ICCO, Institute for Public Relations, PRCA, PRSA and The Global Alliance.
>
> This marks the first update to The Barcelona Principles in the five years since they were launched at the AMEC International Summit in Barcelona in 2010 as the first global standard of effective public relations measurement. The new changes come only two months after delegates at AMEC's International Summit in Stockholm called for the Barcelona Principles to be reviewed. [. . .]
>
> David Rockland said: "In 2010, the development of the Barcelona Principles was a powerful moment in time in the development of public relations.
>
> "The original set of Principles was never intended to be a final or complete solution, but simply a place for us

to start. What AMEC and our partners have now done is refresh the Barcelona Principles to reflect the significant changes we have seen in the media landscape and the emergence of integrated communications."

Rockland believes that if the original set of Principles focused more on "what not to do," the updated Barcelona Principles of 2015 now provide more guidance on "what to do."[3]

And without further ado, here are the new principles:[4]

BARCELONA PRINCIPLES 2.0

Principle 1: Goal Setting and Measurement Are Fundamental to Communication and Public Relations

- Conduct measurement and evaluation against defined goals and SMART (Specific, Measurable, Attainable, Relevant, Time Based)
- Make goals quantitative or qualitative, but still identify who, what, how much, by when
- Be holistic: traditional and social media; changes in awareness among key stakeholders, comprehension, attitude, and behavior; and impact on organizational results. Campaigns or ongoing are both relevant
- Be integrated and aligned across paid, earned, shared and owned channels where possible

3 Reprinted here with permission from AMEC. AMEC, "International Industry Collaboration Results in Barcelona Principles 2.0," September 3, 2015, https://amecorg.com/new-look-communications-measurement-benchmark-launched/.

4 Reprinted here with permission from AMEC. AMEC, "Barcelona Principles 2.0" (PowerPoint presentation), September 3, 2015, https://amecorg.com/wp-content/uploads/2015/09/Barcelona-Principles-2.pdf.

Principle 2: Measuring Communication Outcomes Is Recommended versus Only Measuring Outputs

- Tailor practices for measuring the effect on outcomes to the objectives of the communication program
- Consider both quantitative and qualitative methods
- Apply standard best practices in target audience research

Principle 3: The Effect on Organizational Performance Can and Should Be Measured Where Possible

- To measure results from communication for an organization, models that determine the effects of the quantity and quality of communication outputs on organizational metrics, while accounting for other variables, are a preferred choice
- Use models that determine the effects of the quantity and quality of communication outputs on organizational metrics (e.g., Demand for models to evaluate the impact on target audiences, survey research)
- Develop communication measures that can provide reliable input into integrated marketing and communication models, including through advanced econometrics and advanced survey analysis

Principle 4: Measurement and Evaluation Require Both Qualitative and Quantitative Methods

- Consider qualitative methods to better explain the quantitative (or to replace, in some cases)
- Media measurement, whether in traditional or online channels, should account for:
    - Impressions among the stakeholder or target audience

- Quality of the media coverage including, but not limited to:
    - Tone
    - Credibility and relevance message delivery
    - Third party or company spokesperson
    - Prominence as relevant to the medium
- Remember that we are measuring results and progress, not necessarily success
    - Quality measures can be negative, positive, or neutral

Principle 5: AVEs Are Not the Value of Communication

- Do not use Advertising Value Equivalents (AVEs)
- Do not use multipliers for "pass-along values" for earned versus paid media (unless proven to exist)
- If you must make a comparison between the cost of space or time from earned versus paid media, use:
    - Negotiated advertising rates relevant to the client
    - Quality of the coverage (see Principle 4), including negative results; and
    - Physical space or time of the coverage related to the portion of the coverage that is relevant

Principle 6: Social Media Can and Should Be Measured Consistently with Other Media Channels

- Define clear goals and outcomes for social media
- Include measurement methods such as:
    - Media content analysis
    - Web and search analytics
    - Sales and CRM data
    - Survey data
- Evaluate the quality and quantity of social media (just like with conventional media)

- Focus measurement on engagement, "conversation" and "communities," not just "coverage" or vanity metrics such as "likes"

Principle 7: Measurement and Evaluation Should Be Transparent, Consistent, and Valid

- Ensure integrity, honesty, openness and ethical practices
- Use valid methods
    - Quantitative = Reliable and replicable
    - Qualitative = Trustworthy
- Consider other relevant standards, like:
    - For Media Measurement:
        - Source of the content along with criteria used for collection
        - Analysis methodology
    - For Primary Research:
        - Methodology
        - Verbatim questions
        - Statistical methodology
- Recognize any potential biasing effects
    - In the research itself, or
    - Broader societal context

THE HELSINKI DECLARATION[5]

Mindful of the considerable and increasing influence and importance of public relations, ICCO members commit at all times to abide by the following ten principles:

1. To work ethically and in accordance with applicable laws;
2. To observe the highest professional standards in the practice of public relations and communications;
3. To respect the truth, dealing honestly and transparently with employees, colleagues, clients, the media, government, and the public;
4. To protect the privacy rights of clients, organizations, and individuals by safeguarding confidential information;
5. To be mindful of their duty to uphold the reputation of the industry;
6. To be forthcoming about sponsors of causes and interests and never engage in misleading practices such as "astroturfing";
7. To be aware of the power of social media, and use it responsibly;
8. To never engage in the creation of or knowingly circulate fake news;
9. To adhere to their Association's Code of Conduct, be mindful of the Codes of Conduct of other countries, and show professional respect at all times;
10. To take care that their professional duties are conducted without causing offense on the grounds of gender, ethnicity, origin, religion, disability, or any other form of discrimination.

---

5 Reprinted here with permission from ICCO. Adopted by the ICCO Global Summit in October 2017, in Helsinki, Finland. Source: International Communications Consultancy Organisation, "Helsinki Declaration," accessed April 12, 2019, https://iccopr.com/helsinki-declaration/.

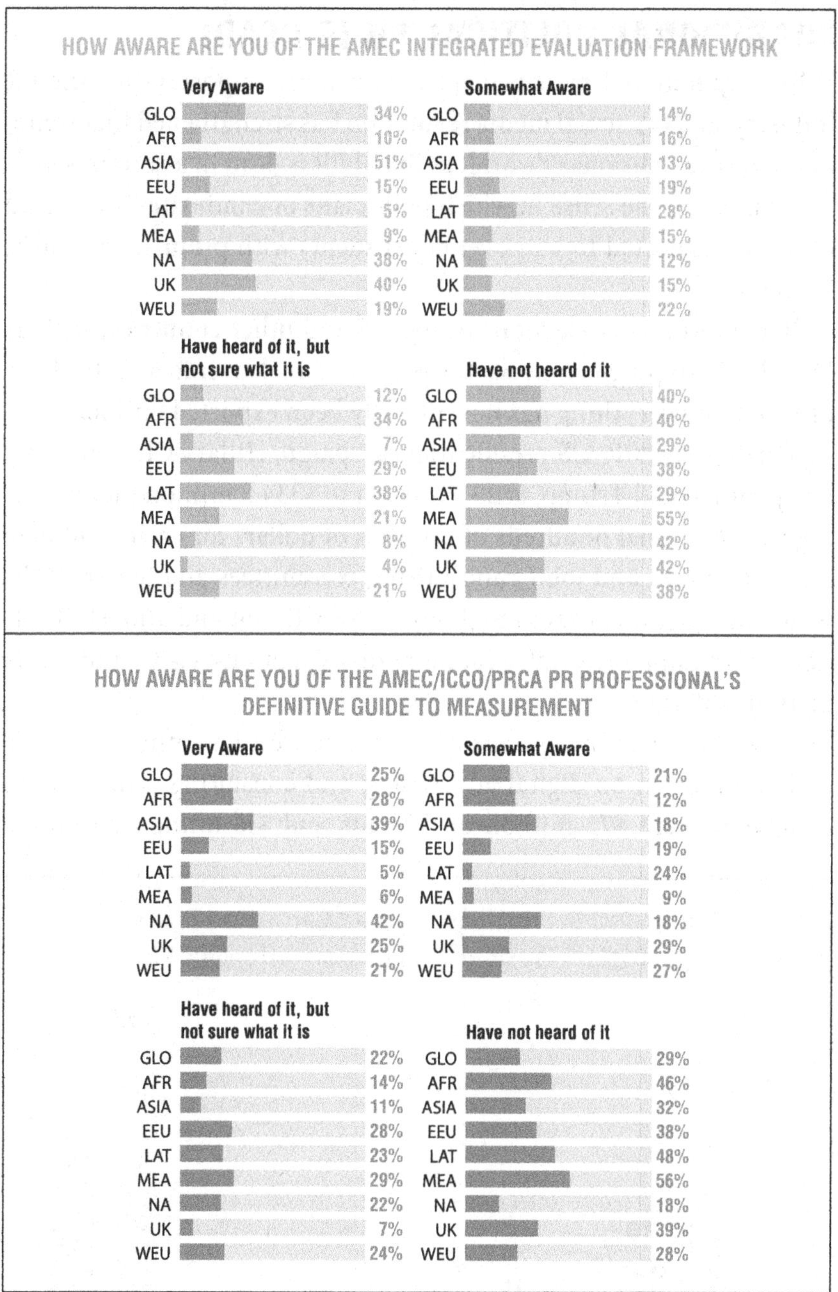

Source: 2018 World PR Report by the International Communications Consultancy Organisation (ICCO)

TRADITIONAL POLITICAL PR IS DEAD!

While reputational management is ever more important for the PR industry, and the social media revolution has strengthened that trend, in the postrevolutionary world, political PR is dead in a certain sense.

Namely, in the sense in which politicians or candidates for elected office are expected to win over constituents with promises and long speeches.

The most recent elections in the US and other countries, such as Donald Trump's election as US president in November 2016, have proven that everything has now literally been exported online.

During the 2016 US presidential campaign, Hillary Clinton vastly outspent Donald Trump, $623.1 million to $334.8 million (not counting the additional hundreds of millions of dollars for each candidate raised by party and joint fund-raising committees and Super PACs, which brought the total to $1.4 billion for Clinton and almost $1 billion for Trump), investing a lot more in TV ads, city visits, and information materials.

The Trump campaign spent $39 million on last-minute TV ads and $29 million on digital advertising and consulting. The Clinton campaign spent $72 million on TV ads and $16 million on online

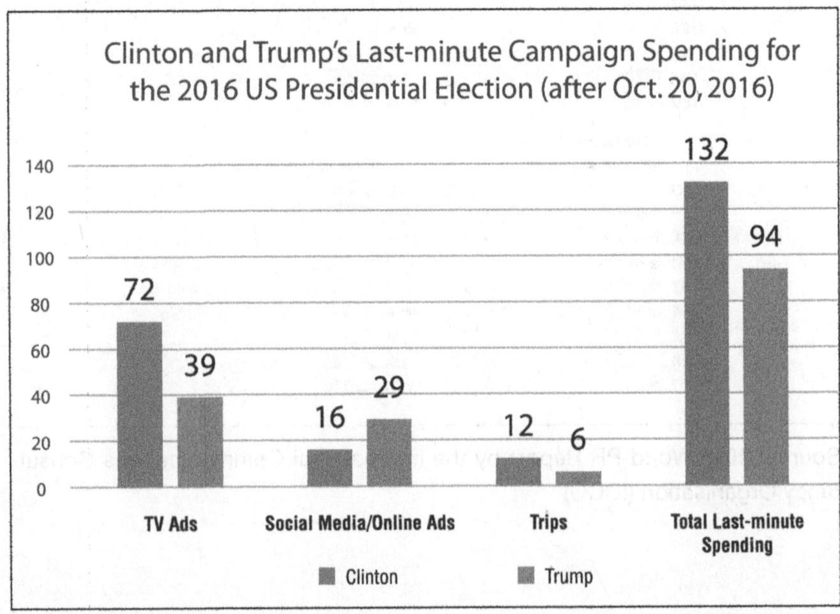

Source: US Federal Election Commission.

ads in the final weeks. So Trump actually outspent Clinton online in digital advertising.

Clinton also spent $12 million on travel, nearly double what Trump spent.

The last-minute spending did reflect the trends of the entire presidential campaign: Clinton massively outspent Trump.

So what?

Clinton still lost.

Trump triumphed largely because everything has already been moved to the internet, to social media in particular, and everything has become really, truly personal.

What Trump has been doing on Twitter—I wouldn't call that "political marketing."

That's something I would call "Trump on Twitter"—an entirely new discipline! (Which, interestingly enough, can also be abbreviated to TT, just like "Total Transparency" . . .)

Whatever it is, it's *not* political PR.

Not a single expert in political PR and marketing, not even the best expert, not even a genius in PR can come up with the things that Trump himself writes and posts on Twitter. It's not that these things are extremely smart—it's just that they seem to have been working.

What's more, social media gives much greater opportunities for understanding whether a certain person is good for the job or good for nothing based on their thoughts and reactions.

Not a single PR company can create truly authentic messages like that. Sure, in the old days before the social media revolution, that was possible. Experts in political PR could write a great speech for you, put up nice billboards, or teach you how to use your hands in public speaking.

However, nowadays, no PR company can build a social media image for you, a reputation using such a short form of communication as tweets, in which in each of the 140 characters must convey your personality. Each character must convey your own meaning—that can't be the PR company.

This development, generating the conclusion that old-style political PR is dead, is not negative for the PR industry.

It just means that the PR industry now has entirely different dimensions and entirely different tasks from a professional point of view.

These tasks mostly boil down to working with the truth itself.

Because that is the paramount idea of PR!

If you have got to manage a reputational crisis, you can do it only with the truth, the whole truth, and nothing but the truth. Nothing more, nothing less.

Going back to the Weinstein scandal—that man never denied. Technically, there aren't exactly pieces of hard evidence about the things he was accused of. Nobody took photos or video footage, nobody was in those hotel rooms, nobody saw him, nobody tested bodily fluids, etc.

Yet this man didn't even try to deny the accusations against him; not even for a second did he try to say that any of those claims were not true. He didn't argue that his alleged victims went to his room, got undressed, and lay on the bed voluntarily.

Why didn't he? First, because nobody is going to believe him. Second, because there is no point in denying when somebody makes a blunder.

When you've blundered, you shut your mouth. Of course, you must at least apologize, and that's it.

However, if you haven't done anything wrong and you are the target of a malicious, evil attack, you voice the truth, the whole truth, and nothing but the truth.

That's why I began this book with that definition of PR, and I keep thinking more than ever that it is the most accurate one: telling the truth in a way so that people would understand it.

"Truth" is the keyword in PR.

Because of the dreadfully large amount of media out there, and the confusion caused by all of those billions of words and sentences that we are bombarded with every day, if PR tells the truth, it will be unbeatable—its competition won't stand a chance.

This is one reason why old-style political PR or political marketing is dead: with all the experience that we have, we know that many of the messages the politicians send out are lies.

And the PR business cannot work with lies!

PR, TRUMP STYLE

While Donald Trump has been a public figure for decades, his first two years as president of the United States are what's put him on the map with his Trump-style PR. What is Trump-style PR? I would define it so: "Saying what YOU deem true in an arrogant way."

Trump's vocabulary is such that, on the one hand, it tolerates no objections, and on the other hand, it's the vocabulary that many Americans use in the street and probably at home. One of his greatest qualities that was totally underestimated by his rivals is that Trump is natural in that regard—that's what he's like. He didn't learn this style of communication. He probably has an army of consultants around him, though I'm not sure he ever listens to them. Probably some things he's told get into his head from time to time, but the language he speaks seems to be the language that many, if not most, Americans seem to identify themselves with. In other words, they go home, chug a couple of beers, turn on the TV, and see a guy who talks just like them. What Trump uses is the language of the working-class and middle-class American that you can hear in any American bar. Trump is most striking with his language, more so than with his actions. Perhaps if you go to some art café in Manhattan or some skyscraper office building filled with people in suits and ties, they won't like Trump because he's too direct and abrupt and vulgar.

But I think Trump and his PR style fit perfectly in the world we live in today, in 2019. Trump makes fast decisions. He doesn't think much—and that's categorically a typical characteristic of global modern life today. He speaks briefly. He doesn't use long, complex sentences at all. Sometimes he says with three words things that his predecessors would need a five- or ten-minute speech for.

But he is very abrupt, and what doesn't do him any favors is the fact that he is hyper-self-absorbed, way too much in love with himself. But who knows, people might like precisely that—just as they spend a lot of time in front of mirrors. The more time they spend posting photos on Facebook, the more they like themselves, and the more they boost their own feeling that they are pretty and intelligent.

However, it is essential to note that the reactionary nature of Trump's style has no place in the PR industry, because there is no way to be arrogant in our business—you can't even be emotional. Only very rarely can you afford to be emotional when you are solving a crisis.

Of course, Barack Obama, en route to his first term, was the person who discovered social media and the strong influence it can exert on the voters. Trump's social media campaign was no less efficient than Obama's, but it was also very different. While Obama had rather sophisticated messages, Trump's social media campaign was slam-bang. Nonetheless, Trump is the first US president, the first extremely influential public figure, who turned social media into a cult with his Twitter usage.

While he's not often live on Facebook, it is the way he's been active on Twitter that's emblematic. There is hardly any world leader today—be it a president, prime minister, king, queen, or emperor—who doesn't start their morning by asking their advisers to bring them a printout of Trump's tweets overnight.

Trump's proven that he knows his way around social media, and his posts, or tweets, are the envy of a lot of people, even in the PR industry, who are trying to say a lot with just a few words.

But what's most characteristic of Trump's PR style is his absolute imperturbability, ruthlessness, and arrogance—and while his approach doesn't always sway the public in his favor, it certainly keeps him on everyone's radar at all times.

For better or worse, PR, Trump style, seems like it is here to stay, because more and more people like the brevity of this type of public communication: they prefer to be told the truth—or a version of the truth they deem right—in just five words, rather than have somebody explain the nuances to them in thirty sentences, with many failing to understand what they are actually told.

With Trump, you at least know for sure what he's telling you, and what he wants—there is no doubt about that. After that, you don't have to scratch your head and wonder, "He spoke for so long, what the heck was he trying to say?"

Arrogance aside, Trump's PR style should not be discarded, because it's worth using brief and clear sentences to make your honest views known.

BREXIT AND THE EU: MANIPULATION AND INEPTITUDE

The UK's decision to leave the European Union is no doubt the other global public affairs event, alongside Donald Trump's election as president of the United States, that has not only shaken up local, regional, and global politics, but also has far-reaching ramifications for public communications.

Brexit, first and foremost, is a lie, a fake, and all materials, stories, and films about it increasingly point in one direction: how a dozen people, using the power of social media as well as traditional media (in Britain, both TV and the press are extremely powerful, sophisticated, and still superinfluential), managed to lie to a lot of people by telling them things that are just incorrect.

It is a whole other story whether the Brits would feel better once they depart from the EU, whether they would be able to use the money they would save from EU payments and put it in their National Health Service, and whether the over 1 million Eastern Europeans who do menial labor in the UK won't leave the country. There are still a million unknowns, but the fact is that Brexit as a voting campaign for the referendum was just a very strong parade of lies and frauds by those who promised almost literally that when the UK quit the EU, it would again become a great empire.

Once Leave prevailed in the Brexit referendum, these top Leave campaigners just about vanished. When the UK actually leaves the EU, they will probably become even more invisible.

Of course, the whole campaign in favor of Brexit was not actually PR, because, as noted at the beginning of this book, the most precise definition of PR is to tell the truth so that people will understand it. In the case of Leave, they told not the truth, but a million lies. All they did was demonstrate the power of social media as well as traditional media, and how it can be abused to trick the public—it's all up to how "good" you are at such abuses. In that regard, those pro-Brexit figures were indeed very efficient.

The European Union, on the other hand, isn't just bad at PR, it is devastatingly horrendous at it. Part of its PR problem is that it doesn't take much for things to unravel—you just need to spend a day at the

EU headquarters in Brussels, watching thousands of glassy-eyed bureaucrats toss folders back and forth, drink coffee, and feel self-important. It's not so much that they squander public money as it is a question of how they irritate everybody, especially those who toil to make a living.

Episodes such as the one in which the president of the European Commission seemed as though he were drunk don't help, either. There seem to be EU bureaucrats at all levels who are unable to communicate. The president of the European Council, Donald Tusk, has been somewhat of an exception, but even he couldn't make much of a positive impression, because his position doesn't have that much to communicate.

The European Union is a wonderful concept of the free movement of people, goods, services, and capital—so that Germany wouldn't be foreign to French people, or Belgium to the Czechs, or Poland to the Bulgarians. However, the people who have been implementing this concept with their background of bureaucracy, party meetings, little real-life experience, and huge publicly funded salaries and benefits appear very demoralizing. Such a bureaucratic elite wouldn't be tolerated at all had it not been for the two pillars of the EU: first, Germany's money; second, the Europeans' desire to have free movement and thus easier and better lives.

If there is an example of bad PR anywhere in the world, it's the communication by the EU institutions with its target audiences. That is especially disheartening given how at one point before Brexit, the EU was the world's largest economy.

FACEBOOK'S RESTRICTIONS: WRONG MEDICINE FOR THE FAKE NEWS DISEASE!

I think the global revolution in public communications occurred in the years between 2005 and 2010. However, we are still getting used to living under the new conditions. I don't think the essence of the revolution is going to see drastic changes for a while, except that in 2018 governments (in free and democratic countries!) are trying to subordinate social media and limit their influence as the wrong medicine for some diseases.

The total shift in Facebook that occurred in 2017–2018, allegedly as a means to fight fake news, was absurd. I consider the total restriction of influence and access of any media by anybody to be absurd.

All of a sudden, the US Senate looked Zuckerberg directly in the eye—and that refers to the entire concept of social media—and said, "Do what you want, but stay out of politics! Post your mawkish lifestyle stories, let your three billion users showcase their new suits, or shows, or jewels, or watches, and which plane or bus got delayed, and be disgruntled by this or that person. But don't touch politics. Keep your databases safe, they may not be shared, they may not influence in any way, and certain political messages shouldn't make their way to your users through them."

MARK ZUCKERBERG'S TESTIMONY TO THE US CONGRESS: TOP QUOTES

Facebook's chief executive, Mark Zuckerberg, faced the US Congress in April 2018, answering questions on privacy, data mining, regulations, Cambridge Analytica, fake news, and Russian cyberwar during a five-hour hearing. Following are the top quotes:

On Privacy:

> I believe it's important to tell people exactly how the information that they share on Facebook is going to be used.
>
> That's why, every single time you go to share something on Facebook, whether it's a photo on Facebook, or a message, every single time, there's a control right there about who you're going to be sharing it with . . . and you can change that and control that in line.
>
> To your broader point about the privacy policy . . . long privacy policies are very confusing. And if you make it long and spell out all the detail,

then you're probably going to reduce the percentage of people who read it and make it accessible to them."

[Asked if he would be comfortable sharing the name of the hotel he stayed in last night]: No. I would probably not choose to do that publicly, here. I think everyone should have control over how their information is used.[6]

On Cambridge Analytica:

"Cambridge Analytica wasn't using our services in 2015, as far as we can tell . . . They weren't an advertiser. They weren't running pages. So we actually had nothing to ban. [. . .]

I want to correct one thing that I said earlier in response to a question . . . [on] why we didn't ban Cambridge Analytica at the time when we learned about them in 2015.

[From] what my understanding was . . . they were not on the platform, [they] were not an app developer or advertiser. When I went back and met with my team afterward, they let me know that Cambridge Analytica actually did start as an advertiser later in 2015.

So we could have in theory banned them then. We made a mistake by not doing so. But I just wanted to make sure that I updated that because of I . . . I . . . I misspoke or got that wrong earlier.

When we heard back from Cambridge Analytica that they had told us that they weren't using the data

6 Chloe Watson, "The Key Moments from Mark Zuckerberg's Testimony to Congress," *The Guardian*, April 11, 2018, https://www.theguardian.com/technology/2018/apr/11/mark-zuckerbergs-testimony-to-congress-the-key-moments.

and deleted it, we considered it a closed case. In retrospect, that was clearly a mistake. We shouldn't have taken their word for it. We've updated our policy to make sure we don't make that mistake again.[7]

On Personal Data:

Yes, we store data . . . some of that content with people's permission.

There's a very common misconception that we sell data to advertisers. We do not sell data to advertisers.

What we allow is for advertisers to tell us who they want to reach, and then we do the placement... That's a very fundamental part of how our model works and something that is often misunderstood.

[When asked if the Cambridge University neuroscientist Aleksandr Kogan sold the Facebook data to anyone besides Cambridge Analytica] Yes, he did.

We're investigating every single app that had access to a large amount of information in the past. And if we find that someone improperly used data, we're going to ban them from Facebook and tell everyone affected.

My position is not that there should be no regulation.

I think the real question, as the Internet becomes more important in people's lives, is what is the right regulation, not whether there should be or not.[8]

On Russia's cyberwar:

One of my greatest regrets in running the company is that we were slow in identifying the Russian information operations in 2016.

7 Watson, "The Key Moments . . ."
8 Watson, "The Key Moments . . ."

> We have kicked off an investigation . . . I imagine we'll find some things.
>
> There are people in Russia whose job it is to try to exploit our systems and other internet systems and other systems as well.
>
> This is an ongoing arms race. As long as there are people sitting in Russia whose job is it to try to interfere in elections around the world, this is going to be an ongoing conflict."
>
> It was my mistake, and I'm sorry.
>
> I started Facebook, I run it, and I'm responsible for what happens here.
>
> It's clear now that we didn't do enough to prevent these tools from being used for harm. That goes for fake news, foreign interference in elections, and hate speech, as well as developers and data privacy.[8]

Fair enough as far as the databases are concerned! There are privacy issues, such as the EU regulation GDPR, which will be traced differently in different countries. But taking away somebody's right to be informed, their access to information, everybody's right to share whatever position they wish, even political, is unacceptable.

We all know that social media platforms, especially Facebook, Instagram, and Twitter, have developed their own mechanisms for banning certain words and positions, and as a result, there have been absurd situations in which somebody gets banned simply for mentioning some indecent word, even in a joke, or in something positive.

I am in favor of being able to suspend fake profiles, which Twitter did recently. Even if this sounds a little extreme, it is advisable to ban the profiles of real people who are hiding behind pseudonyms in order to be able to slander somebody or to spread some political view that they might otherwise be afraid to share. (These fake profiles are common on Twitter, a platform that thrives on strangers following

8 Watson, "The Key Moments . . ."

one another. However, on Facebook, where the vast majority of users appear with their own photos and names for the purpose of digitally connecting with people they already know, users are far less likely to accept friend requests from someone unfamiliar. While you *could* have a fake profile on Facebook, it's much harder to gain friends and followers if the other users don't recognize you, so this is less common.)

Restricting and banning, forbidding people to deal with politics, striking at large old-school media by forbidding them to share their news on social media just because you think they should be paying or can't have access because they compete with Facebook's users as news sources or statements—I think that's just not right, it's not fair. I think all media should be granted absolute access to Facebook, but this isn't exactly the case at the moment.

It should be a hyperopen network without any limitations. The only restrictions should be the law, not somebody's whims, or the fact that some founder was summoned before some committee somewhere.

Didn't they limit the impact of fake news substantially this way? They forced Facebook to shift their algorithms, so instead of media content, users got more content from their friends in their feeds. Those users were unable to differentiate between real media and Russian trolls, for example.

Perhaps something was achieved in that regard, but I think the fight against fake news shouldn't be through algorithms or limitations that restrict one's access to potential fake news or real news.

If you wish to learn something from CNN, for example, if it doesn't reach you in your feed—you would have to make the extra effort to visit their website.

Social media needs to be a platform that's open to everybody and allows the exchange of news, views, opinions, positions.

So why are we putting all media under restriction because some of them have fake news?

Don't Facebook users also spread fake news? Don't they do it every single day? Say, whether you read a story from a user or from some third-rate media source, or from a profile of Ivan Petrov or John Sullivan, there is actually a much greater chance you would believe

John Sullivan because he's got his photo up there, with his family, his smiles, and his experiences, and all the other news they shared, whereas if it is a media source that is not even authoritative, you can also cast doubt on them and say they are lying to you. But how can John Sullivan lie to you?

Maybe a lot of people don't differentiate between real news and fake news—or between the *Washington Post* and, say, the *Washington Daily Express* (a fake newspaper for the sake of illustrating my point). Nonetheless, brutal top-down restrictions are not justified.

If the *Washington Daily Express* doesn't have exposure on Facebook, they might have exposure on Twitter, or on their own site, or in search engines, or in a million other ways, and when you limit it on the most popular platform, Facebook, that doesn't mean you are shutting it down; you're not shutting down its fake news.

So if we know that the *Washington Daily Express* is a proven source of fake news, site administrators could slap a "Fake News" label, or a "Be careful, possible fake news" label on its social media profiles and pages. They had better place a tag on it, so everybody will know that this media source spreads fake news. That will be a hundred times more effective than just banning its access.

So alongside all those fake news media, all proper media suffer, and they are the vast majority who suffers.

This means that real news, which is important and interesting, can't reach social media users. Why? Because somebody somewhere dares to publish fake news and lies? They are able to cause even greater damage that way! Instead of just spreading fake news, they have succeeded in limiting everybody's right to information.

Even in the present state of affairs—because of 10 percent who are liars, the other 90 percent who aren't also suffering are partly stripped of their right to be informed.

If the *Washington Post* has 1 million users on its own website, and Facebook has 3 billion users, and the *Washington Post* would like to inform those 3 billion, or the 100 million Americans who are on Facebook, of something important, they can't. They don't reach them. Why not? Because of the *Washington Daily Express*—one person lies and nine more are also treated as liars.

The mechanism for coping with this grave problem should be entirely different: through labeling and exposing. Of course, three things are totally banned, and there can be no compromise about those: child pornography, aggression, and drugs. But those are known and clear.

But if somebody writes in a post, "Steal ten dollars from your neighbor!"—that doesn't mean they are a thief or have stolen it. These are conversations online that need freedom. The more democracy and opinion exchanges there are on social media, the better and more informed the people in the world will be.

Informed people will be more resistant to violations by their opponents, partners, and friends. If certain sources are restricted on social media, they will just go somewhere else. In today's world, if a person wants to release a piece of fake news, there is no way they would be unable to do that.

The methods for coping with this should be different, and they should support our business, because our industry has to do with fast communication. Very often, we solve crises and inform the public about new products, or new and interesting things that can be useful for them. So proper media sources would be unable to inform users of great discoveries and advances, or, God forbid, armed conflict, just because a small percentage are fake news-makers?

There must be another system to sort this out. I am absolutely a proponent of criminalizing fake news. Do you write fake news? There has to be a law where you get sentenced. A lot of countries and legal systems are actually already doing that or trying to do that.

You lied, violated somebody's rights, somebody lost their business because of you, their branding, image, self-confidence and all that—you get sentenced and your paper or site gets shut down.

It is a known fact that probably Russian trolls and Russian cyber geniuses took advantage of the vulnerabilities of social media. What are you going to do? Ban the Russians from the internet? They already don't have access to LinkedIn. (Russia banned LinkedIn, but they did it because they wanted the servers to be on its territory. Perhaps LinkedIn should have tried to achieve some kind of a compromise.) What Google's former CEO Eric Schmidt predicted—that the internet would split in two—is already happening. You go to Russia, you have no LinkedIn; you go to China, there is no YouTube or Google. This is totally absurd. There is no way that one day LinkedIn won't return to Russia. When you ban a business media source, especially such a useful and intelligent one as LinkedIn, you make Russia even more isolated. The Communist-minded population who hates the free market becomes even stronger. You solidify Putin even more.

I think any single ban—except for those that can be imposed by a court of law—only leads to damages. And of course, it is hurting our business, because if I'd like to use Facebook to promote something for our clients, that's a lot harder than it was just a year ago. That is because every single story, even purely commercial ones, can fall under a ban.

I expect that these bans would be lifted within a couple of years, as by then every major social media would have come up with effective ways to limit fake profiles as well as aggression, arrogance, and fake news. That is already happening.

In a free and democratic environment, bans are no solution. They just demonstrate powerlessness.

PROF. SCOTT E. FAHLMAN, INVENTOR OF THE "SMILEY" EMOTICON, ON THE NEW ENVIRONMENT

I've got no office, clients, or market, but regarding changes, I have observed in the media in the US:

When I first heard about Twitter, I thought that the idea of communicating by spewing 140-character snippets to all your "followers" was the worst idea I had ever heard and that Twitter could never catch on. Now I only believe half of that. :-) On Twitter, almost any thoughtful comment gets mangled by compression. Poets and very thoughtful writers can perhaps turn this brevity to their advantage. But for the rest of us, Twitter should never be used to communicate ideas of any complexity. Add to that the fact that most tweets are sent with only a few seconds of thought by the author, and you have a recipe for great embarrassment, and a powerful force for dumbing down complicated issues into quips and slogans.

The current US president has played a major role in [the newly emerged erosion of truth]. By constantly spewing false information and outright lies, he has called into question the very concept of objective truth. Government spokespeople have been forced to follow this lead, and a total disregard for objective truth is now spreading to other media.

The implications of this for the PR profession are hard to imagine. It used to be said (half in jest, but only half) that if you try to persuade others by lying, that's called "fraud." If you try to persuade others by (selectively) telling the truth, that's called PR. But in a world where truth is no longer a valued concept, what does that mean for the idea of "ethical PR"? So this is also revolutionary in a bad way. In a world with just a few media outlets and very powerful gatekeepers, bad things could happen. A classic example was in the 1890s when the Hearst chain of newspapers whipped up a frenzy, based in large part on lies and speculation, for the US to go to war with Spain over Cuba. But I think that fully democratic media, in which the very concept of truth is blurry, is more dangerous.

On the plus side, it is now possible to access some real expertise when you have a question about something. As a small example, I like the website Quora, in which people ask questions and others try to answer them. There is a lot of garbage there, but very often a question will be answered by someone who actually is an expert in that area. I have posted several hundred answers there in two areas: my own professional field of AI research, and answers about what graduate admissions committees at top schools are looking for when we evaluate the applications from students. (I have been on graduate admissions committees at Carnegie Mellon University for many years.) Something like four million students and others around the world have read these answers, and many have told me that this affected their desire to come to CMU and their success in getting in. So that sort of thing can be very helpful: the best kind of social media presence is real, useful information from real experts who are genuinely trying to help. But sorting good answers out from all the garbage is difficult for readers, and we need better ways to do that. This too is revolutionary, I think, and mostly in a good way.

An anecdote that illustrates why an online AI-powered customer service agent might make a big difference:

As it happened, my wife and I were trying to fly from Boston to Glasgow via Heathrow on British Airways last May 28—the date of the systemwide computer outage that crashed BA's entire system for more than a day, causing utter chaos at Heathrow. That's just not acceptable—that this could happen at all is a huge, costly, and infuriating screw-up that should result in a bunch of people getting fired. But the worse problem was that BA was totally uncommunicative during this crisis. We couldn't reach them by phone (even via the "frequent traveler" numbers) and their website had no useful information—and then it went down.

We finally decided to go to the airport in Boston to see if we could sort out our bookings and missed connections. We had to wait hours in line. They had only one check-in desk open, and some guy from Africa with really complicated problems tied up the line for more than an hour while fifty people behind him fumed. Then they opened a second station but started ushering all manner of higher-priority passengers to the front of the line, nearly causing a riot among the rest of us.

Well, we did finally get to Glasgow at about 8 p.m., instead of the planned arrival time of noon, angry and tired. During the Glasgow flight, they brought around a refreshment cart: two club sodas and two bags of pretzels cost ten dollars, adding insult to injury. Suggestion: When you are running eight hours late, everyone on the plane is furious, and many have missed meals, maybe the soft drinks and snacks should be free, or at least not priced in a predatory way.

Thanks to EU regulations, we did eventually get a nice compensation check, essentially paying for both of our round-trip tickets. And (amazingly) BA paid up without us having to threaten legal action. But I don't plan to ever fly on BA again unless there is absolutely no alternative. BA used to be my usual airline for travel from the US to the UK, but that's over. Lots of my friends have heard this story. And I think that thousands of other travelers have made the same vow as a result of this incident—and again, the total lack of communication was much worse than the shutdown itself.

So there is one example of a situation where an AI-powered customer service line would have been *much* better than nothing at all.

CHAPTER 7

THE INDUSTRY AFTER THE REVOLUTION

THE TRANSFORMATION OF THE PR OFFICE

Every revolution devastates the structures that existed beforehand, making room for new structures to arise from the revolutionary ashes.

The social media revolution in the PR industry is no exception. It is safe to say it has largely demolished the previous state of the typical PR office, resulting in the need to build many news structures from scratch.

In this sense, our offices are being redeveloped and rebuilt to a great extent, both in terms of technology and of a redistribution of responsibilities.

A few years ago, my company had ten graphic designers on staff—now we've only got one or two, who on top of that have to be able to work with social media.

We used to have four people dealing with event management—now we have only one, and that employee's schedule isn't even full on some days.

We used to have more proofreaders because we used to make brochures, leaflets, and other print editions, and we used to have people in charge of printing, but we don't anymore. Instead, we have only one proofreader, who deals exclusively with social media.

On the other hand, we have just as many people who deal with social media as those who deal with clients.

That is because every single client has social media in their PR strategy. It will be even more present in future PR strategies.

I recently had this funny case with a client who called me and said, "Another company is going to take care of our social media channels for us, you will be in charge of the PR only."

Imagine my response: "What am I going to do, then? What will you be paying me for? PR is social media!"

A couple of days later the client called back, saying, "Actually, you are absolutely right. Whatever it is—it is all connected with social media."

On one hand, PR companies are becoming more technologically advanced inside their offices, especially when it comes to staff being increasingly tech-savvy.

On the other, PR companies have become, or are in the process of becoming, a lot more journalistic.

A few years ago, our company had several people whose only job was to write press releases, but now each and every member of our staff deals with the written word.

That means that all of them must all be erudite, and very skilled and quick in language communication.

These new necessities demonstrate once again that the PR industry has been transformed by the social media revolution into an entirely different business field from the one it used to be.

And I've got a real proof of that. Following you will find the opinions of some of the world's top PR experts about changes in their offices and their business environments in the era of social media and technological developments in the past five years.

Question: What has changed for the past five years—in your office, in your market, with your clients, or in the media in your country?

ADAM BENSON, Managing Director, Recognition PR (Brisbane, Australia)

Australia's media has continued to consolidate, which means fewer publications and full-time journalists for traditional PR consultancies to engage with. At the same time, more organizations use content marketing, social, and other digital channels to directly influence stakeholders. To stay in business, PR firms have had to evolve rapidly to solve our clients' total communication challenge—not just the media relations component.

ADRIANA VIEIRA, CEO, InterMídia Comunicação Integrada (São Paulo, Brazil)

In Brazil, . . . [we are seeing] more events and relationship with the public and less advertisement. The brands no longer need to "tell for sell," but to "listen to understand and deliver what the public opinion is/what clients wish and believe." The public opinion is now a fast judge who no longer accepts lies and mistakes; more transparency and ethics is also a must-have for the brands now.

AGNIESZKA DZIEDZIC, Managing Partner, Weber Shandwick (Warsaw, Poland)

PR is definitely less viewed as strictly media relations or events, as was the case some years ago. Because of changes in the media landscape—online overcoming print—and of the growing role of influencer marketing, most PR briefs now cover a large portion of digital work: managing influencer relations, social media communication, and blogger relations. This means a convergence between PR agencies and digital agencies. Succeeding in the market are those agencies that have managed to develop a strong digital offering to complement their traditional PR offer.

AHMED JANABI, CEO, Harf Promotions (Baghdad, Iraq)

The increasing influence of social media hubs on brands ultimately made the digital identity the core of the brand identity. Brands used to talk one-way to the audience. Nowadays, the audience has the final word by the way they respond, and on many occasions, the comments, shares, and likes are forming the final perception of any brand, instead of the main content shared by brands themselves.

AIVE HIIEPUU, President, Estonian PR Association (Tallinn, Estonia)
Today we talk not only about traditional PR tools, but mainly integration with other marketing and media areas. PR has a transfunctional role. This is the art of how to integrate four media types—paid, earned, shared, and owned—to help a client achieve real success.

AKI KUBO, Managing Director, North Asia, Williams Lea Tag (Tokyo, Japan)
I consider no significant change in the local PR business, while the way people consume information changed dramatically.

ALISON CLARKE, Founder, Alison Clarke Consulting (London, UK)
Change is the constant in our industry. The past five years have seen a far greater focus on and use of data to give insights that help inform strategies. Integration communications are the way forward, ensuring creatively relevant content works across multiple platforms.

ALMA GERXHANI, CEO, Manderina Promotions (Tirana, Albania)
In less than five years, the change has been dramatic. We have shifted from drafting press releases to distribute to media and then to the public to writing statuses on social media and communicating directly. For better or worse, we are more exposed to the consumer, while we are carefully crafting our status, somewhere one unhappy customer can ruin everything. Today is about being 100 percent alert and responding quickly and accurately 100 percent of the time. This is more important than what we produce to polish our image.

ALTHAF JALALDEEN, General Manager, Phoenix Ogilvy—PR & Influence (Colombo, Sri Lanka)
A lot has changed in the past five years. The main change is how we define journalism and the birth of the informal journalist (mainly

consumers of brands). This is mainly due to the rise of various social media platforms—from the revolution of Facebook and Twitter to Snapchat and Instagram and many more. It is said that 68 percent of Americans get their news from social media platforms. With this much news being consumed from social media and with accessibility, everyone is a journalist now. This I see as one of the major developments of public relations and its behavior overall.

AMIR RASTEGAR, Director of International Affairs, Arman Public Relations Institute (Tehran, Iran)

During the past five years, thanks to technological progress, the focus of PR business has changed from traditional tools to modern tools, especially digital and social platforms. The most prominent feature of traditional PR in Iran is press outreach with the focus of newspapers, television, radio, etc., but the focus of modern PR is online, digital, and social media.

ANDRAS SZTANISZLAV, Senior Consultant and Managing Director, PersonaR (Budapest, Hungary)

Physically, we have fewer wires and cables and more wireless connections; we store more on the cloud than in our computers and servers; and we use significantly less paper, notebooks, and flip charts, and a lot more online project management and communication software. We also do a lot more work remotely (not at our clients and not even in the office) and work with more freelancers. For our own marketing, we use more online marketing tools and basically nothing with traditional media (not even trade media).

ANDREW BONE, Chief Strategy Officer, Middle East and Africa, Hill+Knowlton Strategies (Riyadh, Saudi Arabia)

The rise of "content publishing." PR has transitioned from media relations through "digital" to becoming a content publishing operation, whether that is through owned, earned, shared, or paid channels. This means that professionals with a much wider skill set—video production, editing, graphics design, SEO, etc.—have become the people currency for communications consultancies.

ANDREY BARANNIKOV, CEO, SPN Communications (Moscow, Russia)

The communications industry is undergoing serious changes caused by new economic realities. Mass media used to be the main tool to deliver your message, but now channels of communication have changed completely and speed of reaction has increased a lot. Social media are the main media today. Facebook has won.

ARUN SUDHAMAN, CEO and Editor in Chief, The Holmes Report (Hong Kong/China)
The past five years have seen considerable disruption of the PR industry, as communicators and agencies have realized that they can no longer attempt to control the narrative. Instead, it is clearer now more than ever that reality outweighs rhetoric, that organizations must behave responsibly and deliver value to all stakeholders rather than just tell a good story.

ASSEL KARAULOVA, President, Kazakhstan Press Club and National PR Association (Nur-Sultan, Kazakhstan)
The biggest changes we have seen are in social media development and digital communications. It has transformed completely the way businesses and some government representatives communicate—24/7 direct communication with customers and citizens implies different thinking, mentality, approaches, and speed of feedback.

BASHAR ALKADHI, CEO, Middle East, North Africa, and Turkey, Hill+Knowlton Strategies (Dubai, United Arab Emirates)
We are seeing colleagues entering the firm and the industry from different careers and backgrounds. Whereas it was predominantly from the industry itself or the media previously, we now have ex-bankers, sportspeople, management consultants, healthcare professionals, and so on coming into the firm. This can only be good for our company and the industry as a whole. These colleagues bring new insights and fresh perspectives, which make us better consultants to our clients.

BOŽIDAR NOVAK, Owner, SPEM Communications (Ljubljana, Slovenia)
More small agencies. Prices have fallen.

BRIDGET VON HOLDT, Business Director, Burson Cohn & Wolfe (Johannesburg, South Africa)
Public relations has come of age! Public relations has crept into the boardroom, and it seems that it is there to stay. More and more CEOs are adamant that it is important to have public relations represented

at the boardroom table. Companies listed on stock exchanges seem to be leading in this arena. There is still work to be done, but it is encouraging.

Second, digital has been integrated into most campaigns, and this is now the norm rather than the exception. Content management is paramount and is owned by the PR practitioner. Owning the content, links into key messaging, and consistency across all channels and platforms.

The absence of relying on the newsroom to convey content about a client, a product, a service, or a person is becoming more and more evident! "Citizen Journalist" is now charging to the fore and releasing information to an audience via the digital platforms. In fact, many journalists now get their news leads from social media platforms.

The use of video has been a huge step in reaching all target audiences. In the past, we used to say that "a picture is worth a thousand words"; now we have a video relaying the message. It's vibrant, it's storytelling, and it's now.

CATALINA ROUSSEAU, President and CEO, BDR Associates (Bucharest, Romania)

We focused on developing both strategic communications' most sophisticated components and in developing internal digital PR capabilities, investing in talents, and bringing on board new terminology like Professionals, Wordsmatchmakers, Drummers, or Masters of Disaster when dealing with clients' needs. Clients' demand has increased, yet budgets are limited for PR actions. This reality forced us to enroll ourselves in what could be called the PR revolution, and to rethink the classic approach, making more room for creating scenarios and being very quick in reactions. Social media has become a revolutionary tool for PR.

CESARE VALLI, Former Managing Director, SEC (Milan, Italy)

The Public Relations business is undergoing a profound reshaping. You will not find anyone who may deny this. The trigger of the change is obviously digitalization—based on growing computer power, faster interconnecting networks, big data, artificial intelligence. Quantum computers are on their way. This has imposed the first pattern of the chance, the digitalization of our life (PCs, tablets, and smartphones are part of our daily use), but the other one is speed. Communication nowadays, influenced by the latter, is much, much faster and wide reaching than it ever was in the past. Everyone is connected in real time; everyone can be a source of information; news dissemination is immediate.

CHRISTOPHE GINISTY, Head of Digital Engagement, OECD (Paris, France/Brussels, Belgium)
Within PR agencies, people have started to integrate back the former separate digital/social practices. After years of considering these practices as addressing challenges from a world apart, PR practitioners have started to assume that everything has to be managed simultaneously. It has become obvious that you can't anymore have an impact on the stakeholder's state of mind by activating one channel only (could be print, online, or social). Digital savvy account leaders are now part of broader teams.

CIRO DIAS REIS, CEO, Imagem Corporativa (São Paulo, Brazil)
Digitalization has been the most important topic over the past five years in Brazil regarding the PR business. Agencies that did not dedicate efforts in this field have suffered losses in terms of business because clients want more and more integrated offerings, which comprises the traditional press services + institutional PR + digital services. Agencies that move forward in digitalization can now even compete against advertising agencies in many high-level campaigns.

CLARA LY-LE, Managing Director, EloQ Communications (Ho Chi Minh, Vietnam)
Social media and online traditional media are taking over print traditional media, thus changing the whole media landscape and PR practice in Vietnam. Social media is more particularly under focus: the social media penetration rate in the country is more than 43 percent, with more than 40 million active social media users.

DAPHNA TRIWAKS, CEO, Triwaks PR (Tel Aviv, Israel)
Clients ask for more new services and expect the agent to bring new tools to the table. Storytelling and traditional PR are just not enough. PR is a service in Israel that is usually underpaid, so the competition is very strong.

DAVID GALLAGHER, President, International Growth and Development, Omnicom PR Group (London, UK)
The first truly (or nearly truly) global generation has come of age, connected by technology and all that it enables, and they're beginning to alter the way we do everything—think, work, consume, manage, and govern. For PR, this shifts our value from "who we know"—decision-makers in media, business, or government—to how people connect, why, and what that means for organizations.

DAVID GORDON, Managing Partner, Cohn & Wolfe Canada (Toronto, Canada)
With the rise in "influencer" communication, traditional journalism has evolved—newsrooms are tracking the most "read" or "engaged" news stories from their electronic feeds, and journalists are ranked on their resonance with the public—shifting the role of the journalist from an arbiter of news to fulfillment of consumer demand.

By extension—the skills required to be successful in modern communications have also evolved, with e-skills and content capabilities that sidestep the traditional channels becoming increasingly important and reflective of success.

DIMITRIS ROULIAS, Managing Partner, Out of the Box PR (Athens, Greece)
The technology explosion, mainly expressed by social media, changed fundamentally the way individuals, organizations, and corporations produce, share, and consume content. This deeply influenced Public Relations practices and—paradoxically—put forward, although totally revamped, the core element of our profession: storytelling.

EITAN HERSHCO, Chairman, Israeli PR Association (Tel Aviv, Israel)
In order to combine PR with sponsored content, we've added employees who specialize in content writing specifically to customers and their products. Today, customers are showing a high demand for an overall solution that includes marketing of their brand and products.

ELISE MITCHELL, Founder and CEO, Mitchell Communications Group (Fayetteville, Arkansas, USA)
The agency moved from a centralized "department" model to an integrated model with creative, content, and digital skills embedded in client teams.

ELIZABETH GOENAWAN ANANTO, Founding Director, International Public Relations Summit (Jakarta, Indonesia)
The digital technology has forced public relations and strategic communication practice to redefine their strategy and tactics. In this digital era, stakeholders are more fragmented with various kinds of interests. The public is more flooded with twenty-four-hour news and hundreds of channels and resources. Thus, the practice of public relations should be more targeted and effective; content is more valuable than channels if the social impact is the objective.

ERIK CORNELIUS, Cofounder and COO, G3 Partners (Seoul, South Korea)
Korea has been ahead of most of the world in digital adoption, since the 1990s, when wired broadband became ubiquitous. In the past five years, online media have become even more important, especially on mobile platforms.

FABIÁN MOTTA, Director, Smart PR (Bogota, Colombia)
The most notable change the public relations business has had is related to the way people acquire information. This has to do, mainly, with the connectivity our era offers. We are facing much larger digital audiences, which pose a greater challenge of being able to connect them in shorter time, with better content, and in different platforms. In short, we are dealing with omnichannel consumers.

FILOMENA ROSATO, CEO, FiloComunicazione (Milan, Italy)
I had to transform the entire way of thinking on the job and organizing the structure with the creation of new professional skills. It was both financially onerous and mentally stressful, as we couldn't find on-the-market and ready-to-use solutions nor defined skills. Nonetheless, it was a fundamental step.

GABRIEL PASLARU, General Manager, Perfect Co. (Bucharest, Romania)

We now rely to a much greater extent on outsourcing. To better meet the varied needs of a changing market, we have developed a vast network of professionals ranging from top-notch ones to just enthusiastic yet very resourceful beginners. "Flexibility" has become the keyword, with an emphasis on integrating more and more of the growing number of communication channels.

GERMAN SAA, Group Director, Kyodo PR (Tokyo, Japan)

In the Japanese PR industry, the biggest change is of course how mass media has changed in the form it is consumed by Japanese audiences. Although its main role has NOT changed and it continues to be as influential as ever, the emergence of digital media and the marked decline of printed copies (newspapers and magazines) have caused PR agencies to rethink how we distribute information to them, from content to actual news angles and key messages. Now we even have a new category of media (social media), which, depending on the clients (B2C) and their targets (under 25), we need to use almost exclusively in order to reach our target audiences!

HALIM WALID ABOU SEIF, Senior PR Consultant, Rada Research & PR (Cairo, Egypt)

The staff became much younger. We were always debating if we need to hire experienced (older) executives to handle clients and PR work. Also, social media usage and friendliness have become the most important assets of our staff. The language has changed, from the formal writing and editing to a more slang episode that proved to be more appealing to our stakeholders. Clients have been more and more demanding. Their understanding of PR and strategic communication improved, and now they want more than media coverage.

ILARIJA BAŠIĆ, PR Director, MITA Group (Sarajevo, Bosnia and Herzegovina)

More and more companies are looking for agency services, but unfortunately, all the budgets are getting smaller and expectations of clients are exceptionally high. I also see the problem in the fact that today everyone thinks they can deal with PR. There are also a lot of those who fail to make a good and quality PR story and have begun to pay for the announcements. This puts us true professionals in an unenviable position.

JAFAR MANSIMI, Cofounder, PRoloq Magazine (Baku, Azerbaijan)
Changes are tremendous, indeed. People and businesses started paying much more attention to their brands, and it created completely different necessities for crisis management and a completely different style of communication. Interactive media also brought a completely new style of communication, and it is visibly quite strong even in my home country, Azerbaijan, where people started being active on social media, and it brought a lot of challenges to the PR business. More creative communication is expected.

JAROSLAV MAJOR, Senior Consultant, Hill+Knowlton Strategies (Prague, Czech Republic)
Social media is now considered a serious marketing tool in the PR business, while five years ago, it was just a fun toy for kids. Nowadays, we are using social media for marketing purposes mainly. But there are still some limitations. Due to the strict contracts and confidentiality agreements with our clients, we are not entitled to comment on our work for them in social media.

JOAN RAMON VILAMITJANA, CEO, Hill+Knowlton Strategies (Madrid, Spain)
The three most critical aspects that transformed H+K Spain over the last five years: diversity, creativity, and speed. Diversity: we're now much more diverse than five years ago with many different profiles and specialties, from creatives to analysts, healthcare professionals, or former politicians. Creativity: we're now 100 percent creative—not a creative agency (ad agency), but a PR agency that builds and executes creative strategies for its clients. Speed: our ability to make decisions and implement them extremely fast is extraordinary, compared to five years ago.

JOHN SAUNDERS, CEO and President, FleishmanHillard (Dublin, Ireland/St. Louis, USA)
Consumers' expectations of businesses, in general, are changing. We've seen erosion in public confidence in government and social institutions, with people looking to the business community to fill that void. In many cases, corporations are being forced to take a stand, and that has brought PR to the table in a new way, as strategic advisers

who can provide a holistic view of which actions will be best aligned with their consumers' expectations.

JÜRGEN H. GANGOLY, Managing Partner and CEO, The Skills Group (Vienna, Austria)
On the staff side, a new generation of consultants has been hired. More technical and hands-on IT and social media know-how are required at all positions nowadays. Also, the agency infrastructure faced heavy changes and investments in mobile working, process digitization, and—of course—also data security, storage, and cloud services, digital archive, etc.

"Speed kills"—a lightning speed at reaction time, project implementation, and 24/7 reachability are required by basically all agency clients nowadays. This is probably a result of the client's very own increasing pressure faced from markets, consumers, NGOs, and media.

KAMAL TAIBI, Founder and CEO, Stratëus Group (Casablanca, Morocco)
Interaction with and behavior toward institutions, brands, and leaders have dramatically changed over the last five years. The relationships have become extremely complex, and only public relations has the understanding and background to deal with this.

KHALID BADDOU, President, Moroccan Association of Marketing and Communication (Casablanca, Morocco)
The senior leadership of companies are becoming increasingly aware of the strategic role that communications in general—and PR in particular—could play in building up thought leadership and protecting brands' reputations. While this position has been considered a support function for years, today communications directors are part of the decision-making process, instead of being involved only in crisis management.

KIM NYBERG, Chairman, M-Brain, and Special Advisor, Hill+Knowlton Strategies (Helsinki, Finland)
The biggest change has happened in the way that technology has made it possible for each and every one to communicate directly with one's target groups. There is a common belief that technology takes care of it all, and even if it is true that tech has enabled us to have faster interactive communications with an abundance of information to back it

up, it definitely does not mean that tech is the holy grail of PR: you still need to think issues through, you still need old-fashioned professionalism and planning to get your messages across.

KRESTEN SCHULTZ-JØRGENSEN, CEO, Oxymoron (Copenhagen, Denmark)
Trade and industry barriers are shifting—management consulting investing in coms, coms in analysis, ad agencies in PR, etc.

LARS ERIK GRØNNTUN, Global President, Hill+Knowlton Strategies (Oslo, Norway)
I believe the biggest change is the increasing complexity for our clients and for us. Macro trends like the declining trust in institutions and elites, the crisis the media industry is going through, and the rise of social media as well as the public increasingly expecting companies and organization to have a larger goal than just creating value for shareholders have profound implications. It translates into a larger need for clients to acknowledge and address their role in society and relate to a more complex stakeholder landscape than before, as well as be more creative and emotional to cut through the contextual noise.

For our market and our operations, this also has some profound effects. It drives convergence, where different disciplines like marketing, communications, advertising, data analytics, etc., converge together. It also drives the need for new talent on our side, recruiting data scientists, more content producers (designers, journalists, etc.), as well as more creative people—in addition to our usual talent profiles.

LORENA CARREÑO, President, Confederation of Communication Marketing Industry (Mexico City, Mexico)
Technology has undoubtedly changed the way we do public relations, but deep down it's still the same.

LOULA ZAKLAMA, President, Rada Research & PR (Cairo, Egypt)
The public relations profession has witnessed great changes during the past few years. These changes took the PR profession from its old vision to a new and broad one that embraces the term "Corporate Diplomacy," a term that is rapidly rising.

Corporate diplomacy incorporates both countries and corporations. Since the foreign policies of a country could put a damper on its international commerce, multinational corporations must have their own corporate diplomats and protocol officers for business development abroad. Business engagement supplements rather than replaces a government's work in public diplomacy.

The rapid technology evolution changes the traditional way of practicing the public relations profession. Press releases are no longer as effective as before; we do not have the luxury of time. Facebook, Twitter, and all other social media tools can spread the news in a fraction of seconds.

Therefore, as PR professionals and practitioners, we have to adapt ourselves to these quick changes and in the meantime change our practice of PR in a way to incorporate the faster evolution in technology.

MARTIN PETERSON, President and CEO, H&H Group (Stockholm, Sweden)

The significance and value of trust have become brutally obvious. Building, defending, and maintaining our clients' trust capital is at the core of what we do as communication advisers. Hence, our industry has gained a more senior seat at the table.

MARTIN SLATER, CEO, Noesis PR (Milan, Italy)

We need a different set of skills, so we have had to employ creatives, analysts, etc., alongside the event managers, press officers, public affairs specialists, etc. We continue to need account handlers.

The personal relationship continues to be important, but clients expect high-quality service. This expectation is an advantage for us, in that agencies that relied only on personal relationships are increasingly less likely to make the grade. There are always exceptions, particularly in a country like Italy, where personal relationships are more important than in some other markets.

MASSIMO MORICONI, General Manager and CEO, Omnicom Public Relations Group (Milan, Italy)

PR and communications are more and more seen as business enablers. PR experts are also required to create innovation by advising on technologies/software that can be embraced by clients. There are also a lot more requests for in-house support. This is a good sign, as this means we are seen as real partners.

MICHAEL THOMAS SCHRÖDER, CEO, ORCA Affairs (Berlin, Germany)
Credibility/reputation: as consultants, we work in a trust relationship. The great art is to inspire people without stifling them. Mobile communications: in mobile communications, the pace is constantly increasing. To be present and relevant on all platforms and sometimes funny? Twenty-four hours a day? Mobile communications requires good resource management. Integrated communication across all channels: the visibility and retrievability of the content have the highest priority in the implementation of a successful online PR strategy. It is not enough to place the content on your own website.

MICHAELA BENEDIGOVÁ, Managing Director and Partner, Seesame (Bratislava, Slovakia)
I very much believe that the fundament of PR remains unchanged—our role is to create stable and harmonic relations to our clients, brands, companies, and communities with their various stakeholders and constituencies. We do it ethically and with respect for all parties involved. Speaking of the digital revolution, the environment and technology made a remarkable change. When Facebook entered the PR industry, it enabled any user to be a journalist, to spread their ideas and get feedback. And this had a profound impact on our work. Until then, we had communicated with a smaller group of people, with journalists or closed on-site or online communities that were usually fairly limited.

MINA NAZARI, Public Relations Expert, Tabriz Electric Power Distribution Company (Tehran, Iran)
I must say that these changes are regional and different in all countries of the world. In Iran, due to the advancement of the theory of PR, unfortunately, in the field of practice, there have not been any significant changes in the last five years.

MYKOLAS KATKUS, Chairman of the Board, FABULA (Vilnius, Lithuania)
Everything. We used to be quite diversified before—we have had strategists, public affairs persons, and others—but these specialists amounted to one-eighth of the total workforce; the rest were consultants and account managers. Now, more than half of all teams are people

specializing in digital, social, content, training, and other things. Our mindset has also changed a lot—we became real channel agnostics.

MYRON WASYLYK, CEO, PBN Hill+Knowlton Strategies (Moscow, Russia)
Without a doubt, the biggest change has to do with the changing media landscape and the adaptation of PR agencies to digitalization and social media. Virtually all campaigns—whether they are public affairs, PR, or marketing—now have a very large digital component, as the majority of the readers and viewers receive information on their smartphones, laptops, iPads, etc.

In the office, this has meant that we have had to specialize our personnel to become community managers, video bloggers, content creators, etc., to ensure that messages are delivered to the targets in the proper formats and templates.

NITIN MANTRI, Group CEO, AvianWE (New Delhi, India)
We have learned how to harness the powers of digital media: the initial fumbling in the dark is over, and the industry now knows how to use digital tools to its advantage. PR firms are creating opportunities for brands to stand for something meaningful through digital campaigns. Since PR firms have learned how to capitalize on emerging technologies, the focus has shifted from the medium to the messaging. Firms are cutting through the noise by creating high-quality, authentic content—editorial, social media, graphics, and video—that connects with audiences emotionally and inspires them to care and share, thus changing behavior. Leveraging the power of big data analytics has also improved our social listening skills, which has had a direct impact on sales, especially in the B2B sector.

NURUL SHAMSURI, Project Director, Yayasan Juwita (Kuala Lumpur, Malaysia)
In Malaysia, just like the rest of the world, public relations faces a turbulent future. The media landscape has never been so fragmented, and this is caused by massive digital revolutions that happen so fast.

In comparison with the past, there are only a handful of traditional media companies you have to deal with; however, now you have hundreds of alternative online media such as bloggers and social media influencers who are sometimes as powerful as the mainstream media, if not more. The result is that it's now very hard to make an impact.

OKSANA MONASTYRSKA, Managing Director, PBN Hill+Knowlton Strategies (Kiev, Ukraine)
In the past five years, we have been living in a fast-moving, information-overloaded, untrustworthy, and unpredictable environment where speed and the ability to learn and effectively communicate are the deal-breakers. PR has become a business of ideas and strategies, solutions and approaches, with a focus on tangible results, a business of relations with consumers, employees, partners, governments, and communities.

PATRIK SCHOBER, CEO, PRAM Consulting (Prague, Czech Republic)
Like everyone, we started to hire millennials and have to learn how to cowork with them. These days, we have about 30 percent of them in my agency. Nowadays, we have more people who are working remotely, from home offices, and these are mostly women on or right after maternity leave.

Clients are more mature; they understand more how the PR job has been done, which means big pressure on agencies' performance. Unfortunately, many clients are pushing prices down, and there are uneducated agencies that are willing to work for a small amount of money.

PELIN KOCAALP, General Manager, Hill+Knowlton Strategies (Istanbul, Turkey)
Content management has been the most important part of communications. The channels and tools have also changed in the past five years, and creativity has become more important than ever. The change from either writing a press release and distributing it to the media or doing a pitch has all changed drastically. We have all updated our services in the new era, such as social media and tech changes, to remain relevant in today's digital world. For instance, today, a short video tells a story on Instagram and promotes brand awareness at the same time.

PETER MUTIE, CEO, Peterson Integrated Communications (Nairobi, Kenya)
We have gone more paperless. The mode of communication has also changed, with most of the meetings being held virtually. Also, several

of our staff are working away from the office, meaning we need less office space. Our clients are more informed and demand more information on our services.

PHILIPPE BORREMANS, Independent PR Consultant, Reputation & Co. (Casablanca, Morocco)
Nothing much for myself, as I am a one-man organization. Although when I worked in an agency I saw a frantic rush to get "digital services" integrated into classic PR. PR agencies today are waking up to the fact that they are (and have been) missing out on many changes and opportunities in the digital space and that once again our cousins in advertising and marketing have been eating away the pie.

Clients are more and more looking for a "flexible specialty approach" as they understand that no one agency can do everything they need (media relations, strategy, digital, paid, etc.). They also start to understand the importance of strategic advice and the need for good crisis communications. It is a slow change, but it is happening. Probably the reputation crises that happened over the last couple of years have played a role.

RANA NEJEM, Founding Director, Yarnu: The Art of Social Intelligence (Amman, Jordan)
It used to be that everything was private until I decided to make it public, but now everything is public until I decide to make it private. Media became a very fuzzy term. Everyone is a journalist now, so the result is the loosening of standards. Complete loss of control over the media and what is published over social media. So the only thing I can control as a company is my behavior and my statements.

From my small office in Amman, Jordan, I can market my services and reach potential clients at no additional cost by using LinkedIn, Twitter, and Facebook.

RETO WILHELM, Managing Director, Panta Rhei PR (Zurich, Switzerland)
We have a new workspace—more teams and subteams. We also have new working agreements—we have people working part-time or from home. We are a lot like freelancers. We also collaborate a lot with third parties via online collaboration tools (such as Slack).

RHINGO MUTAMBO, Chief PR Officer, Prime Minister's Bureau (Windhoek, Namibia)
Information and communication technology has transformed the mediums and modes of communication. It has further shifted engagement from traditional means of communication to a virtual space. That has been replaced by social media, where almost all institutions have a media WhatsApp group through which all pictures, statements, media releases are shared instantly. Ironically, faxes have become white elephants and scanners are overloaded, as most documents are scanned, uploaded on mobile devices, and shared on virtual platforms.

RICHARD MILLAR, Global President, Hill+Knowlton Strategies (London, UK)
I've (we've) seen more change in the past five years than in any preceding period of my more than thirty years in the profession. The fundamental shift in power and influence away from the institutions of the state, from business, and from a once objective and impartial media into the hands of the public. The public now has the power to make and break reputations and at a speed once unimaginable in the days before the internet.

SARI-LIIA TONTTILA, Founder, Ahjo Communications Oy (Helsinki, Finland)
Empathy and purpose have changed the way of thinking about communications. Strategy is about how. Purpose is about why. If the purpose is missing, the strategy is sure to miss, as well. Strategy is how to get where purpose is taking you.

SAURABH UBOWEJA, CEO, Brands of Desire (New Delhi, India)
We have experienced two significant changes in our workplace. Instead of hierarchical systems with well-defined reporting structures, we now have a flat organization structure, where everyone is a leader, not of people, but of their respective area of expertise. There are juniors and seniors, but not people leaders anymore.

In the last five years, we have seen clients becoming more aware of what they want from agencies, obviously with some assistance from experts. They are also learning to work with multiple partners who are domain experts rather than working with one organization that claims to know and do all.

SERGE BECKERS, Managing Partner, Wisse Kommunkatie (Arnhem, Netherlands)

As the PR activities became more focused, more targeted, and more effective, we have had more difficulties in finding the right staff. We now have a good feeling for finding true PR professionals that are committed to this line of work. We no longer simply hire people "who love to write" but do not have knowledge of the work we actually do on a daily basis.

Clients have become more critical; the majority no longer hire a PR agency without knowing what to expect. Budgets have become tighter, but clients seem to be more aware of the benefits of good PR.

SERGEY ZVEREV, CEO, Cross Communications (Moscow, Russia)

We have been restructuring our team and competence in accordance with the new market requirements. We have become younger, more flexible, digital, and mobile. We try to think beyond standard paradigms and create unique scenarios, which let us develop and execute projects that have already set benchmarks for the industry.

Now clients don't request just corporate communications or creative support. They give us tasks, which are often impossible to structure. And to solve these problems, we lack the standard PR toolkit; we have to learn new technologies.

SHAMIL TUMISANG AGOSI, Director, Square Gate Holdings (Gaborone, Botswana)

Over the years, there has been a rise of citizen journalism and brand publishing, which has brought an end to the current-day mainstream media. We now have audiences digesting content real time and from multiple interactive sources, virtual press releases, embedding images, graphics alongside short text carefully customized and speaking to audience need.

SOLLY MOENG, Convenor, SA Brand Summit & Awards (Cape Town, South Africa)

We've found that the PR professional of the future must know how to think "integrated" in terms of media, and understand data mining, analytics, and application. What has changed is the need to integrate and almost work on more platforms than it was the case, traditionally.

Clients ask more questions, they want to know more and cannot be taken for a ride. They might not always know how to articulate their needs, but that doesn't mean they can be taken for granted. But clients also need to be helped to understand the key trends in the industry. For instance, many clients still place too much value on the use of AVEs (Advertising Value Equivalents) for PR measurements. They rely on us to understand when AVEs are applicable and when they're not.

SOPHYA BALAKINA, Cofounder and CEO, Bureau of Communications TAGS (Bishkek, Kyrgyzstan)
The approach to the profession of both PR specialists and business executives has changed. First, the tools and responsibility were significantly expanded—PR professionals began paying more attention to the efficiency of their activities, which is caused by the advent of new technologies and the increase of new possibilities and tools for evaluation process. The status of PR consultants increased. Many of them take higher positions in companies (the level of CEO), enter the management board, and their opinions became significant in strategic planning of the business. Of course, it also affected salaries, which have grown significantly in the last five years. In general, it can be said that the PR market of Central Asia is developing dynamically, although it still lags far behind global trends in terms of the technologies used, the boldness, the scope of the campaigns, and the overall creative approaches.

STUART BRUCE, Managing Consultant, Stuart Bruce Associates (Leeds, UK)
The biggest change I have witnessed in the last five years is a far greater recognition by clients that things can't go on as they are. Most of my clients are large corporations or government organizations that have traditionally had a very conservative approach to public relations and communications. Now they are willing to not only listen to me explain why they need to modernize, but are actually starting to implement change.

SVETLANA JAPALĂU, Managing Director, BDR Associates—Strategic Communication (Kishinev, Moldova)
Our sector may be compared with the geopolitical status of Moldova, which actually represents a mix of influence from EU, US, and

post-Soviet countries. In other words, the style of strategies applied in the post-Soviet countries (except the Balkans) fits well the famous saying: "All is fair in love and war." On the other hand, PR and strategic communications in the EU and US are governed by ethics in the first place. To conclude, in the past five years, the Republic of Moldova has become a "fertile" region for propaganda and "abundant" usage of false information (by political parties, geopolitical organizations, and others). On the other hand, PR campaigns have shifted from traditional to digital media (online and social media).

TAMARA BEKČIĆ, Managing Director, Chapter 4 Communications (Belgrade, Serbia)
PR business is highly dynamic, although I am a firm believer that the profession itself does not change—our principal goals are the same. However, the channels and tools we opt for have changed over the course of past years significantly, as a direct and consequent result of technology development. I also think our view of the world has changed, and we always have to have a broader perspective now.

TATEVIK PIRUMYAN, Communication Key Expert, EU Assistance to Armenia Project (Yerevan, Armenia)
We have more freelancers now than we had five years ago. Clients became more "aware" and "educated." Additionally, we have a lot more clients from abroad—foreign companies operating in Armenia.

TATJANA LOPARSKI, CEO, Element PR (Skopje, Macedonia)
The channels of communication, the media landscape, and the storytelling has changed a lot. The information is fast, and the need to get the story public quickly has become essential. Internet and social media have changed the scope of the work in public relations.

THIERRY WELLHOFF, President & CEO, Wellcom (Paris, France)
PR is back! Changes in the PR business occurred in three stages: (1) The internet gave access to everything, at any time, from anywhere in the world; (2) with social media, communication isn't vertical anymore but has also become horizontal; and (3) there has been a decrease in trust for every form of authority (politicians, press, companies). And in the past five years, we have seen in a change in the scope of our profession with the permeability of all the communication professions: PR no longer only covers Owned and Earned, but also Paid. We are back

to an integrated communication where PR is just a part of the other professions (advertising, marketing, events). Today, PR and the quality of relations are key to communications and trust creation—PR is back!

THOMAS TINDEMANS, Chairman, Hill+Knowlton Strategies (Brussels, Belgium)
The distrust of the public in all forms of sleek communication has greatly increased. Many people seem to believe only information received from sources they personally relate to and do not accept authoritative sources—especially not government sources. Fake news, unfounded accusations, and whispers increasingly shape public opinion and reputations, more than fact-based, verifiable, and reliable messaging. A communications overdose risks killing PR impact because of spreading popular disbelief.

VIVIAN LINES, Global Vice Chairman, Hill+Knowlton Strategies (Singapore)
Clients need us to be their communications partners more so today than ever before. They look to us to guide, to advise, and to help them navigate ever more treacherous waters of public accountability. They need us to bring solutions to the table that traverse business consultancy as much as communications support. And they expect us to be experts across multiple disciplines and to be able to dissect, strategize, and implement solutions online, offline, above the line, and below the line.

YASEMIN EDIGE ÖZTUNC, Group Coordinator, Lobby PR (Istanbul, Turkey)
You never step into the same river twice—now more than ever. Five years is a very long time in today's world, especially for counting the number of changes. But I believe the "being always online" capability of people all around the world is at the very center of all the change happening. We can call it the deus ex machina. Internet, broadband networks, and handheld mobile devices have changed everything in the last twenty years. Big data changed everything and also radically changed how we do our business.

YOMI BADEJO-OKUSANYA, CEO, CMC Connect Burson Cohn & Wolfe (Lagos, Nigeria)
The deepening of its practice through specialization as organizations and clients demand more proven value from budgets. No doubt

technology and social media have had the most significant impact on how PR services are being delivered or consumed across the board.

ZDENEK LOKAJ, Former Managing Director, Hill+Knowlton Strategies (Prague, Czech Republic)
The change is in technology and people's mindsets. We are more focusing on the content of the work than on some formalities: with advancing technology, people can more easily work from home or their favorite locations, which brings new enthusiasm, lots of creativity, and lowers must-do-place-and-time tensions. People are more flexible, and it eases workflow and service. Clients are more focused, both on quality of content (as opposed to an overall number of published articles) and on more precise targeting—even if they use traditional media. Clients are planning more on an ad hoc basis, and the "good ol' days" of monthly retainers are disappearing, yielding to performance-based remuneration. This is on one side a challenge, but on the other, it is an opportunity motivating us to perform better and in more creative ways.

ZSOFIA LAKATOS, CEO, Emerald Communications (Budapest, Hungary)
I started my own agency as H+K was closing. Same client portfolio, but they spent much less money. Multinationals spend a fraction of what they used to; they intend to stay "under the radar."

THE SKILLS OF TODAY

Which are the most valuable skills for a PR expert against the backdrop of this transformation of the PR office?

This book has already emphasized my Rule Number One: that even the worst decision is better than no decision at all, a decision that hasn't been made.

One of the most cherished skills and qualities of a PR expert today is a quick reaction, the ability to assume responsibility very quickly!

This is because everything has become a function of time; everything is connected with time. That goes for any kind of regular communication, not just for crisis management.

If you have to react on behalf of your client, to defend your client, or to promote your client, time is of the utmost essence.

If you take your time, or delay thinking or coordinating the response with your client, a lot more things might happen in the meantime.

This is why nowadays we bear a much greater responsibility; we are much more important decision-makers, than we were before the social media revolution.

You must react as quickly as you would if you were your own client. Cases when you actually have time to consult with your client are exceedingly rare today, because news and comment feeds keep rolling in the meantime.

This book never set out to paint too rosy a picture of the PR industry after the social media revolution. There are seemingly negative consequences of this revolutionary change. One, of course, is the incessant danger of getting fooled and tricked by fake news, of not having sufficient time to verify whether a news story is true, to fact-check its details.

However, I am certain that fake news is going to begin to die, because at the end of the day, social media is getting so personalized that nobody will dare produce fake news anymore because they might go to prison.

Fake news remains a major risk, though, which is why people need to be much more erudite, educated, and knowledgeable, which requires much better training and preparation.

Regardless of how good you are at googling things, or doing more sophisticated online research in the oceans of available information, as a PR expert of today's reality, your head must be full of knowledge, thanks to which you would be able to make a very fast but adequate decision.

That is why I think that now is the time of the knowledgeable people in PR.

Now is not the time of the "searching" people or those who can google something, because today even a three-year-old kid could do that.

Now is the time of knowledgeable people who have received a good education, and have undergone proper training, and are mentally prepared to assume responsibility for making immediate decisions.

PR EXPERTS OR EDITORS?

As a result of the social media revolution, PR has now started overlapping substantially with the management of media to such a degree that the clear-cut difference between a media editor and a PR expert might seem blurred.

Yet the title "PR expert" presumes a very substantial upgrade from the role of an editor.

An editor needs to have knowledge of the topic they tackle, and proper writing and text-editing skills, whereas a PR expert should have all of that plus much wider knowledge and should also be able to communicate with clients.

So a PR expert is supposed to have a lot more skills than an editor, even though a big part of a modern-day PR expert's work is to be able to edit well, and especially to write well.

THE PR LANGUAGE—DO WE UNDERSTAND IT?

Language in today's world has changed a lot since the advent of social media, but in the PR industry, the changes in language style have been drastic.

This is because we are not allowed to write in a language (style) that isn't easily comprehensible to everyone.

Back in the good old pre-social media days, the most meaningful verbal/written way that PR professionals communicated was by writing and sending out press releases to journalists.

Now we are in contact not just with journalists, but with a wide "readership," or clients' clients. Journalists used to be able to take your dumb or badly written press release and rewrite it in their own style to make it understandable for the readers, but now you are the person who communicates directly with the readership.

Therefore, PR professionals are now obliged to focus a lot more on language skills, and especially on being able to write concisely, intriguingly, and accurately, while also finding the right dynamic of the title sentences.

HOW TO SWAY PEOPLE TODAY

No matter how traditional it might sound, the main way to sway people still remains the personal experience. It is about your own skills in doing things from which your colleagues can learn.

In the public relations business, people you work with are influenced by two things.

One is salary, and the other is working conditions (including teamwork, the boss, the team leader, where they work, how they work, the clients they are assigned to work with, and the atmosphere in the office).

The good manager must balance nonstop between these two.

You can't enjoy a very high salary but work in an office that is a nightmare, or the other way around.

You can have great clients, everything at the office might be very organized, but if your salary is low, you will not be overjoyed with your job.

And of course, you need conceptual thinking, a vision guiding your work and leading you forward.

IN-HOUSE CLIENTS' TRENDS: CHEMISTRY OR THE LACK THEREOF

In today's revolutionary business environment, having good chemistry with the client is more key than ever for the success of a PR company, which is why the role of a client's in-house PR department is essential. In-house PR departments often do more harm than good, and it is safe to say not only that they should disappear, but also that they *will* disappear in the near to medium term.

During a recent discussion in France on the difference between advertising and PR, I spoke out in favor of the notion that "PR earns media, while advertising buys media." I was quickly corrected.

"No," some of the other participants in the discussion told me, "the difference is that the CEO of the advertising company meets with the marketing manager of the client company, whereas the CEO of the PR company meets with its CEO of the client company! That is the main difference!"

We, the managers of PR companies, are indeed in contact with the CEOs of our clients. Partly as a result of that, we know our clients' businesses better than advertising agencies do.

However, this situation very often generates resistance from the midlevel executives of a corporation's in-house PR department against the external PR agency hired by that corporation.

We, and many other PR companies from around the world, have had problems with in-house PR departments, and always will.

A large corporation wouldn't employ twenty PR experts. It's normal to hire an external PR company to do much of the job of its in-house department.

Therefore, the in-house PR executives feel threatened, and on the other hand, they have their own concept about the approaches to take and how to get things done.

The external PR agency very often has an entirely different concept. More often than not, it is much more accurate and adequate, because the PR company has a lot more experience, it works with more clients, and it sees the bigger picture.

Of course, the CEO or manager of the PR company is in contact with the CEO of the client corporation, which naturally generates a great deal of jealousy among the corporation's PR staff. Jealousy from in-house PR departments is one of the huge issues that we are trying to surmount every day, and it is an issue that has to do with trust or lack thereof.

The moment you manage to establish trust with the in-house staff, that's when the best projects get done. And a client's entire staff should theoretically have trust in you by default because you work with their CEO!

In other words, chemistry.

Because of the not infrequent jealousy and resistance on the part of the in-house PR departments, it is probably much more logical for them to be gone, rather than to stay there.

In-house PR departments should have solely coordinative functions. Under no circumstances should they be trusted with decision-making functions.

If that sounds extreme, consider the following: many large companies own a fleet of cars and have drivers, but they don't own their own car service companies. Why? Because having your own car service is pretty expensive and unnecessary.

In-house PR departments increasingly resemble such service stations. Not to mention, of course, that they can never be as good as an

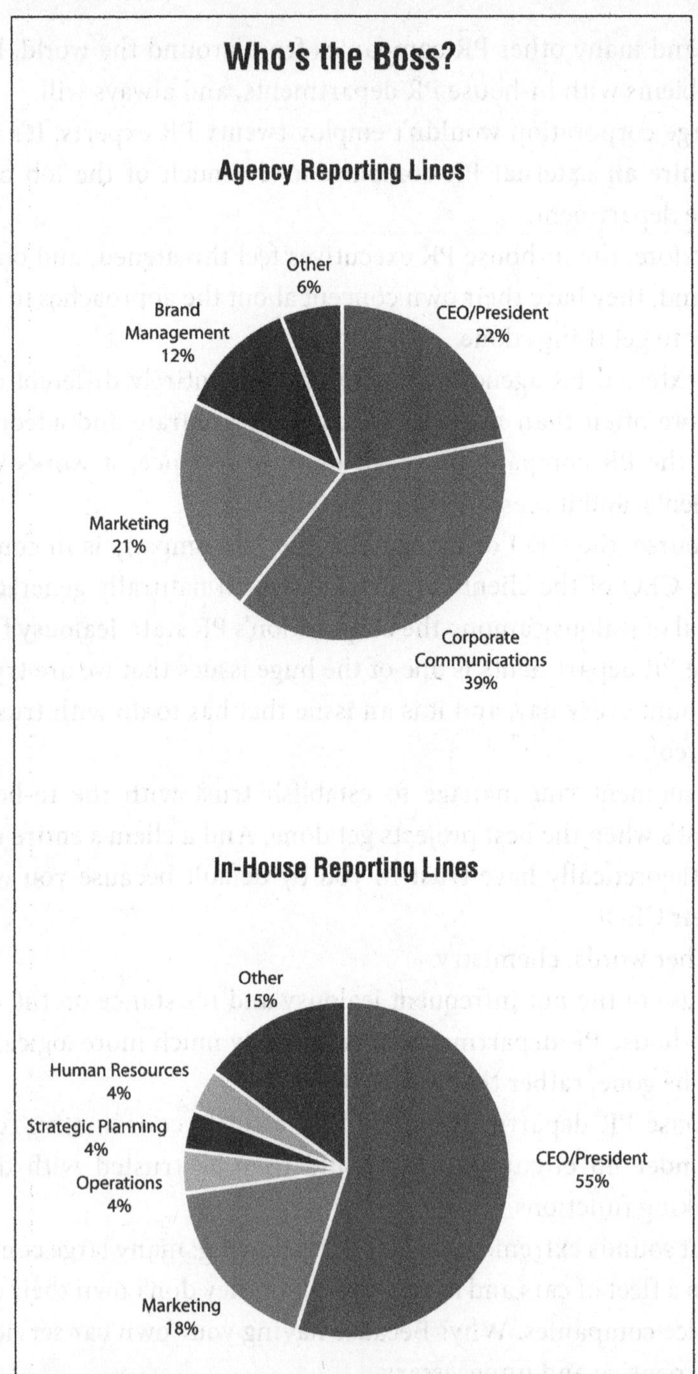

Source: 2017 Global Communications Report of the USC Annenberg School for Communication and Journalism.

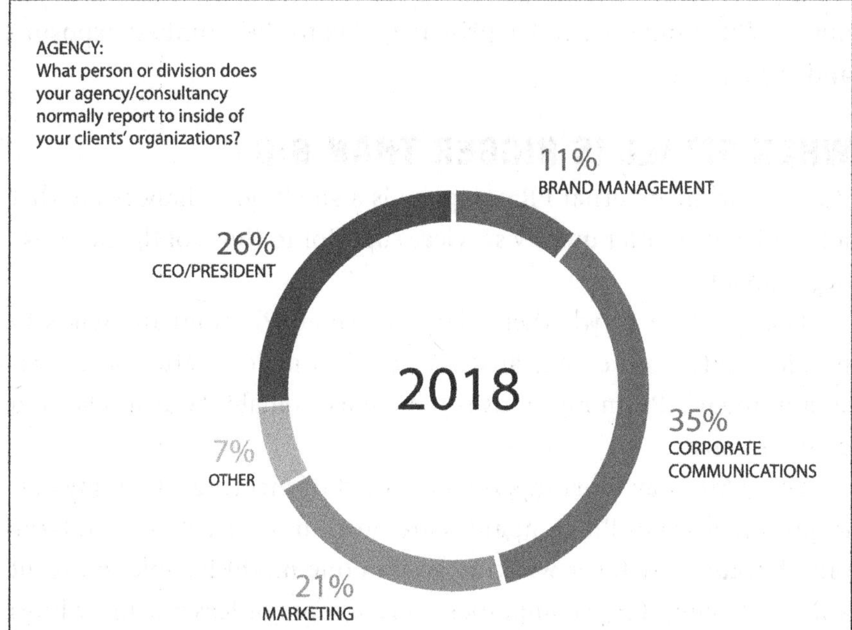

Source: 2018 Global Communications Report of the USC Annenberg School for Communication and Journalism.

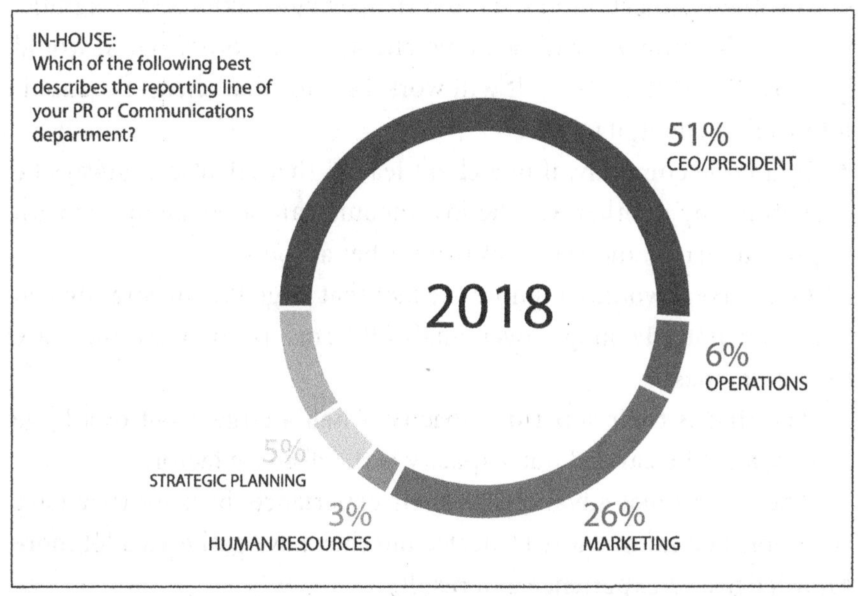

Source: 2018 Global Communications Report of the USC Annenberg School for Communication and Journalism.

outside PR company can be, primarily due to their limited exposure and experience.

WHEN SMALL IS BIGGER THAN BIG

But even if the external PR company is a small one, chances are that it is still able to offer quality services superior to those of the in-house department.

The question of whether a large or small PR company tends to provide better, more dedicated services is a major matter of discussion in today's PR industry, as is the issue of reliability as it relates to company size.

Every Monday morning, during our staff meetings, I tell my colleagues that small PR companies are much more creative than large ones because whatever working system one might be able to invent and implement, large companies remain more or less assembly lines for projects and ideas, albeit usually insightful and efficient ones.

Many of the things they do and the way they do them are heavily uniform because of the vast commitments they have, the volume of each of their projects, and the often staggering workload they handle.

A small company with a single client, on the other hand, would literally die for that client. It will work 24/7 for that client. Because if it loses that client, it's gone.

In a large company, if one client leaves, that client can always be substituted by another. Or the lost income can be made up for with improved results and revenues from other accounts.

Of course, I wouldn't ignore the fact that large PR corporations do possess major advantages over small PR firms. In my view, there are two main ones.

The first is their superior capacity: when a large event or a large project must be carried out, capacity is the decisive factor.

The other great advantage is their experience, because they have accomplished many more projects, and they have gathered a lot more knowledge and experience as a result.

The experience of small PR companies shouldn't be underestimated, though, because every single large PR company used to be a small one before it grew.

I do have major respect for small PR companies, because very often they give birth to notably outstanding ideas.

An in-house PR department in a large corporation, however, could hardly ever come up with such comprehensive, wide-ranging, and appropriately applicable ideas as an outside PR company could, regardless of its size.

It is probably safe to view even the smallest PR company as more efficient than an in-house PR department, plus in-house departments often suffer from a myriad of dependencies on bosses and other departments, and all kinds of domestic corporate rules, intrigues, and other complicated internal relations, whereas an outside PR consultant should not be interested in any of those things apart from the corporate standards.

All an external PR company needs to be interested in is the client's success.

SPEED, SIMPLICITY, SELF-CONFIDENCE: THE RULE

I formulated the Three S's Rule many years ago, and it is even more valid today: Speed, Simplicity, Self-Confidence.

Not one of them is the most important, or more important than the others. They form an equilateral triangle.

The Three S's Rule:

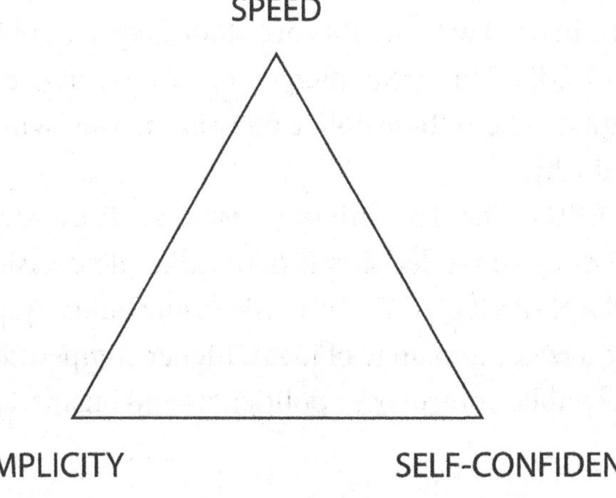

First of all, speed is extremely important. The impact of dynamics cannot be exaggerated and should never be underestimated.

Second, the world is so sophisticated today, and our tasks are so complicated, that we must have very clear priorities and a simple agenda as to how to achieve them, hence simplicity.

Third, I don't know a single successful person who achieved anything without self-confidence and a desire to do their job perfectly and responsibly.

I think this rule of Speed, Simplicity, and Self-Confidence applies to everything in the PR industry, to every step you take.

The three S's, however, cannot just be a motivation tool. Rather, they should be something like a rule of law in your office, dictating how you organize your team and communicate with your clients: you must always remember that the speed of decision-making and doing your job is crucial, that you need to have priorities and simplify things, and that you need to have self-confidence.

TOP 10 WORDS OF THE GLOBAL PR REVOLUTION!

1. **CHANGE**—Different media environment, different tools, offices, structures and abilities, a need for both different managers and different management.
2. **MEDIA**—We are the media. Public figures, journalists, newspapers may exist, but without advertisers. So now instead of being PR consultants, we are publishers!
3. **MERGE**—The great merger of advertising, PR, and digital. The billion-dollar question is who will lead it and why.
4. **SPEED**—The five-minute response time standard: even the worst decision is better than no decision.
5. **TRANSPARENCY**—Intrinsic to our industry, providing a faster exchange of ideas, higher competition, and *full* public control over politicians and businesspeople.

Creates an excellent environment for ethical business, development, and fair competition.

6. **INTEGRITY**—A very important keyword. We are machines for news, we are publishers. If anything goes wrong, it's our fault!
7. **EDUCATION**—We must bridge the big gap between theory and practice; we must address the overwhelming prevalence of the latter over the former.
8. **MEASUREMENT**—Our clients used to complain of a lack of clear evaluation principles. No more.
9. **LANGUAGE**—The worldwide language of PR business is "clear"!
10. **RISKS**—Transparency brings all kinds of risks—fake news, trolls, and attacks on reputation—but these are much more easily manageable if we are prepared.

NEW TOOLS, OLD VALUES

Regardless of the wide-ranging reach of the new PR tools generated by the social media revolution, the fundamental values of the PR business are going to survive 100 percent unchanged.

These fundamentals are honesty, accuracy, ethics, professionalism, and knowledge. Without any one of those values, the PR industry itself would not exist.

People working in PR today need to internalize those values even more than companies do, because the greater transparency of public and social relations makes ethics and morals more and more prominent.

This has been exemplified by the Harvey Weinstein case and the other recent Hollywood sex scandals, many including stories from twenty or thirty years ago that have only just come to light. Once made known, the public awareness of these events spread rapidly thanks to social media and everyone's access to it. A few years ago, it would not have been that easy for any actor or TV host to go to the traditional media and beg to be allowed to reveal something on air about Dustin Hoffman or Kevin Spacey. But now that they have ready access to social media, it is a whole other story. We are now much more vulnerable in that anyone can check to see if our actions are up to high ethical standards.

So the greater the ethics in the PR business, yours and everybody else's, the more peacefully and confidently you will be able to do your creative job.

MEASURING: EASIER THAN EVER!

As noted in Chapter 1, thanks to social media, measurement of PR's achievements and efficiency has become easier than ever. This is a good indicator of how the business will develop in the future.

No human factor can interfere with your data when it comes to knowing how many people shared that article of yours or of your client.

Here and there, someone might try to cheat using bots, but that can be found out easily.

Facebook, Google, and other social media platforms offer you a very clear picture about your users (readers, consumers) as to who read the article concerning your client, and when, and for how long. There is no way to falsify that.

The one thing that cannot be measured is mood. There is no way to measure the readers' moods, unless you film everyone with a camera.

Even though Facebook's improved "Like" button, with its multiple reactions, could be a good indicator, I am skeptical of "Likes" in general, because my experience has led me to conclude that at least half of the people who "like" something do so to show off, become known, or demonstrate their presence, and not because they actually like it. The more detailed "Like" options could theoretically provide some additional information, but the picture they paint probably isn't that realistic.

What's realistic is the accurate data about the number of people, their origin, gender, age, and interests. These are the data that can be tracked. The significance of PR's newly acquired ability to use highly accurate data measurement cannot be exaggerated.

The 2017 report on "The Evolution of Public Relations" by the US Association of National Advertisers (ANA) and the USC Center for

Public Relations at the Annenberg School for Communication and Journalism found most respondents, who are client-side marketers, deem that demonstrating how PR programs achieve *measurable* business results is how the PR industry can validate its value.

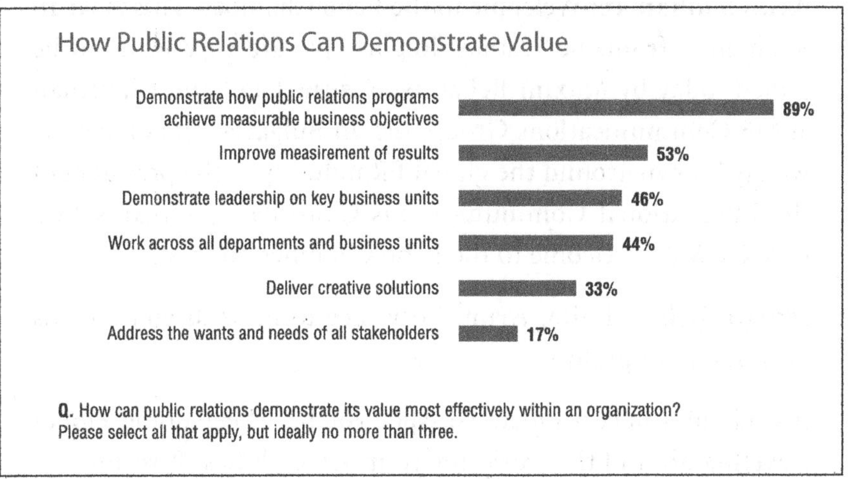

Source: 2017 Report of the Evolution of PR by the US Association of National Advertisers (ANA) and the USC Center for Public Relations at the Annenberg School for Communication and Journalism.

RISKS: MORE THAN EVER!

The risks spurred by the social media revolution for the PR industry and the other communication fields are becoming more, not less. They cannot be prevented because of the essence of social media.

The only way to neutralize the emerging risks is with sufficient in-depth preparation for any eventuality. That way you will be able to appropriately react to anything.

Some might see a discrepancy between the conclusion that risks are growing and my earlier argument that the PR industry has become much better thanks to social media.

One has nothing to do with the other, even though both are consequences of the social media revolution.

PR has become a much better industry because it has become more measurable, more transparent, more creative, and faster.

It is *also* becoming much better *because* risks are increasing. This new and ever riskier environment forces us to organize our offices and client relations better and to think more deeply about how to do things better.

PR BUSINESS NEEDS PEOPLE WITH "SPARKS IN THEIR EYES": MAXIM BEHAR'S INTERVIEW FOR THE HOLMES REPORT[1]

Arun Sudhaman: Welcome to the Echo Chamber. This is Arun Sudhaman from the Holmes Report. We are very lucky to be joined today by Maxim Behar, who is the CEO and Chairman at M3 Communications Group, Inc. in Bulgaria, and of course, widely known around the global PR industry as the president of the International Communications Consultancy Organisation (ICCO). Max, welcome to the Echo Chamber podcast.

Maxim Behar: Hello, Arun. Very nice to be with you on this prominent program.

AS: Thank you very much. So, Max, you have been doing a lot of traveling around the world for your ICCO duties. It seems you have been speaking at most of the conferences on PR in various countries. I am curious to know how you are seeing the growth of the global PR industry from your perspective.

MB: I don't call it growth, I would call it, rather, change. Because in some countries, which are more advanced in social media and in some countries where people do understand the market as general, understand the changes in our business, there might be growth. But in other countries where people are not so advanced to change rapidly the way they do their business, the approach to their customers, it is not necessary to be growth. But the fact is that nowadays PR business is the most dynamic business in the world, having in mind that since many, many years, more than 100 years since this business existed, there is one change, which happened several years ago and has never ever happened before. And this is the ownership of media. You

1 "Podcast: David Singleton on UK Politics; Maxim Behar on Global PR," The Holmes Report, The Echo Chamber podcast, March 2, 2017, https://www.holmesreport.com/latest/podcast/article/podcast-david-singleton-on-uk-politics-maxim-behar-on-global-pr.

remember, Arun, something like ten years ago the clients were coming to our offices, they entered our big conference rooms, they sat down and said: "Mr. PR expert, please, help us to get our product to the media." Because that was our main business—how to get to the media, how to make it more attractive, more interesting, what would be our approach to the journalists, how to attract them. But these days they don't need to do this and we don't need to do this, because of we all own media. The first and most important change to our business, which happened recently, is that from mediators, from bridges between media and our clients, now we are much more managers or publishers than mediators. So, it means that in our offices, we should start learning how to manage media, how to make content, how to put this content in a way that it is not controversial, it is honest, ethical, and also influential. So, this is really the first important change—the change of the ownership of the media. But the second change is happening these days and this is the very fast, almost invisible, but existing merger between the three main elements of our PR business—and this is advertising, digital, and public relations. And there are many, many opinions among experts, which of those three businesses will lead the future business, the future merged business. And I really think it will be the public relations.

AS: Now, it is interesting what you have talked about in terms of the change. But I wonder in some of the less mature PR markets, that you and I are both familiar with, is it that much of a change, or is it just kind of what they have known about what has the PR started with? Perhaps they are more comfortable with this new reality, because they haven't had to change.

MB: It is a change. It is a big change. Sometimes, even very often, the clients don't understand that we operate in a different communications environment, because the commercial environment very often is the same. And when they approach us and negotiate with us, PR companies or experts, they really prefer that we operate with the same old-fashioned ways and instruments and tools—just to invite journalists, to have a media breakfast, to start convincing them how good is the product or service, but in fact this is a change. Because even the traditional media, they take their news from the social media, as social media are much faster, much more independent, which is their biggest advantage, and also I would say much more influential than the traditional media.

AS: It is interesting because it seems to me that these changes require in many PR markets perhaps a different consideration of the types of skills, and the types of talent, that work within whether it is PR agencies or communications departments. How do you see in that play out? Do you feel like that the industry is doing a good job in bringing in different skills?

MB: You are absolutely right. In our offices, we observe total change of the skills which the stuff or the managers should have regarding the new way of doing business. First of all, we should emphasize very much the speed. In order to react in a high speed in a PR situation or crisis, we must be absolutely well prepared. Something which happened ten years ago in ten minutes now we don't even have ten seconds to solve it. It requires a lot of preparation and a lot of simulation training of different PR cases which may happen. And another example, ten or twelve years ago the clients were having a crisis in the morning in the newspaper and then usually we had about ten hours to solve this crisis—to have a press conference or a press message, meet the client, discuss with the team. But if we had ten hours in the past, now we don't have even ten seconds. Once the bad news is online it may spread in a way that it will go beyond our expectation, it will go internationally, it will reach many more countries, it may hurt the international business plans of the client. So the advanced preparation is one of the most needed requirements, which we have in our offices. Secondly, simplicity is something which is very crucial. Nowadays we are overloaded with international news, different information, social media; some of this information is fake, if not the majority of it, depending on the case. So we must create a very simple way to differentiate the most important news, the priorities we have, in a way that our clients feel they are in good, secure hands. So providing very fast service to them, emphasizing the priorities of the projects, is something which is the base of modern PR, not to mention a strong knowledge of how to create content, how to create a story, how to make this story a real one, an influential one, but also very interesting and serving the client. Because I know a lot of people are dealing now with storytelling and in every other forum or summit or conference I go to, storytelling is obligatory, one of the main topics, but at the end of the day, storytelling is nothing other than journalism. Because we are journalists. I used to be a journalist for about twenty years. And what were we doing in the newspapers, radio stations, or TV channels? We were creating stories—nice stories, good stories, interesting, catchy. So that is the job of the PR expert these days. And going back to my vision or point of view that now we should be masters of the content, it covers really the biggest change.

AS: It seems that in the kind of skills that are required there are as you mentioned a change. As it may not always be that easy to find people who can do all of those things. What does it look like when you hire new people?

MB: Usually I am training them because I don't think the old-school PR professionals or experts might be changed very easily. So the new generation, the Generation F, which I call them in the title of my book a couple of years ago, *Generation F*, which comes from "Facebook," "Fear," and one more word with four letters. A lot of young people say, "We don't care." They say (sorry for the language), "Fuck off. We don't care. We don't want to live in this world, we would like to live in another world with different relations, we don't want to be approached by fake profiles, by fake news, by trolls." So the second word was "fear" because a lot of people experience a lot of fear from the new media environment. Because they are not used to this. In the past, we used to have one TV channel and one newspaper, and that was it. But Generation F, the new generation, which manages very well with the new environment—I think is very easy to be trained. And also in our business, I see a very weak enlargement of the need of professionals in different fields. And I usually say I can make a doctor a good PR expert in six months. But I cannot make a PR expert a doctor. So it means that I hire doctors, engineers, financial experts, and train them in our offices to learn how to manage social media and public communications and it is a much easier way than to rely on (sorry to say this) a university education. What I see recently is a huge gap between a university education in PR or marketing and our practice. And this is because, as a trend all over the world, education is moving twenty miles an hour and in our offices, in case of studies, in practice, we are moving with 100 miles an hour. And it is not the problem of two speeds, it is a problem of the fact that if they are moving at twenty miles an hour and we are moving at 100 miles an hour, then this gap between us is getting bigger and bigger and bigger, so in any case we hire a person who graduated in marketing or PR anywhere in the world, and I still need to train this person six to eight months in the office, to explain the practical approaches, the practical ways to make PR successful and to make our clients happy.

AS: So when you are looking for someone to hire, even if you are going to train them, what are the characteristics of the people you are looking for?

MB: It might be weird for you, but I will tell you now. When I have an interview I usually look at the eyes of the candidate and I have one and only one request to the candidate—and this is "sparks in the eyes." Because if the young man or woman has these sparks in the eyes—it means they are ambitious to make a career, to handle the business, to be better and better professionals. It means that everything might be fixed. Because I can make an amateur a professional in six to eight months, but I cannot make a lazy person a hardworking one. I cannot make someone who creates intrigues within the team a team worker. So these are characteristics that most probably cannot be changed. So for me, of course the English language and some communication skills are the basics, which I am not even talking about, but when I see that a person has a good attitude toward the business, which I called "sparks in the eyes," and would like to make a successful career, then for me it is more than enough. Nowadays you can teach very easily your employees.

AS: Is this something that you are looking to do via ICCO because it seems that it would be a good vehicle to develop this kind of a code of conduct?

MB: We have a draft code of conduct written by me to discuss within the Executive Committee, and I would like to bring it to the attention of the board very soon. I also had long and extensive talks with my colleague from IPRA—who you know very well—Bart de Vries, the president 2016–2018 of IPRA, so we agreed both ICCO and IPRA, that if we have a good basis for such a code of conduct we will sign it together. ICCO and IPRA, I guess, can cover something like 60–70 percent of the PR business all over the world. And it would be a good message. But again I don't expect that the politicians will sign and promise something. I don't expect that the media will say we will keep the ethical standards, we will write only the good truth and the reality. Or they can say it is OK and they fully support this. But I think that also it is a code of the PR business to say a word, to make an international appeal that we should keep the standards of honest and ethical business.

AS: Tell us a little bit about your work at ICCO. I think it would be useful perhaps for our listeners to get a better understanding of what ICCO does and perhaps what benefits it could bring to agencies that are part of the organization.

MB: The International Communications Consultancy Organisation is a great community, for which I am involved with the Executive Committee and the board for the past twelve or thirteen years. And I had the privilege and the amazing chance to follow the development of ICCO, which nowadays unites forty-eight countries. And we unite the PR associations with more than four thousand company's members of these associations. Which means that our voice is getting stronger and stronger every year. And I think that we really do represent the PR communities all over the world. And it is very worthwhile for whatever country or organization or PR agency joins us, even just the fact of being a member of this big group of experts and professionals. With our awards, ICCO Global Awards, we gather more and more excellent projects every year, as you do in the Holmes Awards and the Holmes Project, which is much more advanced than ours in ICCO, not only because of the years but because of the coverage of the topics. I think that we have good chemistry and a good way to work together, to cooperate. So all those contests, all those award ceremonies at the end of the day are good benchmarks, public and professional benchmarks, for all our members to know how their achievements are progressive and innovative. Secondly, we are organizing every year the ICCO Summit. A lot of people, hundreds of people are joining the Summit exchanging their opinions, but also meeting and exchanging business cards, talking to each other, getting to know the latest trends in the business. So belonging to the voice of the international PR community, keeping good professional and ethical standards, is a big advantage for each company or national association.

AS: Max, thank you so much, not just for taking part in this podcast, but frankly for all the work you do on behalf of the global PR community. I am aware that you do most of this for no payment at all, and that is very important work. I hope to see you soon and indeed it is good news that, of course, the Holmes Report is working closely with ICCO now in terms of our own global events calendar.

MB: I would like to thank you personally and also to my good friend Paul Holmes for the excellent cooperation, for what you are doing for the PR community, because you are amazing innovators, for the event management and also for the networking between the communities. So without you guys, maybe without us as well, but without you, the PR business in the world would be completely different.

CHAPTER 8

THE PR REVOLUTION: REGIONAL TIPS

THE WORLD'S REGIONS

Under authoritarian regimes, those who criticize them on social media do so very publicly and with their names—otherwise, there is no point in criticizing a one-party regime that controls the entire state with various levers. If you do criticize such a regime anonymously, it would be absurd, because it would not generate any effect. A case in point is the protest movement in Russia led by Alexei Navalny, a lawyer, long-time blogger, and anticorruption activist who seems to have established himself as perhaps the most recognizable face of the country's nonparliamentary opposition.

I am going to take this stance—even though many of my friends and colleagues around the world might not like that this book talks about those countries with free media and with developed or at least emerging and developing market economies. I am a bit cautious of using the actual word "democracy," because, since the October Revolution in Russia 100 years ago, all sorts of totalitarian and authoritarian regimes have been styling themselves "democracies."

The Index of Economic Freedom of the Heritage Foundation and the Index of World Press Freedom of Reporters without Borders are the most important indicators as to what extent the PR industry (and many others) can develop in a certain country.

When you have free media in a given country, that means the government does not control the dissemination of information. The media cannot be punished or rewarded for publishing this or that, which creates a healthy environment for the real PR industry.

PR does exist and is developing in partly free or nonfree countries and economies, but that is a whole other world where the rules of the PR game are quite different.

If the world were divided into regions isolated from social media, we would be speaking different languages. Those without access to the global social media will think that what they do is PR, but it won't be what we discuss here.

I was extremely surprised by a country such as Georgia, for example. I had no idea what type of a regime is in place there.

I attended a PR forum in Georgia, and there was a top-ten list of PR blunders, and they were all blunders of the government, ministries, and institutions. The ranking was very critical of the government.

That was markedly different from similar events in Moscow or St. Petersburg. In those, there is still criticism of the government—but since I spent half of my life under Communism, I know how criticism used to work back then—you know where to stop.

For instance, I have been attending the PR Baltics forum in St. Petersburg for three or four years now, and there is zero government criticism there. Everyone is very positive. If there is any criticism, it is humorous in the style of Soviet writers Ilf and Petrov, or the longtime Bulgarian weekly *Starshel* ("Hornet"), for those who are familiar with their work.

HONESTY IN MEDIA

In my early years in PR, new or prospective clients' invariable first question was "Do you have connections in the media, do you know any journalists?"

I have never done that. Everybody knows that I have never picked up the phone to intercede for a client of mine (or solicit the media for something), and I would never do that, because this would make the industry pointless.

It would assassinate the essence of our industry—to be creative in order to generate interest.

Years ago, there was a difference between advertising and public relations: while PR wins media, advertising buys media.

One consequence of the great power and influence of social media is that the differences between different cultures and markets are being wiped out.

Every distinct culture, every country certainly retains some particular ways in which people perceive messages, which should be kept in mind by the that country's PR companies.

However, because of the social media revolution, we are witnessing unification, or rather uniformity, of the communication tools.

Social media communication tools are becoming the same everywhere, even in China, where WeChat and Baidu are the strongest social media, or even in Russia, where Vkontakte and Yandex are the strongest.

The communication instruments offered by the major social media platforms work in basically the same way everywhere in the world.

To a great extent, this uniformity of communication tools is gradually starting to wipe out the differences among cultures and countries and to make the way PR is done around the world very similar.

I don't currently see the possibility of an integrated global social media market, because in addition to globalized Western-led markets, there are other huge markets that more or less stand on their own—China, Russia, and to some extent India and Brazil—that have their specifics and especially their different ways of political management.

If the political management of these countries becomes uniform, then the social media will probably also become uniform or unified—but I don't see the former, and therefore the latter, happening any time soon. All the more so since Russia and China have managed to establish such positions by having their own social media.

Facebook is almost everywhere as a global social media platform, but there will always be the ever-growing resistance from the different markets where they want to prevent outside influence.

Unless some miracle happens, the current social media pioneers—and now giants—such as Facebook, Twitter, YouTube, LinkedIn, and Instagram are going to remain market leaders for a long time.

Facebook already has two billion users, and India has just surpassed the United States as the country having the largest number of Facebook users. The platforms are also huge in other key countries of developing or emerging markets such as Indonesia, Brazil, and Turkey.

In Chapter 6 above, I already voiced my categorical position that bans are no solution to problems stemming from the public vulnerabilities exposed by the vast opportunities offered by social media, and that they are indicative of a failure to truly tackle the issues at hand. That understanding refers to bans in the democratic and free world. Of course, there are a number of countries where it is well known that the government has total control over the media—Cuba, North Korea, and China, for example. Although I have been told that people in China are allowed to have rather open and free discussions on WeChat and Weibo, but only within China. Whatever happens there stays there.

There have been reports about Google's alleged "Dragonfly" project to launch its own search engine in China, but in a censored version, in cooperation with the Chinese government. This is an attempt at a compromise to allow Google into the Chinese market. It doesn't seem justified, however. You either do something properly, or you don't. Putting Google with its global brand, a global media platform—because Google is a media platform even if it is usually thought of as a search engine—to mutilate its most powerful brand just to gain footing in the market of one country, even if that's China . . . it is not justified. The Chinese already have too many search engines of their own to welcome another one, which they would probably still view with suspicion.

Whether that really is a PR gaffe, a real information leak, or just Google theorizing as a way to probe for public reaction is another story. Google invests gigantic sums of money in communications, so it would be no surprise if they just sounded out the public with this "leak."

Apple does such tricks quote often, though. They decide to do something, leak information to the media or leave a forgotten iPhone somewhere in some public restroom, the consumers react, as in "We love it" or "We hate it," and subsequently Apple might decide not to do it at all.

When everybody is fighting for market share and new markets, compromises are often unjustified.

Here are the opinions of some of the world's top PR experts as to how they see the PR industry in the age of the social media revolution in their countries and regions.

ADAM BENSON, Managing Director, Recognition PR (Brisbane, Australia)

Australia's media has continued to consolidate, which means fewer publications and full-time journalists for traditional PR consultancies to engage with. At the same time, more organizations use content marketing, social, and other digital channels to directly influence stakeholders . . .

Apart from certain specialist PR firms, many across Australia have been pivoting for the past five years and now compete directly with social agencies, advertising agencies, content writers, design studios, marketing consultancies, and others.

ADRIANA VIEIRA, CEO, InterMídia Comunicação Integrada (São Paulo, Brazil)

In Brazil, we are facing the social media era and the digital influencers; the phenomenon of fake news as well as the decrease of high budgets for traditional advertisement (TV/newspapers/magazines). For PRs it is a great opportunity to go "outside of the box." More creative strategies and guaranteed ROI with less money.

AMIR RASTEGAR, Director of International Affairs, Arman Public Relations Institute (Tehran, Iran)

The most prominent feature of traditional PR in Iran is press outreach with the focus of newspapers, television, radio, etc., but the focus of modern PR is online, digital, and social media.

Although technology has changed the way of PR performance due to digital and social media, changes are occurring with difficulty regarding the PR business in Iran. We must keep up with the times, so revolution is about to happen.

ANDRAS SZTANISZLAV, Senior Consultant and Managing Director, PersonaR (Budapest, Hungary)

The Hungarian market has changed. After the financial crisis, big budgets and cross-year projects have disappeared. Economic unpredictability and the loss of this market's strategic role in Central Eastern Europe significantly reduced the strategic consultancy role of the PR industry. Despite the lower budgets, the opportunity for more creativity, more targeted campaigns (thanks to the increase of social media and decrease of traditional), is necessary to survive and prosper. More and more PR or content-based agencies start their business and more startups and SMEs need communication support, which is healthy for the market. Since the market is mainly based on multinational companies, we see the effect of global growth and in-house PR teams and competencies are growing, while agencies have to focus more on specific needs rather than big client management account teams.

In the meantime, the rise of freelancers and small niche-focused boutique agencies is inevitable.

ASSEL KARAULOVA, President, Kazakhstan Press Club & National PR Association (Nur-Sultan, Kazakhstan)

Our country is a so-called emerging market, meaning that PR business is also emerging . . . Kazakhstan is a catching-up country, not a trendsetter, so for our market, it is critically important to become more transparent, to stop using paid journalism, to raise professional and ethical standards, and to improve government communications. In other words, it is crucial for countries like Kazakhstan to build open and transparent societies and independent media.

BASHAR ALKADHI, CEO, Middle East, North Africa, and Turkey, Hill+Knowlton Strategies (Dubai, United Arab Emirates)
Clearly the impact of social media has been absolutely huge. YouTube and Twitter, for instance, have the largest penetration per capita in the world in countries such as Saudi Arabia and Kuwait. Facebook is massive in Egypt.

Governments in the region are now utilizing these media to communicate directly with their constituents; the United Arab Emirates is a prime example of that. Many other regional governments, too.

CATALINA ROUSSEAU, President and CEO, BDR Associates (Bucharest, Romania)
Such environments like Eastern European countries in which we operate seem to generate a crisis per day lately. This fact has changed both clients' communication needs and their priorities. This reality forced us to enroll ourselves in what could be called the PR revolution, and to rethink the classic approach, making more room for creating scenarios and for being very quick in reactions.

CHRISTOPHE GINISTY, Head of Digital Engagement, OECD (Paris, France/Brussels, Belgium)
The markets where I am operating are the theater of an intense race between PR agencies, advertising agencies, marketing, and digital agencies. The influence cake is a big one, and lots of players not only want their piece, but the biggest one. Because it involves much more than just traditional PR, because it involves more and more investment, because it requires more skills than just the ones needed to be a good public relations practitioner, PR agencies are constantly challenged. And they are not assured of winning that race.

Digital has become the mainstream channel, and media companies try to find smart ways to have people pay for it, without succeeding at this stage. On another side, we see more and more publications emerging in the market with a quarterly frequency.

CIRO DIAS REIS, CEO, Imagem Corporativa (São Paulo, Brazil)
Digitalization has been the most important topic in Brazil regarding the PR business. There is a tendency of a wave of merger and acquisitions in the PR field in Brazil. In addition to that, being able to offer

more and more integrated services and solutions will be a must in our market.

CLARA LY-LE, Managing Director, EloQ Communications (Ho Chi Minh, Vietnam)
In the past five years, Vietnam has witnessed many organizational or brand crises that started on social media platforms. In such instances, through extensive online sharing of a single stakeholder post about an organizational issue, social media users attracted enough attention to the issue to turn it into a full crisis.

DANIJEL KOLETIC, CEO, Apriori World (Zagreb, Croatia)
The markets that we work on are changing their directions to specialized agencies for managing digital strategies on social networks. Large corporations have opened new positions such as departments for digital communication.

The media image is constantly changing. New information and media platforms are emerging. The media are changing their content. New technologies are constantly seeking new investments. Worldwide platforms become part of media outlets such as Facebook, Twitter, Instagram, and the media invest lot in mobile applications. The radio has come back as a medium that, along with digital media platforms, becomes a respectable source of information.

DAPHNA TRIWAKS, CEO, Triwaks PR (Tel Aviv, Israel)
While printed media is still very strong in Israel, the mass market websites are getting stronger. What we see more and more is that consumers are getting the news on their mobile devices rather than on their laptops or computers. Mobile is the new king. Bloggers and influencers are also getting stronger.

EITAN HERSHCO, Chairman, Israeli PR Association (Tel Aviv, Israel)
The PR market in Israel is becoming more competitive due to the increased growth of new PR offices of individuals whose specialty is social and digital media and branding via marketing content creation. It seems that the media have also changed their strategy and are working online and in real time using the internet, which is full of new and unique systems and content pages.

I am certain that the PR field in Israel has gone through many changes along with the people who work in the field and gained new and advanced skills. Overall, digital and social media campaigns are considered very successful as soon as they manage to propel the traditional media to report and cover the social and digital campaigns.

ELIZABETH GOENAWAN ANANTO, Founding Director, International Public Relations Summit (Jakarta, Indonesia)
The point is that—Are we driving the change, or are we driven by change? My venture, EGA Briefings, is the agent of change. We have been functioning as an early warning system by organizing strategic meetings in the form of Public Relations Week Indonesia, a decade of an educational campaign (2005–2014) that leads to the International Public Relations Summit, since 2012.

ERIK CORNELIUS, Cofounder and COO, G3 Partners (Seoul, South Korea)
Korea's big three newspapers (Chosun Ilbo, Joonang Ilbo, and Dong-a Ilbo), along with the major broadcasters (MBC, SBS, KBS), still set the agenda on major national issues, but online influencers and online media have become especially important for brands. These influencers tend to be on global channels like Instagram, as well as local channels like Brunch, a Korean language competitor to Instagram.

In Korea, most people consume their news online and especially on mobile devices. A few years ago, Naver, the main search portal in Korea, began to exclude reprints of press releases in their news aggregator. This meant that brands could no longer just pay to get a press release covered verbatim by multiple outlets. They actually had to work with reporters to craft relevant stories.

Another big change in Korea has been thanks to a recent anti-corruption law that prohibits gifts to journalists of more than about $30. This has meant that companies can no longer host lavish press conferences or send journalists on expensive junkets. In some ways, this has made media fairer, but it has been accompanied by a rise in native advertising by media companies, so the cost of doing business is not really any lower.

. . . Right now, Korean news outlets give heavy coverage to major companies like Samsung, LG, and Hyundai. It makes sense.

Samsung has a nearly $1 trillion market cap. Right now, Korea's startup ecosystem is maturing, which means that more mainstream publications will soon be covering these new giants of Korea's tech world.

FILOMENA ROSATO, CEO, FiloComunicazione (Milan, Italy)
It has changed the relationship between journalist and communicator. It has changed the role of a journalist at the desk. Journalists today have to face problems like the native advertising and the programmatic. The media are under pressure following the crisis and are now dealing with communication and not with information anymore. The media have become content producers and event organizers.

GABRIEL PASLARU, General Manager, Perfect Co. (Bucharest, Romania)
Printed media has been losing ground with circulations nose-diving from five to merely three digits. Tabloids are gaining ground, and even previously solid business publications are now moving in this direction in order to survive. All of the printed newspapers now also have electronic editions. TV and radio have similar issues while vloggers and bloggers now add to the picture.

It also makes communication a round-the-clock business. You have to take positions in real time, 24/7, sometimes in just minutes, so farewell to the luxury of sleeping on it until tomorrow's news program.

GUNTRAM KAISER, Managing Partner, Kaiser Communication (Berlin, Germany)
Over the last twenty-five years, the requirements to PR have entirely changed as the whole media environment has changed. Also, in Germany, the role of print media is consistently going down, while social media and all other forms of digital communication are becoming more and more important. This has had a clear impact on the people we need as the orders from the clients reflect the changing communication. As a medium-sized agency, you have to decide whether you prefer a higher specialization or you continue offering the full range of PR services, which is becoming more and more difficult as it is becoming more and more difficult to find people who can cover the whole range of skills that is needed.

JAROSLAV MAJOR, Senior Consultant, Hill+Knowlton Strategies (Prague, Czech Republic)

The number of social media users has dramatically increased. In 2012, about 35 percent of the Czech population was on Facebook, currently about 50 percent (monthly users). Social networks are the fastest way to mobilize people for a variety of social events, such as culture, sport, leisure.

The credibility of Czech mainstream media has fallen to a very low level. This is due (mainly) to the biased and untrue way of informing about the so-called Refugee Crisis, Brexit, 2016 US presidential election, etc. People increasingly believe in so-called alternative media, whose information value is highly dubious, too. Social media successfully divided society into two hostile camps.

JÜRGEN H. GANGOLY, Managing Partner and CEO, The Skills Group (Vienna, Austria)

Shutdowns of traditional media are a sad regularity for a couple of years now. As a result of the digitization and new consumer behavior, we constantly lose important newspapers and with them our natural-born partners in PR. Corporate publications are booming as a result of the shutdown of independent business media.

KARA ALAIMO, Assistant Professor of Public Relations, Hofstra University, and CNN contributor (New York City, USA)

The election of President Trump has revolutionized the landscape here in the US. Now, businesses are worried about being attacked by the president on Twitter and becoming the victims of fake news. Businesses are also increasingly being called upon to take stances on controversial political issues and even being criticized for their positions by their own employees and endorsers.

KHALID BADDOU, President, Moroccan Association of Marketing and Communication (Casablanca, Morocco)

In emerging markets, and due to the restricted budgets allocated to communications and PR, clients are looking for more efficiency and coherence from their agencies and consultants. They are keen to be supported by communicators who have the right market outlook and understanding of business challenges, rather than handling only the execution of operational communications (writing and editing press releases, inviting journalists).

This clients' attitude is game-changing, especially in markets like Morocco and Africa. For the past two decades, the communication industry was heading toward specialty (advertising, digital, events, PR), obliging the client to speak to different partners, while losing precious time, effort, and money. Today, agencies are asked to offer a one-stop shop to clients, with the right understanding of business, problematic customer needs, and how to address them.

KHRISTO AYAD, Senior Director, BLJ Worldwide (Doha, Qatar)
Traditional media with local reach in Qatar ultimately always remain in line with overall government direction but provide a decent mix of local and international news, sports, current affairs, and so on. The volume of classical media in Qatar is thin, particularly in terms of specialized trade titles. This, on the one hand, is a reflection of a small market, hence already small readership; on the other, it is a consequence of the very high growth rates in terms of social media use and consumption across the entire region.

Digital media is overtaking (not to say, "has overtaken") classical media in terms of visibility and relevance in the mainstream, as well as in niche areas. This is particularly true for young people in the Gulf, among whom news consumption and two-way engagement are predominantly happening on social media in the meantime. For the Arab world, engagement on such platforms may be especially compelling by default. Communication here is perceived as fun, free, most current, direct, unfiltered, and, if wanted, anonymous.

LARS ERIK GRØNNTUN, Global President, Hill+Knowlton Strategies (Oslo, Norway)
The public is increasingly expecting companies and organizations to have a larger goal than just creating value for shareholders, which has profound implications. It translates into a larger need for clients to acknowledge and address their role in society and relate to a more complex stakeholder landscape than before, as well as to be more creative and emotional to cut through the contextual noise. The changes bring along new opportunities, though, too. The biggest one is most likely the content revolution, the ability for everyone, including our

clients, to be publishers and have an impact without going through traditional media gatekeepers. The growth in the access of data also brings along new opportunities both to measure the impact and effect of communications and to use big data to understand the world around us better.

MARTIN SLATER, CEO, Noesis PR (Milan, Italy)
There has been a drastic decline in the circulation of national dailies in Italy. Most of these dailies have provided online versions that have enjoyed growing success. Free press and local dailies remain popular. TV is big in Italy, though new generations are increasingly getting their news and their entertainment online, especially through social media.

SIR MARTIN SORRELL, Founder, WPP and S4Capital PLC (London, UK)
The key changes in the market and within our own business are reflected in our four strategic priorities: horizontality, fast-growth markets, digital, and data.

We are far more integrated into our approach than we were five years ago. Our core strategic priority is horizontality, which means placing great emphasis on collaboration and providing seamless solutions for our clients.

In media, the biggest change is that the world's most powerful publishers are now to be found in Silicon Valley. And they are only just beginning to come to grips with the challenges and responsibilities that status brings.

MASSIMO MORICONI, General Manager and CEO, Omnicom Public Relations Group (Milan, Italy)
Basic PR is becoming a commodity, and advisory PR services are creating value and quality. Also, there is a big war for talent—agencies lack PR professionals and people who are prepared for the job.

With regard to the media, there has been a big integration (media, advertising, PR) creating new services and igniting competition. Journalists nowadays are becoming influencers and key opinion leaders. Therefore, there has been a war between the media and fake news.

MYKOLAS KATKUS, Chairman of the Board, FABULA (Vilnius, Lithuania)
Around 70 percent of our clients used us primarily for corporate communications. While the corporate comms and public affairs angle remain strong, now around 50 percent of our projects deal with integrated communications, where we use more than two disciplines to reach goals.

The PR agencies that failed to realize the change are slowly fading, and around half of them now depend on the state sector clients and EU funding, which will dry out after three years. While we still compete with them for some clients, our main competition now comes from some advertising agencies that have embraced the change, media agencies, and young and trendy social media and content marketing shops.

NITIN MANTRI, Group CEO, AvianWE (New Delhi, India)
Crisis counseling has emerged as a critical function. This comes as no surprise, as fake news is a cause for concern for many countries, especially India, where the 4G revolution has created plenty of first-time users of WhatsApp and Facebook who do not know much about verified news/information. PR practitioners are the privileged few who know how to guide brands in a world where you can't tell the truth from a lie.

Public policy has gained in importance, especially in the APAC region, because brands cannot build a moneyed business here without an in-depth understanding of the politics, aggressive markets, sociocultural fabric, and nuances of the countries that make up the region. APAC's history and geography mean that there are far greater differences between markets in the region.

PATRIK SCHOBER, CEO, PRAM Consulting (Prague, Czech Republic)
Digital, media, and advertising agencies have found that they cannot live without copywriting, and saying they can do PR is sometimes a must for them, which means that these agencies are sometimes winning PR jobs even if they do not know much about PR.

It was not a problem to find a good PR professional a few years ago. Thanks to the good economic situation and educated clients, there are no PR professionals in the Czech market at all.

PELIN KOCAALP, General Manager, Hill+Knowlton Strategies (Istanbul, Turkey)
PR, advertising and marketing agencies have transformed over the last ten years in Turkey. Change is inevitable everywhere, and Turkey is no exception. Content management has been the most important part of communications.

PETER MUTIE, CEO, Peterson Integrated Communications (Nairobi, Kenya)
The market has become more sophisticated. More players enter the market and offer different services. Social media has taken over. Almost all the news breaks through social media. Newspapers have also gone digital.

PHILIPPE BORREMANS, Independent PR Consultant, Reputation & Co. (Casablanca, Morocco)
Africa has a certain way to go in the professionalization of the PR industry, but the opportunities are enormous on the continent. So big in fact that PR education is seriously lacking, and professionals often do not have an academic background in communications or PR.

CSR communications and media relations are the main services requested in the market, but there is definitely room for creative content strategies and crisis communications. There are many players in the market, from one-man operations to local representations of some of the largest PR agencies. And still, there is room for everyone.

RANA NEJEM, Founding Director, Yarnu: The Art of Social Intelligence (Amman, Jordan)
Openness and transparency and accuracy have become more important than ever. And, of course, speed. Anyone with an internet connection has a platform and a megaphone to shout out, making it harder for companies to work through the noise.

With Queen Rania on Twitter since the start, and also King Abdallah as well as the government—just as in many other Arab countries—officials have become more accessible—or perhaps it is just a perception of accessibility? Companies and government officials can now bypass the mainstream media and put out their messages directly to their audience.

RETO WILHELM, Managing Director, Panta Rhei PR (Zurich, Switzerland)

In Switzerland, we have fewer agencies, but the ones that stay are bigger and they have a 360-degree-service approach. Also, we have become more specialized. For each discipline, we have a specialized agency, which leads to a huge armada of niche experts, but no overall consultants anymore. Additionally, advertising agencies try to get more of the cake by implementing content marketing units.

There is a huge concentration process in the media industry—there are fewer editing houses, fewer newspapers (print under huge pressure), and there is a shift of advertising money toward online and social media channels.

RHINGO MUTAMBO, Chief PR Officer, Prime Minister's Bureau (Windhoek, Namibia)

The public relations (PR) profession in Namibia has evolved so much in the last thirteen years, particularly in terms of scope of work and recognition, especially in the public service, as the largest employer.

For instance, the role of public relations in the public sector in terms of media and public engagement and information dissemination has notably improved over the years.

PR, however, is mostly seen as an operational task in some quarters and a means to a political end, and there is no sufficient prominence placed on the importance of the profession. It is often reduced to a mere information desk, as opposed to a management function with a significant strategic role to play in shaping organizational perceptions and setting public agenda.

PR professional bodies such as PRISA, APRA, and ICCO or Global Alliance could play a critical role in assisting the local profession by addressing the gaps through consultations with government and the PR industry to ensure a broader understanding of the profession, building capacity and raising more thought leaders.

RICHARD MILLAR, Global President, Hill+Knowlton Strategies (London, UK)

The influence of traditional media has diminished. Perhaps that was best seen here in the UK at the recent General Election 2017. Labour's particular courting of the youth vote across social media, tapping into the influencers across that constituency, effectively neutralized the influence of the tabloid media—the *Daily Mail* and *The Sun* most notably—in their attempts to demonize Labour's leadership.

For the agency, it has demanded diversification of the services we provide—building capability in the creation and production of content to tell the client's story direct to their consumers and published across earned, owned, shared, and paid channels as well as developing deeper insights on our audiences and the science of human behavior and placing greater focus on "purpose-driven communications."

SAURABH UBOWEJA, CEO, Brands of Desire (New Delhi, India)
There are two types of forces in action in the market. On one end, there are agencies that are looking to superspecialize; while on the other end, there are agencies that want to become a one-stop solution provider. While there is space for both depending on what clients want, more mature clients are likely to work with several specialist agencies rather than one generalist agency.

There is a proliferation of digital media platforms and experts that is creating a high level of clutter in addition to the commoditization of the media form. Online communities, which were peaking till last year, are now headed toward a decline, as consumer loyalties toward communities are dwindling.

SCOTT E. FAHLMAN, Research Professor, Carnegie Mellon University, and inventor of the "smiley" emoticon (Pittsburgh, USA)
Of course, over the past five years, the growing success of Facebook, Twitter, Instagram, and all the others has surprised us all. And now, unimaginably, we have a US president whose communication with the American people and with the rest of the world is mostly in the form of tweets. It's little wonder that this has been a recipe for disaster, both for that president and for all the rest of us. On top of that, this president steadfastly refused to retract or correct or apologize for anything he has said, even in a 3 a.m. tweet, viewing this as a form of weakness. This is very dangerous for the world. Revolutionary in a bad way.

The other startling development is the erosion of truth, and of trust in the truthfulness of any news source that we happen to disagree with. The implications of this for the PR profession are hard to imagine. It used to be said (half in jest, but only half) that if you try to persuade others by lying, that's called "fraud." If you try to persuade others by (selectively) telling the truth, that's called PR. But in a world where truth is no longer a valued concept, what does that mean for the idea of "ethical PR"?

SERGE BECKERS, Managing Partner, Wisse Kommunkatie (Arnhem, Netherlands)

The Netherlands has increasingly been able to position itself as the gateway to Europe, in my opinion. (This is especially true for our office.) The average Dutchman speaks two or three languages, making him or her a valuable intermediary for international clients. In the past five years, media have had to deal with the shift to online, causing many traditional outlets to disappear. Paid publicity has become more and more important.

SERGEY ZVEREV, CEO, Cross Communications (Moscow, Russia)

The market has become more exacting and demanding of fast and accurate solutions. Every year, we have to look for new niches and blue oceans.

TV is gradually losing its position as the main source of information for Russians. Young people consider social networks and blogs the most important news sources. Messengers are expanding their influence in Russia: it is considered to be a new generation of social networking. Another important trend is that brands are creating their own communication channels.

SOLLY MOENG, Convenor, SA Brand Summit & Awards (Cape Town, South Africa)

More competitive, more players, but sadly, too many new market entrants without requisite qualifications and experience. Industry entry barriers tend to be too low.

Everything is becoming more complex by the week. Online will continue to grow and dominate, but traditional media will remain around for a while still. The key is to integrate the two in a seamless manner.

STUART BRUCE, Managing Consultant, Stuart Bruce Associates (Leeds, UK)

Traditional print media is in trouble. It's in trouble nearly everywhere in the world. But in the UK, by far the most serious is the catastrophic collapse of local newspapers. Regional papers that once sold hundreds of thousands of copies now sell tens of thousands. Those that survive. This is a fundamental threat to democracy, as it is thorough, professional journalism that held the local authority to account.

It was professional journalists who scrutinized local government and politicians to occasionally bring them down. No more. Local newspapers were also the traditional training ground for young journalists who went on to become stars of national and international journalism.

SVETLANA JAPALĂU, Managing Director, BDR Associates—Strategic Communication (Kishinev, Moldova)

In the Republic of Moldova, the main sources for the PR and strategic communication business are the multinational companies that have opened their offices/branches in the country, as well as projects financed by the international donors like EU, US, UN, EBRD, World Bank, or the large business associations like EBA, Amcham. In this context, an important change in the industry refers to the expansion of the market, and, namely, local companies started to understand the role of PR and communication in properly positioning the company and helping the business grow on a market.

. . . The culture of storytelling has been launched in the country. This culture was already embraced by the international donors, multinational companies, state institutions, and, the most important—local producers.

TATEVIK PIRUMYAN, Communication Key Expert, EU Assistance to Armenia Project (Yerevan, Armenia)

In Armenia, there is an increased focus on social media marketing, use of social media platforms as PR and communication channels, more attention to SEO and SEA. Also, there are more in-house specialists.

Another change is the increased role of online media, a constant decrease in the popularity of print media and even TV. Moreover, the role and popularity of social media have also increased, which made traditional media less profitable and forced them to enter into media buying relationships.

ZDENEK LOKAJ, Former Managing Director, Hill+Knowlton Strategies (Prague, Czech Republic)
The market is growing both in total value and in the number of subjects offering PR. Competition is becoming more fierce, clients are demanding faster results. Today, everyone is doing everything; even agencies in one group compete with similar services.

The media is more and more fragmented, and the quality of content is decreasing rapidly. There is less time for fact and source checking, less room for analysis, and media outlets are employing a smaller number of journalists, who have an ever-increasing volume of work. Media are more closely connected with big business, major oligarchs and financial groups owning all major commercial media outlets. Political and oligarch pressure on public broadcasters is increasing both directly and indirectly. In short, professional journalism is not what it used to be. On the other hand, technology and the simplicity of virtual and real-world travel are enabling citizen journalism—anyone who is skillful enough to press a button on a mobile and write a short text can publish.

ZHAO DALI, Secretary General, China International PR Association (Beijing, China)
The start-up company, self-owned brand, and self-media were rocketing in the past five years in China, especially in innovative industry that is based on high-tech and AI. The products and services produce focus on the experience of target clients. The traditional e-commerce is evolving into online to offline business. Media are becoming more diverse. Voices of individuals are becoming louder and more important. The model of cooperation and sharing is diverse also.

ZSOFIA LAKATOS, CEO, Emerald Communications (Budapest, Hungary)
Half of the market was taken away by the government (only government-friendly agencies can work for state-owned entities). The PR profession is in big trouble, as the role of PR is changing. Social media and content marketing has taken over, so classical PR agencies suffer. Ethics is nowhere.

The government has taken over almost 100 percent of the media; there are only a few nongovernment outlets left.

EDUCATION TODAY: THE UNIVERSITY OF LIFE

As pointed out in my "Top 10 Words" (see page 207), which are of crucial significance for PR, education remains a key issue for the PR industry, especially the need to close the gap between theory and practice.

According to the 2017 Global Communications Report of the USC Annenberg School for Communication and Journalism, "finding and retaining the right talent remain the biggest business challenge PR faces." The report goes on to explain this:

> Maybe because less than one-third of PR executives believe the industry is doing a good job of positioning itself as an aspirational career choice. Or maybe because hard-to-find strategic thinking is prized as the most important skill a PR person needs. Outranking writing for the first time in our study!
>
> In our first-ever student survey, we found a diverse group of future PR executives who are tuned in to the trends and technologies impacting communications and are reasonably well prepared to tackle them.
>
> These new recruits also bring a sense of social purpose and pride to the profession. They just want a better definition of their role and a little more money.

The findings of the 2018 World PR Report by the International Communications Consultancy Organisation (ICCO) indicate that the top factor stopping PR from sourcing talent from other industries is the lack of transferrable skills and that agencies are most likely to source talent from other agencies.

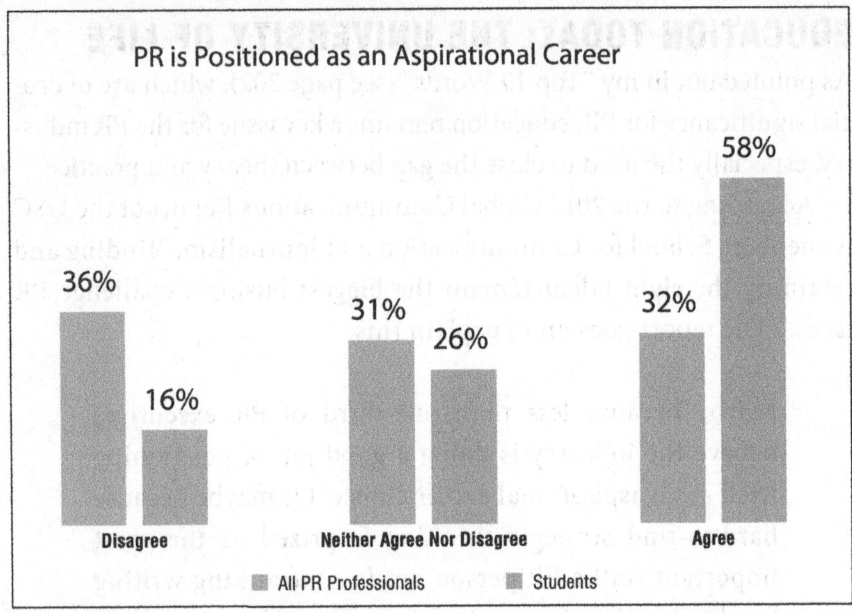

PR is Positioned as an Aspirational Career
36%
16%
31%
26%
32%
58%
Disagree
Neither Agree Nor Disagree
Agree
All PR Professionals
Students

Source: 2017 Global Communications Report of the USC Annenberg School for Communication and Journalism.

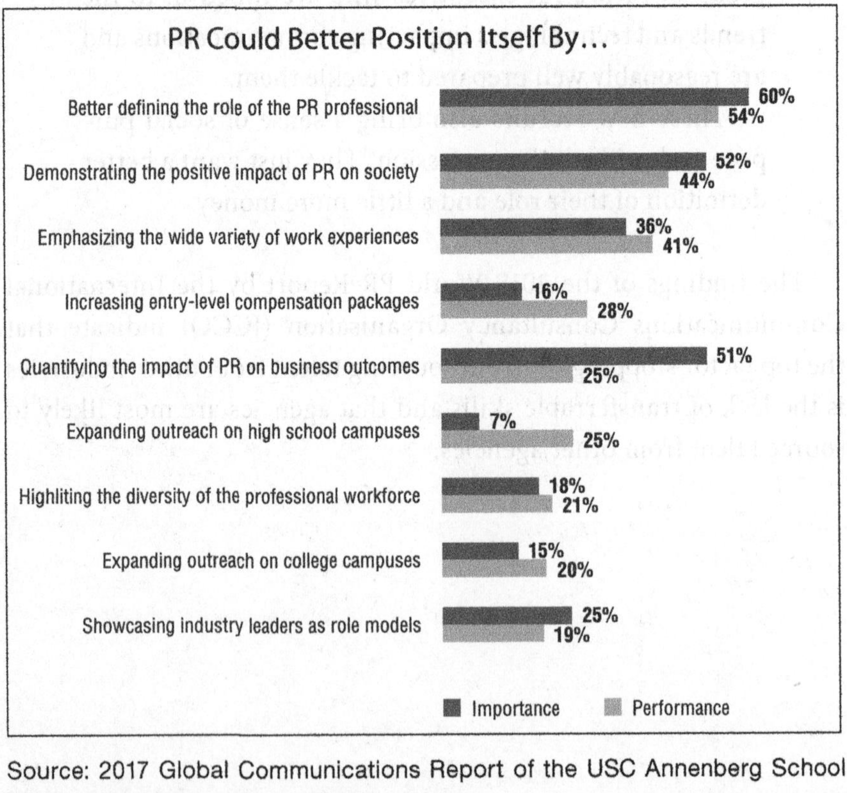

PR Could Better Position Itself By...
Better defining the role of the PR professional
60%
54%
Demonstrating the positive impact of PR on society
52%
44%
Emphasizing the wide variety of work experiences
36%
41%
Increasing entry-level compensation packages
16%
28%
Quantifying the impact of PR on business outcomes
51%
25%
Expanding outreach on high school campuses
7%
25%
Highliting the diversity of the professional workforce
18%
21%
Expanding outreach on college campuses
15%
20%
Showcasing industry leaders as role models
25%
19%
Importance
Performance

Source: 2017 Global Communications Report of the USC Annenberg School for Communication and Journalism.

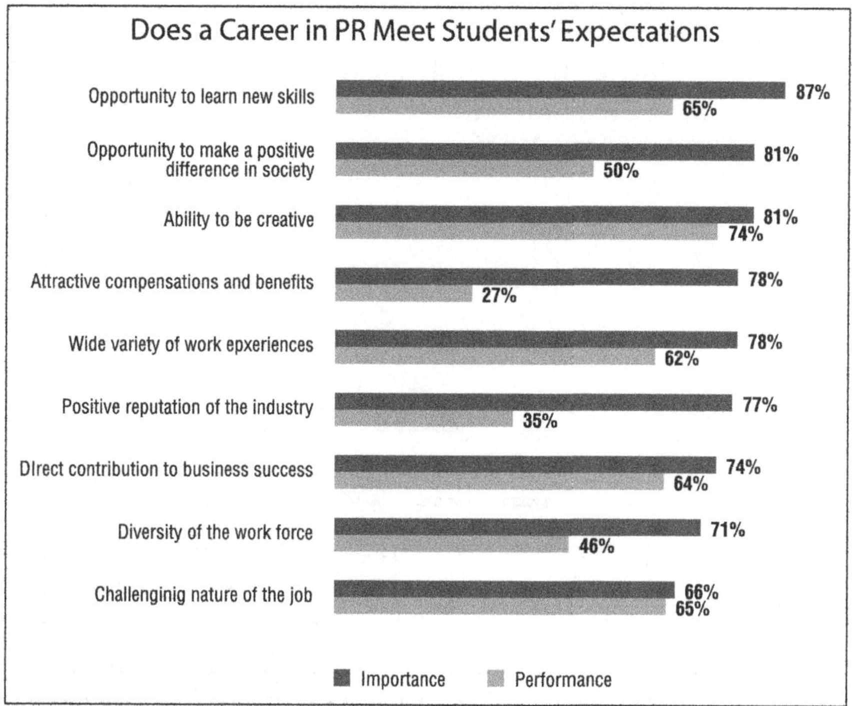

Source: 2017 Global Communications Report of the USC Annenberg School for Communication and Journalism.

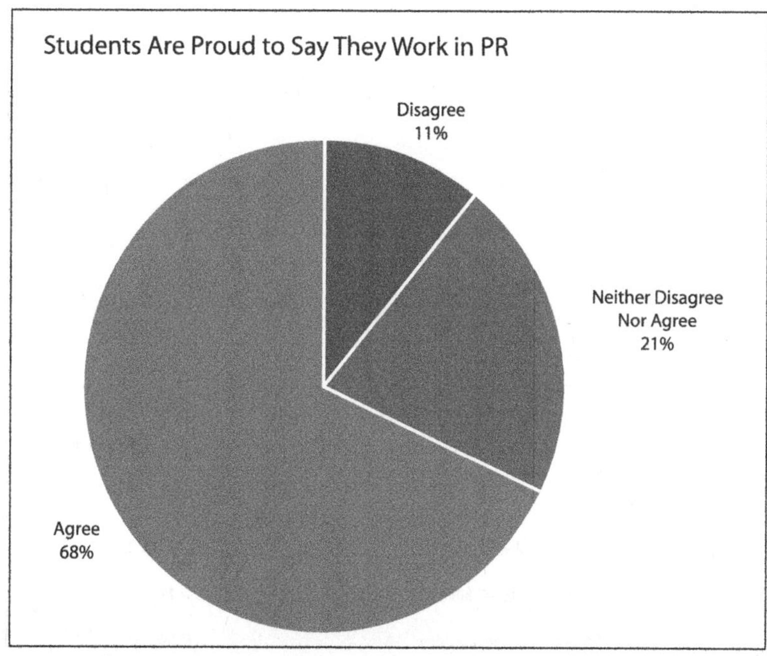

Source: 2017 Global Communications Report of the USC Annenberg School for Communication and Journalism.

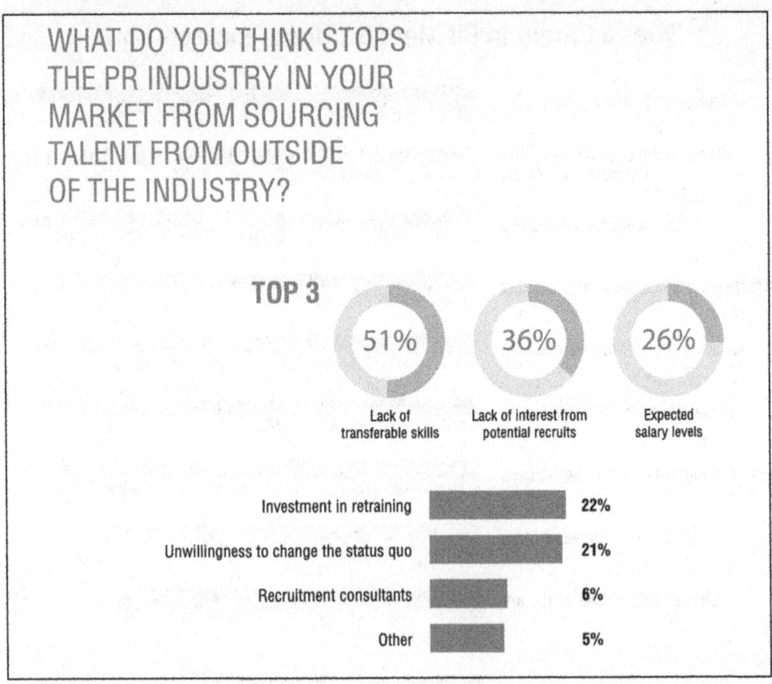

Source: 2018 World PR Report by the International Communications Consultancy Organisation (ICCO).

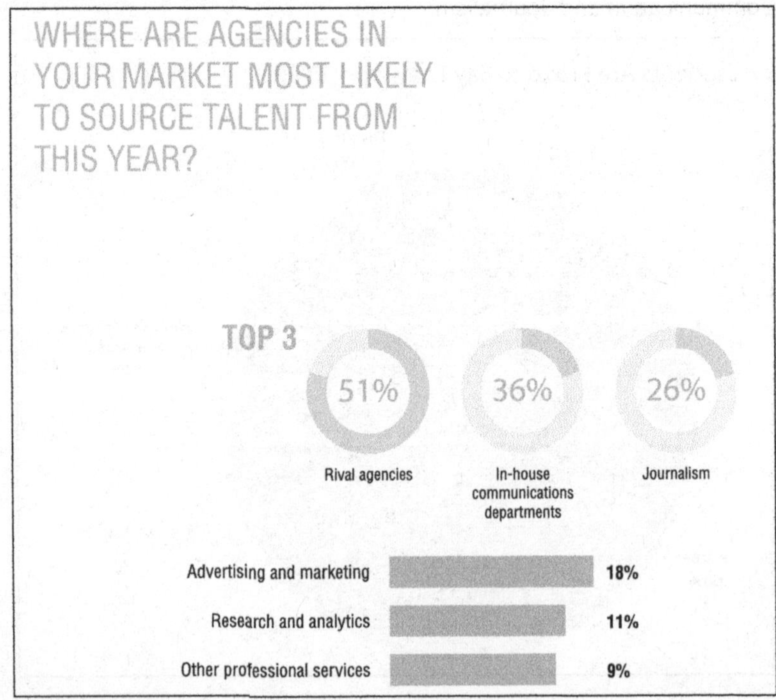

Source: 2018 World PR Report by the International Communications Consultancy Organisation (ICCO).

The ICCO report has also found that retaining key talent is the biggest challenge for PR agencies with respect to their talent strategy.

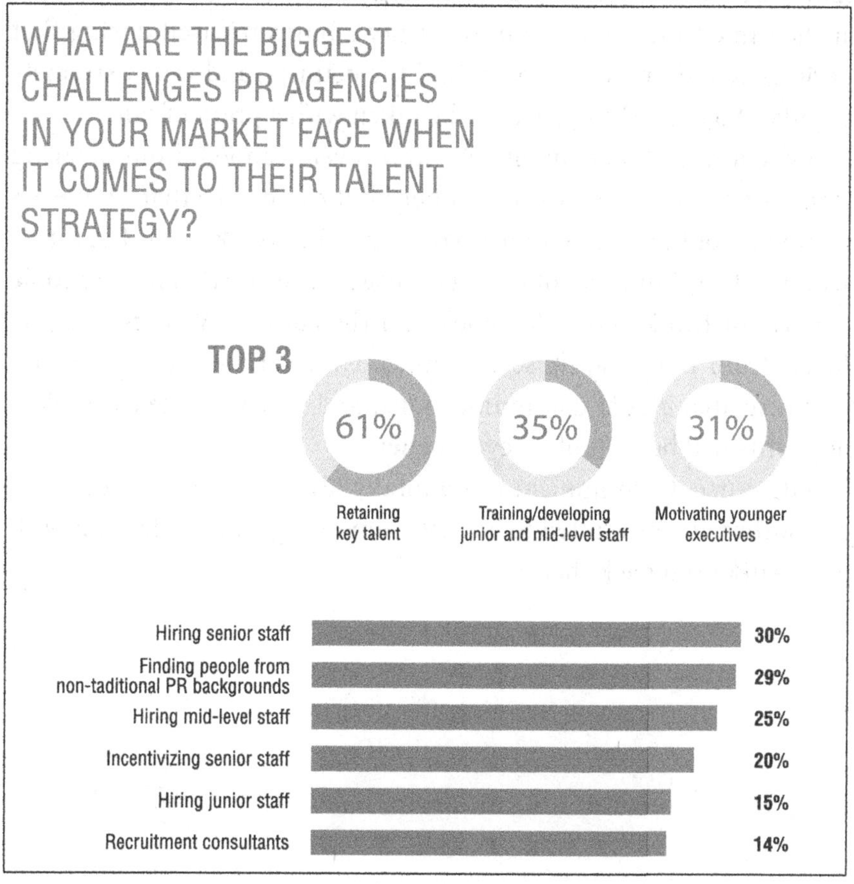

Source: 2017 World PR Report by the International Communications Consultancy Organisation (ICCO).

I never wish to go back to Communism, that dreadful, gray era. But a lot of memories from childhood and youth are really worth sharing—from the neighborhood, the typewriter, the vise in the machine-building factory . . .

Even in the dark age of Communism, we could still do a lot of things. One could get many things done if he or she wanted to. Luckily, most of us weren't in concentration camps.

Repression was present, but not omnipresent. Take the Crickets, one of Bulgaria's top rock bands of all times. Their members still remember the repressions of Communism in media interviews, but at the same time, they had over twenty albums released during that period, went on many tours around the country, and were extremely popular. So everything needs to be taken with a grain of salt.

Of course, at one point, we were even banned from wearing jeans—there was a whole lot of other idiotic stuff like that—but even then you could achieve a lot if you wanted to work hard. I call this section "The University of Life," because I am aware that many people will say or think about this book and the author: "Who is this guy Behar from Bulgaria, those Commies! How can he even talk about global media, global communications, and global challenges?" So I hope this will be a bit of an eye-opener.

Of course, Communism was a totally idiotic system. But one way or another, if you wanted to achieve something, you could do it with hard work even back then.

CHAPTER 9

THE POST-REVOLUTIONARY / EVER MORE REVOLUTIONARY FUTURE

THE FUTURE OF (SOCIAL) MEDIA AND THE FUTURE OF PR

At some point in the not-too-distant future, visuals are going to overtake text as the main means of communication. As I already mentioned, there will be a boom of two industries when this happens—fashion and optical lenses.

Indeed, one day soon, all things will be wrapped inside visuals and audio, not so much in the written word, to such a degree that everything will be real time, live.

It is hard to forecast when exactly visuals will become dominant over text. Everybody is already watching videos on YouTube, Daily Motion, Vimeo, and millions of local video sites.

But the dominant visuals of the future will be different. At some point, holograms and virtual reality will probably also be integrated into them. That is going to be another type of creation and another type of creativity. For example, it will mean being able to convey in a fifteen-second video the information that a person would read in text for a longer period.

That will be vastly useful, since our everyday lives are becoming more and busier. If you have *x* minutes, for this period you can learn a lot more from one video than from reading a specific text. As the saying goes, a picture is worth a thousand words. I think the time factor will be crucial.

The only time I've seen people standing in line for a book in the past twenty years was for a book written by a vlogger popular with teenagers.

I came back to the office and said, "Who the heck is this guy?" I checked out several of his videos, and even though they didn't really get through, I saw that each had one or three or five million views. There are very few writers with that many copies sold.

Apparently, whatever they do, a writer can never convey their messages in the same way as a video can—especially if you're good at this.

When you create PR messages, of course, you have little time, especially in times of crisis. Video is irreplaceable, and it will be perfected as the PR industry develops further.

At some point, a thirty-second video (or another kind of presentation with visuals that has not been invented yet) will serve the role of an entire press release.

AI IN PR

Creative professions should not be threatened by the widely predicted advance of artificial intelligence, but I think that one day, PR can be done through artificial intelligence—possibly even robots.

And I think that it might even be a lot more successful than when done by humans.

For instance, in a crisis situation, a PR company will be able to just set the algorithms for its crisis management software.

There could be, say, twenty to thirty possibilities for about one hundred versions of a potential crisis, and the AI, the algorithm would take just a few seconds to provide you with options about how to react to the emerging crisis.

There would probably be a transition period in which the computer would not yet react automatically on your behalf to a certain situation, but the moment that situation springs up, it will provide you with a couple of decision options, and you as the PR expert would have to choose one of them in seconds.

Such a transition period, in which PR reactions will be managed jointly by humans and computers, will still require a human touch, but such a setup would still save the PR professional a lot of time.

In any case, artificial intelligence is going to enter our industry just as it is entering many other industries and life in general. But it is going to penetrate our field much more deeply, and that is going to make the job of PR experts a lot easier.

With respect to crisis response, the benefits of AI in PR seem evident and self-explanatory. I believe that AI will likely be woven into creativity, critical thinking, and creative solutions in PR even more easily.

One reason is that when it comes to proactive PR, AI can make the process of considering different strategies a lot easier, all the while ensuring that they don't overlap with other global strategies.

Since everything will be transparent and programmed, a software can check within a matter of seconds if anything that it can offer as an option has ever been done anywhere in the world.

Then, its final suggested option could be considered much more carefully and in greater detail by the people developing the public relations strategy.

Yes, there will still be a human touch. Humans are irreplaceable.

But there is no way the intensifying development of technology won't lead to the all-out automation of the consideration of decisions and concepts that a communications company needs to take or adopt.

This would mean that substantially fewer people will be employed in PR. Some new responsibilities of the PR employees of the future might be, for example, to choose the settings of the machines that will process their PR strategies or proposals.

Actually, I am inclined to believe that the total number of people working in PR has already started to decline. Some significant parts of the PR industry have already been automated.

SOFTWARE OR HUMAN BRAIN: YOU CHOOSE (WHILE YOU STILL CAN)!

For the time being, there is still a choice between having humans or computers carry out certain processes in the PR industry. In the not-too-distant future, there probably won't be too much of a choice.

Today, a lot of things in the PR industry can already be done with software, such as editing or translation programs, for instance.

Yet many of our services have to be personalized, tailor-made, and there are many PR companies that prefer to do things on their own.

Following are the opinions of some of the world's best communications experts on the future and predictions for the business.

Question: What are your predictions for the PR industry in the next five years?

AARON KWITTKEN, CEO and Chairman, KWT Global (New York City, USA)

I don't believe specialist agencies will exist in five years. I think specialties will become practice areas of agencies, and vertical practice areas will go away.

ADAM BENSON, Managing Director, Recognition PR (Brisbane, Australia)

From an agency perspective, in order to compete, PR firms will need to get very clear about their unique selling proposition. What we do will become far less important compared to how we do it, and the sectors we choose to serve. Undifferentiated, midsized firms that have been able to trade on their media relations skills and support a wide range of clients are going to find it even tougher now. Successful firms will employ a much broader range of skills, including data scientists, marketing consultants, and digital strategists. The leaders already do.

ADRIANA VIEIRA, CEO, InterMídia Comunicação Integrada (São Paulo, Brazil)

I would recommend a new approach for PR and communication, based on close relationships with the community and clients—events are the best investments for brands, as well as to promote more real experiences for clients and visitors. Stores are no longer places to buy, but places to learn and discover. Clients will no longer be passive consumers, but will be active ambassadors and cocreators for the brands. The content is the new king, and the PRs and marketers will have to work together with digital influencers in order to produce great contents to make a difference for the brands, using AI and big data in the process, more and more.

AGNIESZKA DZIEDZIC, Managing Partner, Weber Shandwick (Warsaw, Poland)
I believe that finally, all these discussions we are having about technology in PR will materialize in Poland, and PR will become more "technological." This means that technology will be present throughout the planning, execution, and evaluation phases. At the moment, the use of technology is quite limited. In future, technology will drive not only the planning and evaluation phases of the campaign, but will be at the root of the big creative idea behind the whole campaign.

AHMED JANABI, CEO, Harf Promotions (Baghdad, Iraq)
In five years, the public will be more aware than ever about the cause-and-effect patterns of the classical PR and advertising businesses. The brands will have more focus on people in a way of manipulating media to look mostly at community-generated positive content while keeping an eye on fighting negative media by implementing it by the brands themselves through third parties before it is being discovered by the uncontrolled public. The governments will be more decentralized while keeping the focus on creating the buzz, because, if not, the public would then create that buzz! The opposition will be a necessity to be created by governments themselves more than ever. The influencers will be caring more about specialized content and brand effect than about generalized content and reach (likes, shares, etc.). The business will be ever-changing to mainly adapt to the changes of factors above.

AIVE HIIEPUU, President, Estonian PR Association (Tallinn, Estonia)
PR business will be driven by technology and mainly by the continuing growth of the popularity of social media. Social media has changed how people communicate, as well as when they communicate, where they communicate, and even who they communicate with. This process will continue.

AKI KUBO, Managing Director, North Asia, Williams Lea Tag (Tokyo, Japan)
Change or die. Many conventional businesses would disappear while new, more digitally savvy, and many-to-many communications-ready PR businesses will emerge.

ALISON CLARKE, Founder, Alison Clarke Consulting (London, UK)
The next five years will see even greater conversion—and our industry achieving the status it deserves in the boardroom as smart businesses really focus on the right way to behave and to engage with all stakeholders.

ALMA GERXHANI, CEO, Manderina Promotions (Tirana, Albania)
With this rhythm of developments, it is hard to predict how will it be. Until now there is a lot out there that businesses are not aware of, and we as professionals should introduce and adopt early. One thing is sure: it will rely heavily on technology. Public speaking will remain useful, especially when done in relevant fields, as will conferences and events that have an international name.

ALTHAF JALALDEEN, General Manager, Phoenix Ogilvy—PR & Influence (Colombo, Sri Lanka)
My main prediction is that most of the disciplines in the agency business will become one when approaching communications. The lines between traditional advertising, PR, and digital are becoming more and more invisible, mainly due to social media. The future PR professional will have to be more multiskilled to adapt to these transformations.

AMIR RASTEGAR, Director of International Affairs, Arman Public Relations Institute (Tehran, Iran)
Social and digital media are changing the future of public relations in Iran; having basic digital skill is an essential requirement for PR professionals. For maximizing the PR campaigns, understanding social media, SEO, digital content creation, etc., is necessary.

ANDRAS SZTANISZLAV, Senior Consultant and Managing Director, PersonaR (Budapest, Hungary)
I am slightly pessimistic. I think that only a very few PR professionals (both in-house and agency leaders) are capable of fulfilling that

very strategic and consultancy role that PR provides. That would mean that other disciplines will lead the market (i.e., digital and social media content creation, targeting, branded content, data-based measurements).

ANDREW BONE, Chief Strategy Officer, Middle East and Africa, Hill+Knowlton Strategies (Riyadh, Saudi Arabia)
I think there will be a much closer alignment, i.e., coming together, of advertising, creative production, and traditional PR agencies as groups of people maximize their individual skills. The traditional PR industry will die, and a new category of firms will arise and be classed as something like "content publishing and marketing communications."

ANDREY BARANNIKOV, CEO, SPN Commmunications (Moscow, Russia)
During the next five years, success will mostly depend on the speed and density of your message. Consumers will be regarded as the center of all communications, and our professional consciousness will change. And the new PR managers will be those who work 24/7 and declare openness.

ARUN SUDHAMAN, CEO and Editor in Chief, The Holmes Report (Hong Kong/China)
Unfortunately, I see only incremental change over the next five years, despite the broader disruption at play across society and the business world. The best PR people will innovate and grasp the new opportunities, but the majority will continue as though little has changed. The best agencies will develop new talent, technology, and products that address the role business must play in the 21st century. And the best organizations will understand the importance of behavior versus messaging.

ASSEL KARAULOVA, President, Kazakhstan Press Club & National PR Association (Nur-Sultan, Kazakhstan)
Speaking globally, technology will drive PR business as well as changes in consumer demand for integrated communications and effective message-delivery channels. Fighting fake news and political challenges faced by the world will have huge impact for governments' and countries' communications.

BRIDGET VON HOLDT, Business Director, Burson Cohn & Wolfe (Johannesburg, South Africa)
Public relations will grow in stature, and so will the practitioner. One thing we are going to have to learn is to think and act very quickly. We are not going to have the luxury of time—it is all going to be in the now.

Crisis communication will continue to be a growing need. Partly attributed to social media and the digital environment. Governance and ethics will be a role that we, as professionals, will need to play more aggressively.

There will not be "one size fits all" campaigns. Tailored campaigns will apply to different countries, to different markets, and to different platform channels. Dedicated monitoring of digital platforms will need to be a necessity. Companies and clients cannot afford not to know what is being said about them—anywhere in the world. PR professionals need to know their stuff! While specializing in practices and sectors may be the current way of operating, I believe that in the future, a practitioner will need to have extensive knowledge of many factors or at least know where to get the information quickly. In many ways, we are going to become like a stock exchange trader—global, knowledgeable, and selling our skills—all in an instant.

CATALINA ROUSSEAU, President and CEO, BDR Associates (Bucharest, Romania)
The future of the PR business can be bright and ever rewarding if we never forget that audiences, from consumers to businesses, are more and more demanding in terms of quality, keeping promises, responsibility, and transparency; if ethics remains the greatest value in dealing with clients and in communicating with public; and if we do not ignore the fact that successful business in PR means investing in human capital and talent.

CESARE VALLI, Former Managing Director, SEC (Milan, Italy)
My view is that the PR business is fantastically well positioned to benefit from this development on the condition that companies and professionals will be able to keep adapting to the new environment. This is not banal. First of all, because changes are always painful for more traditional organizations and human beings, but also because digital PR is still diluting to the bottom line of professional firms. Even in the faster-growing part of the market, the average profit is

still much smaller than the traditional one. This will discourage some from changing, but those who will not change will not survive.

CHRISTOPHE GINISTY, Head of Digital Engagement, OECD (Paris, France/Brussels, Belgium)
I would use the following formula to answer your question: Grow or die. Since the need for influence will continue to grow tremendously, public relations businesses that manage to integrate successfully the new dimensions and skills will grow tremendously, as well. Those sticking to the traditional PR practices will disappear or be bought out for very little money by advertisers or digital agencies.

CIRO DIAS REIS, CEO, Imagem Corporativa (São Paulo, Brazil)
There are a lot of small firms that are not strong enough to go on investing and putting in place new technologies, solutions, and practices. So those ones that cannot move forward in a competitive way tend to lose relevance and be bought by bigger firms, or even worse, simply go out of the business. In addition to that, being able to offer more and more integrated services and solutions will be a must in this market.

CLARA LY-LE, Managing Director, EloQ Communications (Ho Chi Minh, Vietnam)
Social media will still be a prominent platform; audience-share information will replace the (traditional) media-share or business-share. Businesses that are hesitant to expose themselves online will have second thoughts, as social media is where most people are, most of the stakeholders are. Businesses need to become social media-savvy and prepare for two-way communication with stakeholders.

CLAUDINE MOORE, CEO, C. Moore Media International Public Relations (New York City, USA)
We will have to battle fake news and the impact it has on our clients. Also, we will have to navigate the world of artificial intelligence, and the role and place PR has in the mix.

DANIJEL KOLETIC, CEO, Apriori World (Zagreb, Croatia)
Knowledge and creativity in PR will always find its place. Holograms, robotic translators, cyber technologies, and new revolutionary technology products are expected to upgrade media platforms, but depending on which country you are in and the structure of the classical media population, you will always have a role to play.

The PR industry will always count on individuals and agencies. The simple thought of PR is to impose and follow the trends, because ultimately all innovations are communicated by PR experts, and agencies only adopt the methods.

DAPHNA TRIWAKS, CEO, Triwaks PR (Tel Aviv, Israel)
While print media will still survive, most of the consumption will be on mobile and in paid content media collaboration. Creativity will be the name of the new game, as well as an understanding of the digital world with the help of research companies. The traditional PR services will still be practiced by a certain amount of corporates (traded companies, etc).

DAVID GALLAGHER, President, International Growth and Development, Omnicom PR Group (London, UK)
Large agencies will continue to consolidate. Small agencies will continue to specialize. Many professionals will glide between large and smaller consultancies, and handle their own clients, through new "Uber-like" networks. Platforms like Google, Facebook, and Weibo will continue to be sources of competition and collaboration. In-house teams will continue to worry about corporate/brand reputation while shifting resources to social commerce.

DAVID GORDON, Managing Partner, Cohn & Wolfe Canada (Toronto, Canada)
There will be continued evolution—the platform of communication continues to evolve, and the role of the traditional journalists in reaching audiences is lessened, meaning that the industry requires a better understanding of the "public" portion of PR.

DIMITRIS ROULIAS, Managing Partner, Out of the Box PR (Athens, Greece)
The combination of technology evolution and changing social dynamics around the globe leads to a more and more complex communication environment. PR is better positioned to fit in it, mainly because, theoretically, it adapts more easily to change and can attract talent with nontraditional backgrounds. Actually, my prediction is that, if PR responds successfully to these challenges, it will incorporate, gradually, all communication disciplines.

EITAN HERSHCO, Chairman, Israeli PR Association (Tel Aviv, Israel)

PR is becoming a sort of an integrator of the marketing system in large organizations. Therefore, my prediction for the coming years is that PR personnel will be leading the marketing strategy of the company and will play a part in the decision-making process.

ELISE MITCHELL, Founder and CEO, Mitchell Communications Group (Fayetteville, Arkansas, USA)

The most successful PR businesses will be digitally-centric, data-driven, and highly measurable using "micrometrics" to determine effectiveness.

Agencies from a variety of disciplines will be collapsed into and rebranded as integrated agencies with specializations in vertical sectors such as food and beverage or tech. New jobs will spring up in PR to oversee and leverage artificial intelligence-enabled bots, digital assistants, and humanoids, ensuring they interact with audiences in authentic, engaging, and appropriate ways.

ELIZABETH GOENAWAN ANANTO, Founding Director, International Public Relations Summit (Jakarta, Indonesia)

The traditional PR practice is dying, for sure. Leadership and reputation are more important than before. Measurement of PR effectiveness will focus more on creating social impact.

PR agencies will be more competitive in the sense that those who survive will be the ones that could expose values, ethics, and professionalism.

There is a growing need for professional Corporate Communication Officers (CCO) rather than Public Relations Officers (PRO) in any organization—government, private, and NGOs.

ERIK CORNELIUS, Cofounder and COO, G3 Partners (Seoul, South Korea)

While it's far from a bold prediction, I don't foresee major shifts in the way PR is practiced in Korea over the next few years. Companies will follow people to the new channels they use. The biggest change is likely to be the focus of stories.

FABIÁN MOTTA, Director, Smart PR (Bogota, Colombia)
This is a sector, in Colombia, that will grow by ten. Every day, the number of professionals increases; there are more consultants and more multinationals who aim to be in the country to help brands respond to their audiences. Innovation will be one of the greatest challenges in our industry, where automation through AI will allow audiences to have content adapted to their likes and where we will have to prepare companies to create better communication protocols and be one step ahead of any crisis.

FILOMENA ROSATO, CEO, FiloComunicazione (Milan, Italy)
What I see today is that the market needs new stability and looks for quality once again. It has started again to ask for this, as already stated by our recent Nielsen research estimate of +4 percent PR segment in 2017.

Business predictions can be prudent but positive. This is a new revolution of the market, and, entering these new "flows of the river," to quote Heraclitus, PR companies must work to reestablish the ethics of the job and the reputation of the market in general.

GERMAN SAA, Group Director, Kyodo PR (Tokyo, Japan)
Depending on how fast technology is adapted to communications, we will continue to see major changes as the general public gets used to using ONLY digital platforms to get their information. Traditional media will disappear, and old ways such as face-to-face meetings (interviews) and press gatherings will be activities of the past. PR agencies in Japan will offer ONLY integrated programs that rely heavily on digital media that reach all Japanese audiences, regardless of gender, age, or economic status.

GUNTRAM KAISER, Managing Partner, Kaiser Communication (Berlin, Germany)
The change process has just reached its beginning, and it will continue for at least the next ten years. It is difficult to predict everything in detail, but I am afraid that all of us in this business have to be extremely flexible, modern, and dynamic in our thinking and very, very adaptive to the new challenges.

HALIM WALID ABOU SEIF, Senior PR Consultant, Rada Research & PR (Cairo, Egypt)

It is difficult to tell, because we are following the trends, not leading the changes like we used to. We are moving into a more visual world where pictures and videos are much more convincing than words.

So should we focus more on creative work such as video shooting and editing, and photographing skills, more than on our writing skills? PR will never be the same.

ILARIJA BAŠIĆ, PR Director, MITA Group (Sarajevo, Bosnia and Herzegovina)

There will be growing influence of digital media and the ability to spread PR stories through these channels. There will also be increased independence of PR in the sense that in-house PR teams will no longer be part of a marketing department in a company, but an equitable, strategic unit. There will be at least a few PR experts who will be among large companies' management and will really influence strategic decisions.

JACK MARTIN, Former Global Chairman and CEO, Hill+Knowlton Strategies (Austin, USA)

I've found that the best way to answer this question is to restrict one's self to four words: "But wait, there's more!"

JAFAR MANSIMI, Cofounder, PRoloq Magazine (Baku, Azerbaijan)

Education may bring a better future for our business. Universities must cooperate with real practices in a way that students will be much more knowledgeable and ready for future challenges. Public relations professionals should use more creativity. Fewer words, more visual and music . . . And I feel that these challenges will be significant, indeed.

JAROSLAV MAJOR, Senior Consultant, Hill+Knowlton Strategies (Prague, Czech Republic)

Over the next five years, the PR industry will have to change completely. Social media will dominate the public space, YouTube will replace the television, people will be communicating permanently via Twitter, perhaps some innovative networks and ways of communicating will arise. Classic marketing tools will stop working, including PR.

JOAN RAMON VILAMITJANA, CEO, Hill+Knowlton Strategies (Madrid, Spain)
PR will continue to gain relevance (i.e., a share of marketing spent) vis-à-vis other marketing disciplines. Clients will continue to transform themselves towards integrated communications (both in terms of their structure, their budget, and their comms/marketing partners).

The economy will not continue to grow at such a pace forever. We'll see a new recession soon, and its impact on the PR industry will be important. It will be especially negative on those firms that haven't been able to transform themselves and attract the right people, namely, the people their clients need to talk to.

JOHN SAUNDERS, CEO and President, FleishmanHillard (Dublin, Ireland/St. Louis, USA)
I believe the PR industry is in a very good place, with many opportunities in front of us. Our work has never been more important than today—for many organizations, our counsel is having an impact on every decision they're making; I've been told that we're as essential as their right arm. In the future, the winners in our industry will be the firms providing the best strategies and boldest answers to the complex problems faced by our clients.

JÜRGEN H. GANGOLY, Managing Partner and CEO, The Skills Group (Vienna, Austria)
The PR industry will constantly grow in the upcoming years as a result of digitization and increased private, corporate, or institutional communications at all levels. Taking current global and political developments into account, let's hope that crisis communications will not become the biggest subfield in PR.

JUSTIN GREEN, Director, Wide Awake Communications (Dublin, Ireland)
There will be great changes in the wider communications industry. Some will be welcomed, but others will be difficult for some.

KAMAL TAIBI, Founder and CEO, Stratëus Group (Casablanca, Morocco)
With what happened over the last couple of years in the political arena all over the world, things are still getting complex every day from the communications perspective. So the industry has to be bold

in embracing the complexity of communications driven by data and analytics, creativity, technology, and trust-building engagements.

KARA ALAIMO, Assistant Professor of Public Relations, Hofstra University, and CNN contributor (New York City, USA)
Organizations will gain an even greater understanding of the importance of reputation management, and public relations practitioners will become even more valued professionals in C-suites.

KHALID BADDOU, President, Moroccan Association of Marketing and Communication (Casablanca, Morocco)
I reckon that the classical "PR Manager" position will disappear in the next five years, at least in its conventional definition. The PR industry should become more agile, innovative, forward-looking, and much more digital.

KIM NYBERG, Chairman, M-Brain, and Special Advisor, Hill+Knowlton Strategies (Helsinki, Finland)
There will be more "doers" than "thinkers." Communications professionals will be more engaged in choosing channels and means of communication, rather than focusing on substance. Having said that, it also means a new high day for those PR professionals who will at the same time look backward and forward, who will remember that fundamentally we are still the same as 20–30 years ago, and who will understand that PR is and always has been about human relations and that tech is a wonderful enabler, but just that. We will see more use of AI, but an algorithm is only as good as its creator; accordingly, we will see "smarter brains," but also more "legs" in the next five years.

KRESTEN SCHULTZ-JØRGENSEN, CEO, Oxymoron (Copenhagen, Denmark)
I'm a great optimist. Our industry has high trust due to our holistic approaches—but we have to further develop ethical guidelines standards, education and methodology, value creation, measurements, etc.

LARS ERIK GRØNNTUN, Global President, Hill+Knowlton Strategies (Oslo, Norway)
The developments we are seeing presently will continue, and we will see continued convergence. I also believe the increased complexity and

the increased expectations from stakeholders mean that the demand for our services will increase—companies will need to invest more in their reputation and their goals to prevail.

LORENA CARREÑO, President, Confederation of Communication Marketing Industry (Mexico City, Mexico)

The development of governmental communication should encourage the organized industry to offer advice on the professionalization of social communication areas by giving updated courses. In the same way, it should be in tune with transparency and ethics in the development of protocols for the selection of campaigns that support the promotion of various instances of government. In this topic, an advisory council of experts should be created to support the new line of governmental communication.

On the other hand, the private initiative foresees a greater demand for better communication services for brands with a directive and integrating vision, in line with what is happening on a global level. This includes the strategic use of big data, toward a vision of shopper marketing and communication with omnichannel direction. There is an emphasis on corporate reputations tuning into great social causes. There is also a need for the efficient use of the digital ecosystem with an integrated approach—off and online—which will translate the role of communication in obtaining the ROI that is shown in the change of attitudes and consumer behavior. All of this translates into sales and maintaining a level of social dialogue to develop trust and brand credibility.

As never before, market research will be important from an anthropological point of view, which allows deepening in the cultural codes of each target group and gaining insight on consumers' decision-making and their perception of brands.

LOULA ZAKLAMA, President, Rada Research & PR (Cairo, Egypt)

It is hard to predict, as PR is in constant improvement. What I know is that PR is now different and we need to adapt quickly to the change and create new tools to stay in business. It might be easier execution, but for sure more difficult and challenging in strategies, planning, and evaluation.

MARTIN PETERSON, President and CEO, H&H Group (Stockholm, Sweden)
I clearly see that a game changer will be the integration of communication tech in the service delivery models. We will see a higher degree of technology as part of the offering alongside smarter creativity and deeper insights into our clients' business challenges.

MASSIMO MORICONI, General Manager and CEO, Omnicom Public Relations Group (Milan, Italy)
Data science will become more and more relevant. Media analytics players will challenge business consulting firms. Messaging based on real-time data and predictive analysis will be dominating the scenario. In the beginning, PR will act as a filter (interpreter maybe) between data science and media, between data science and companies. The challenges are to make PR take care also of the communication "cascade" that will happen within companies.

MICHAEL THOMAS SCHRÖDER, CEO, ORCA Affairs (Berlin, Germany)
The biggest challenge will be the transition from the PR professional to the social PR manager. Social media is no longer hype, but rather becomes a central component of the communication culture. The political events of the recent past have shown that the communication channels of social media can overcome political censorship and even bring down dictatorships.

The most important task for PR professionals and PR agencies by 2020 will be to familiarize themselves with the new media, communication channels, and technologies and actively use them in their PR strategies and campaigns.

MICHAELA BENEDIGOVÁ, Managing Director and Partner, Seesame (Bratislava, Slovakia)
Both our customers and employees, even more today, want leaders to be role models. They are desperately looking for meaningful conversation, intervention in social issues. This is a tremendous opportunity for the brands and for the comm industry, for us PR professionals, as well. With brands' growing influence over public life, brand managers are finding themselves in brand new roles. While many of them are not even aware of it, there are also those who will try to squeeze this opportunity for their own gains.

MINA NAZARI, Public Relations Expert, Tabriz Electric Power Distribution Company (Tehran, Iran)
The introduction of public relations and communications into the field of artificial intelligence can bring a great transformation for societies in terms of quality, time, and cost.

MYKOLAS KATKUS, Chairman of the Board, FABULA (Vilnius, Lithuania)
The biggest change is what will happen to the TV when the alternative viewership reaches some saturation point. It is obvious that people will still tune in to programmed TV in order to avoid choices, but the current video-viewing platforms like Netflix, Snapchat, or YouTube will change in order to better compete for our attention.

This will further drive the TV ratings down and would have a huge influence on the world of communications. The rise and professionalization of profiling now used in political campaigns by companies like Cambridge Analytica will also move to the mainstream public relations campaigns. But then again, the principles with which we play the persuasion game are the same, and the technological changes will never affect them.

MYRON WASYLYK, CEO, PBN Hill+Knowlton Strategies (Moscow, Russia)
As we move toward the Internet of Things, PR will become more digitalized and more precise in many segments and across many products. PR will become more important with influencers, content, etc.

NITIN MANTRI, Group CEO, AvianWE (New Delhi, India)
I continue to remain bullish on the industry's growth, because it is really up to us to start boosting our value in the boardroom by doing more.

I think we will definitely do more integrated work, which will include a lot of visual and multimedia elements. We will, as organizations, change to become more inclusive of creative people, designers, and planners. Most important, technology is going to play a big role in the way we do things, and influencer marketing will be a big piece of that. One piece of advice in this regard: while our industry's future success will be defined by our ability to stay ahead of the technology curve, we must not lose sight of our core strengths of telling an authentic brand story that connects emotionally with the audience. We have to bring to the table human qualities like trust and empathy to make sure that technology doesn't become the only driving force in this world.

NURUL SHAMSURI, Project Director, Yayasan Juwita (Kuala Lumpur, Malaysia)
PR agencies will have to reinvent themselves rapidly, taking various steps from managing social influencers to engaging freelancers and maximizing digital tools. In order not to suffer, PR companies should embrace the digital revolution instead of resisting it.

OKSANA MONASTYRSKA, Managing Director, PBN Hill+Knowlton Strategies (Kiev, Ukraine)
Communications are going to become smarter and more influential. The pace of technology-driven disruption, particularly in the areas of artificial intelligence, digitalization, and big data, will be driving companies to constantly review and adapt the way they do business and communicate with their stakeholders. Transparency, trust, social responsibility, and authenticity will become the required foundation for any reputable business.

PATRIK SCHOBER, CEO, PRAM Consulting (Prague, Czech Republic)
The biggest challenges for the next several years are to educate clients, to attract new people to PR jobs, and to find the right place to live between media, digital, and advertising agencies.

PELIN KOCAALP, General Manager, Hill+Knowlton Strategies (Istanbul, Turkey)
We have to be more relevant and valuable to the public. This is why we see more attention to content marketing, influencer marketing, and other methods that are designed to deliver actual value to audiences.

Communications consultants should consider integrated campaigns and deliver creative tactics that focus on engaging audiences that their competitors might not be considering. So making something different is the key. That is why it's important for us to be aware of our customers' communications preferences.

PETER MUTIE, CEO, Peterson Integrated Communications (Nairobi, Kenya)
I see the PR business getting more sophisticated. Survival will depend on how innovative PR practitioners will get. Many traditional PR products are getting out of the market. The market is now more open, and clients can access a lot of services online, meaning that competition is no longer local, but global.

PHILIPPE BORREMANS, Independent PR Consultant, Reputation & Co. (Casablanca, Morocco)
There will be a lot of pressure on the industry to come up with true and transparent measurement, cost-efficient ways of operating, and flexible yet specialized teams.

The industry will either welcome this pressure with open arms (by investing in professional education, skills development, and accreditation) or "miss the boat" and be the last in line (again) in the world of modern marketing communication.

RETO WILHELM, Managing Director, Panta Rhei PR (Zurich, Switzerland)
Automatization will continue. The classical distribution of press releases, etc., will disappear. We will also have smart tools in the field of evaluation/data interpretation. New technologies—especially audio-based and video-driven—will create new possibilities for content creation

Glocalization is increasing—people need local news and information again. A new platform for the micro-micro-level will succeed, meaning the creation of integrated media houses as new products.

RHINGO MUTAMBO, Chief PR Officer, Prime Minister's Bureau (Windhoek, Namibia)
Virtual-oriented PR space, especially social media interactions and monitoring, will be on the rise. This is because organizations are realizing the need to have instant communication with the target audience and access to statistics for improved decision-making and to boost business prospects.

SARI-LIIA TONTTILA, Founder, Ahjo Communications Oy (Helsinki, Finland)
I'm predicting that in five years, we will put humanity back in business, and communications will be the tool to lead it.

SERGE BECKERS, Managing Partner, Wisse Kommunkatie (Arnhem, Netherlands)
The PR industry will make a move to digital. In the near future, we will see the emergence of new agencies: "compelling content creators." Whatever that content might look like (social, video, long read, blogs).

SHAMIL TUMISANG AGOSI, Director, Square Gate Holdings (Gaborone, Botswana)
Going forward, 24/7 crisis preparedness strategy will be crucial to respond to negative or incorrect news in a nanosecond. PR and Communications businesses will have to adapt to changing techniques to remain fluid and agile, calling for an outside-in approach to marketing communications and knowledge on bots and AI in order to leverage these changes. R&D, AI, and ML are now kings.

SHELLEY SPECTOR, Founder, Museum of Public Relations (New York City, USA)
There will always be newer and newer channels with which we can communicate coming into play. But the very fundamentals of PR, building and growing public relationships, still remain the same. They're perhaps even more important to consider today, when more attention seems to be paid to getting likes and shares than creating a full-bodied strategic approach to building sustainable relationships with shareholders, customers, employees, et al. In other words—and I'm not discounting social media here—while Twitter and Facebook and Instagram are important, so are employee meetings, analyst shows, articles in the *Times*, and issue advertising. Social media just gives us a few more options we can use in our programs for clients, and they've got to be strategically entwined with everything else we're doing.

SOLLY MOENG, Convenor, SA Brand Summit & Awards (Cape Town, South Africa)
The upcoming years will require growth of online platforms, more need for integration with other elements of the marketing mix, understanding of media, strategic contribution, more emphasis on PR measurements, and contribution to the bottom line. PR must, increasingly, justify its added value.

SOPHYA BALAKINA, Cofounder and CEO, Bureau of Communications TAGS (Bishkek, Kyrgyzstan)
PR specialists will work only with digital tools and use artificial intelligence. Moreover, digitization will affect the functionality of the PR professionals themselves. Robots will take on the logistics, copy-writing, creating visuals, etc. They will perform much faster and will be more creative than a human being. After all, they are not familiar with the creative crisis, fatigue, and other human factors that affect efficiency at work. PR experts will be responsible for process building and management. Due to globalization and increasing access to information, brands will find it easier to organize large-scale PR campaigns, including partner projects, receive feedback from customers, monitor communications, and evaluate the effectiveness of their activities. Traditional media will lose their power and magic; digital interactive multimedia will gain the trust of society.

STUART BRUCE, Managing Consultant, Stuart Bruce Associates (Leeds, UK)
Public relations will become more important than ever. But it might not be called public relations, and it might not be done by PR agencies. In fact, PR agencies don't have much of a future at all if all they do is transactional tactics and traditional activity like pitching media, writing copy, and designing things.

The real money will be adding strategic value that demonstrates a real impact on corporate and organizational success. The danger is that management consultancies, who have now recognized the value of reputation, do it better than PR does. They'll do this by using their high-level processes and taking the best talent from the PR industry, because they can pay bigger salaries as clients pay them bigger fees.

SVETLANA JAPALĂU, Managing Director, BDR Associates—Strategic Communication (Kishinev, Moldova)
In my opinion, the authenticity, innovation, brevity, and social responsibility of the companies will become the main pillars of the PR strategies. I think that traditional mass media (TV, newspapers) may resume their influence and credibility among the public at large. On the other hand, social and online media will become regulated by national legislation, which I'll welcome very much, as now it is like the "Wild West"—social

and online media are riddled with fake news and materials that have controversial objectives, like reputational attacks on specific brands or persons. Finally, yet importantly, I think that everything that has a personal approach or connotation, like direct communication tools, testimonials, etc., will dominate the market in the near future.

TAMARA BEKČIĆ, Managing Director, Chapter 4 Communications (Belgrade, Serbia)
We have the privilege of living in a time of brave ideas and great opportunities, and PR is a valuable partner there. On the other hand, I think we shall have to see a lot more of sustainability and responsibility toward the community and the world we live in, embroidered in practically every element of businesses. This means that more dialogues have to be open as a result of even more vibrant communication. In times of great uncertainty and changes, good or bad, as well as the industrial revolution, communication aims to build bridges between different interest groups. Strategic communication planning can give us a vision of the future and a better team/business/company/world that we are worthy of, yet for which we still have to make a little more effort to accomplish.

TATEVIK PIRUMYAN, Communication Key Expert, EU Assistance to Armenia Project (Yerevan, Armenia)
(1) PR will have to become more creative. (2) Use of social media marketing and communications applications and web analytics tools will become a must in all industries.

TATJANA LOPARSKI, CEO, Element PR (Skopje, Macedonia)
There will be a real struggle with the fake news that became more and more problematic in everyday communication. Also, the crisis scenarios have to have a real impact on social media. Changes are so fast that we have to follow them and be part of them; otherwise, we are losing momentum.

THIERRY WELLHOFF, President and CEO, Wellcom (Paris, France)
In a digital world where the information has become horizontal, PR will keep being essential to communications, as the trust issue will always be the most important. Although competing with digital, media, and consulting actors, we can foresee a strong future for the PR industry.

THOMAS TINDEMANS, Chairman, Hill+Knowlton Strategies (Brussels, Belgium)

Reconquering the trust of public opinion is the greatest challenge for the profession. Asking for the blind faith of audiences produces deception. Day-by-day crafting of truthful reliability will be the industry's critical mission.

VIVIAN LINES, Global Vice Chairman, Hill+Knowlton Strategies (Singapore)

Watch out for artificial intelligence. It is going to transform how and what we do.

YASEMIN EDIGE ÖZTUNC, Group Coordinator, Lobby PR (Istanbul, Turkey)

New digital technologies and the always online economy will transform business, commerce, and society. Reputation will gain importance more than ever.

Digital and analytic functions will be integrated into every facet of organizations. Every PR team will have a tech geek. Companies that embrace the true integration of technology, marketing, and communications will lead in shaping the future of the industry. The communications and marketing organizations workforce of the future will include behavioral economists, computer scientists, programmers, design thinkers, and technology experts. Content will be created by consumers, and, oh yes, we are all consumers.

YOMI BADEJO-OKUSANYA, CEO, CMC Connect Burson Cohn & Wolfe (Lagos, Nigeria)

Artificial intelligence, emotional intelligence, digital PR, specialization, content optimization, big data and research, and innovative media channels will be the order of the day, all driven by technology. The traditional PR consulting structure will decline in revenue, to be replaced by smaller, focused PR hotshops.

ZDENEK LOKAJ, Former Managing Director, Hill+Knowlton Strategies (Prague, Czech Republic)

If PR firms are clever enough (and they always used to be), they will become winners. But it requires extreme flexibility, fast thinking and acting, competence, and very good pricing that is more result-oriented.

Old-school PR based on press releases and having lunch with journalists will become a very minor part of the business.

ZHAO DALI, Secretary General, China International PR Association (Beijing, China)
PR in China will play a more and more important role. The PR industry has a key role and is very necessary for the development of China. PR is necessary for the field of bilateral relations, enterprises development, and human exchanges. The form of PR will have more diversity.

ZSOFIA LAKATOS, CEO, Emerald Communications (Budapest, Hungary)
Either we will find a new role for our profession and get it back to management level, or there will be no PR in a few years.

PR is everything and everywhere. Everything is PR in today's world. That's not destroying it. It's actually making PR more sophisticated, there are greater demands for it, and that's what makes the true professionals in this business stand out more than ever.

Social media has become such a nuanced and dynamic matter that it's no longer as it was ten or even five years ago, when everybody could claim more or less safely that they could handle it.

It was a very different situation: you go to a big accounting firm, they do your financial reports, legal assessments and all, and you ask them about marketing and PR, and they tell you, "But of course! We do marketing and PR." Or even a grocery store could tell you, "We know about PR, we're going to write a press release, etc."

Yet while several years ago the language of social media was all one, now there are probably twenty different "languages" being spoken, and handling them is no picnic. The fact that PR is everything and everywhere does put us PR professionals in a far more beneficial position that empowers us to prove that we can create content as no other social media user can.

Clients keep coming to me and telling me, "Let's do some [good] PR," and I ask, "What do you mean by that?" "You know, to make me look better . . ." In the past, they used to approach journalists with such overtures. They would go to a journalist and ask them, "Would you like to do an interview with me? Would you write something nice about me?" Such pitches are barely the case anymore; they come to PR companies now.

The most important quality in the PR business of today is leadership. Everybody can create content on social media now, but if you can't be a leader in your company, office, or development, if you don't update your leadership qualities every single day, you can't do efficient PR.

By "leader," I mean that every single employee can be a leader: leader to their client, leader in thought, leader most of all in decision-making, because now when you are involved with a client account and you have to make decisions in an instant, you can't go to your boss every five minutes and ask them, "Can I do this?"

Leadership qualities are the most important ones for the PR expert today in the world of the Global PR Revolution.

ACKNOWLEDGMENTS

Special and very cordial thanks to:

All of the **100 top PR experts** from 65 countries for making this book a unique encyclopedia on the development of the public relations business all over the world during these turbulent times.

The team at **Allworth Press** and **Skyhorse Publishing**, who worked hard and dedicated their time to polish every detail of this book and to bring it to the market. In particular, thanks to the one and only Tad Crawford, Chamois Holschuh, Chris Schultz, Hector Carosso, Corinne Enright, Mona Lin, and Cayla Ames.

The great writer **Eric Weiner**, the author of *The Geography of Bliss*, for inspiring in me the idea to give this book a second name: *The Geography of PR*.

The "icon" of Global PR and a good friend for decades, **Paul Holmes**—mentor, teacher, advisor, and someone to quote on many different occasions.

My absolute "#M3DreamTeam" at **M3 Communications Group, Inc.**, in Sofia for the constant support and for giving me the opportunity to "swim" professionally in the ocean of the public relations business.

The first editor of the book, **Ivan Dikov**, for his support and professional advice.

My friends and colleagues from ICCO, **The International Communications Consultancy Organisation**, for their strong support in bringing the organization to a higher level during my presidency and for always giving me "fresh air" and a "strong hand" toward future professional success.

The greatest company to work for, **Hill+Knowlton Strategies**, the leaders in the world's public relations business since 1927.

Two great personalities who are no longer on planet Earth but who were my mentors, friends, and role models: the late **Terence Billing**, who showed me the way to creative PR, and the late **Sir James Mancham**, founding president of the Republic of Seychelles, who brought me into the amazing world of modern diplomacy.

Thank you to the contributors who took the time to answer questions and share their insights:

Aaron Kwittken
Adam Benson
Adriana Vieira
Agnieszka Dziedzic
Ahmed Janabi
Aive Hiiepuu
Aki Kubo
Alan Ogden
Alison Clarke
Alma Gerxhani
Althaf Jalaldeen
Amir Rastegar
Andras Sztaniszlav
Andrew Bone
Andrey Barannikov
Arun Sudhaman
Assel Karaulova
Bashar Alkadhi
Božidar Novak
Bridget von Holdt
Catalina Rousseau
Cesare Valli
Christophe Ginisty
Ciro Dias Reis
Clara Ly-Le
Claudine Moore
Danijel Koletic
Daphna Triwaks
David Gallagher
David Gordon
Dimitris Roulias
Eitan Hershco
Elise Mitchell
Elizabeth Goenawan Ananto
Erik Cornelius
Fabián Motta

Filomena Rosato
Gabriel Paslaru
German Saa
Guntram Kaiser
Halim Walid Abou Seif
Ilarija Bašić
Jack Martin
Jafar Mansimi
Jaroslav Major
Joan Ramon Vilamitjana
John Saunders
Jürgen H. Gangoly
Justin Green
Kamal Taibi
Kara Alaimo
Khalid Baddou
Khristo Ayad
Kim Nyberg
Kresten Schultz-Jørgensen
Lars Erik Grønntun
Lorena Carreño
Loula Zaklama
Martin Peterson
Martin Slater
Martin Sorrell
Massimo Moriconi
Michael Thomas Schrøder
Michaela Benedigová
Mina Nazari
Mykolas Katkus
Myron Wasylyk
Nitin Mantri
Nurul Shamsuri
Oksana Monastyrska
Patrik Schober
Pelin Kocaalp
Peter Mutie
Philippe Borremans
Rana Nejem
Reto Wilhelm
Rhingo Mutambo
Richard Millar
Sari-Liia Tonttila
Saurabh Uboweja
Scott E. Fahlman
Serge Beckers
Sergey Zverev
Shamil Tumisang Agosi
Shelley Spector
Solly Moeng
Sophya Balakina
Stuart Bruce
Svetlana Japalău
Tamara Bekčić
Tatevik Pirumyan
Tatjana Loparski
Thierry Wellhoff
Thomas Tindemans
Vivian Lines
Yasemin Edige Öztunc
Yomi Badejo-Okusanya
Zdenek Lokaj
Zhao Dali
Zsofia Lakatos

ABOUT THE AUTHOR

Photograph by Romeo Cholakov.

Maxim Behar is a globally renowned public relations expert, entrepreneur, writer, and Harvard Kennedy School graduate. He is the founder and CEO of M3 Communications Group, Inc. He is the past president of the International Communications Consultancy Organisation (ICCO) and is currently a member of the executive committee. He has been awarded many titles, among them Global Chairman of the Year by the International Business Stevie Awards and Communicator of the Decade by the Association of Business Communicators of India. Bulgarian born and grown, he considers himself a global citizen.

INDEX

B

C

E

F

H

I

O

P

Y

Z

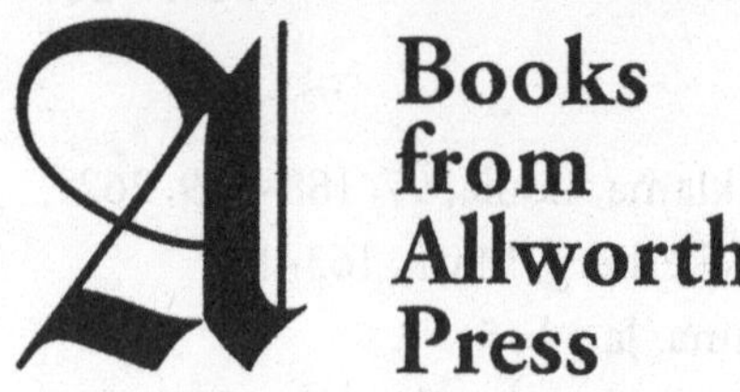

Books from Allworth Press